OUTDOOR PROJECTS IN WOOD

OUTDOOR PROJECTS IN WOOD

Bernie Price

CREATIVE HOMEOWNER PRESS®

Manufactured in United States of America

Current printing (last digit)
10 9 8 7 6 5 4 3 2 1

Produced by Roundtable Press, Inc.

Project editor: Don Nelson
Assistant editor: Marguerite Ross
Illustrations: Norman Nuding
Design: Jeffrey Fitschen
Jacket design: Jerry Demoney
Art production: Nadina Simon
Photography: Jerry Demoney
Photo stylists: Sandra Withers, Ann Demoney
Photographs page 10, top and center, courtesy Black & Decker Manufacturing Co.

LC: 84-17438
ISBN: 0-932944-73-6 (paper)
       0-932944-76-0 (hardcover)

CREATIVE HOMEOWNER PRESS®
BOOK SERIES
A DIVISION OF FEDERAL
MARKETING CORPORATION
24 PARK WAY,
UPPER SADDLE RIVER, NJ 07458

Introduction

All homeowners know that life doesn't end at the patio door. Actually, most of them enjoy the great outdoors. There are picnics and barbecues with family and friends, sitting around the pool or backyard, watching the kids at play or perhaps observing birds or small animals in their daily routines. Homeowners who are also Do-It-Yourselfers are luckier yet. They can reap the esthetic rewards of creating outdoor woodworking projects and then enjoy using their handiwork.

Some of the projects in this book are totally practical such as the duckboards, garbage storage unit, firewood storage bin, lighting enclosure, and umbrella table, while others, which are basically decorative, include the tree surround and the wishing well. Some provide homes for dogs, birds or plants. Another group of projects are entertainment and play centers for people ranging in age from tots to adults. The sandbox, jungle gym, game table, folding picnic table, portable bar, and barbecue cart are good examples. The remaining projects provide a variety of creature comforts for just plain sitting around and soaking up sun.

Most of the projects are constructed with redwood; some use pressure-treated yellow pine or oak. Panels are either A-C plywood or T1-11 textured. All projects are assembled with hardware, except the lighting enclosure louvers, which require glue. All hardware is obtainable at standard lumberyard and hardware stores, except as noted; exterior stains, primers, trim paints, and urethanes are used as finishes.

The first part of the book explains the basic skills and tools required to complete the projects. Read the safety section carefully. Some of the table saw pictures in the project section show the guards removed for clarity. Use saw guards as shown in your saw instruction manual. If in doubt, check with your supplier.

The project section provides shopping lists, cutting schedules, parts lists and details, plus step-by-step illustrated instructions.

Doghouse (pages 58-62). Man's best friend deserves a home of his own where he can shelter from the elements. The base, pressure-treated lumber, will prevent water or insect damage.

CONTENTS

INTRODUCTION 5

TOOLS AND TECHNIQUES

WORK SUPPORTS AND VISES 8
SAWS, SAWING AIDS, AND GUIDES 10
FORMING, SHAPING, AND SMOOTHING 13
ROUTERS 14
JOINTING AND SANDING 15
DRILLS, BITS, AND GUIDES 16
HARDWARE, PAINT, AND STAIN 17
SAFETY FIRST 18

PROJECTS

UMBRELLA TABLE 20
SLING CHAIR 25
GAME TABLE 30
PERIMETER BENCH 34
PORTABLE BAR UNIT 38
BIRDHOUSE 43

GARBAGE STORAGE 48

PORTABLE POTTING UNIT 52

DOGHOUSE 58

BARBECUE CART 63

LIGHTING ENCLOSURE 70

DUCKBOARDS 78

SITTING PLANTERS 81

SANDBOX 85

FIREWOOD STORAGE BIN 89

DECK CHAIR 93

FOLDING PICNIC TABLE 113

TREE SURROUND 117

WISHING WELL 123

SLAT CHAIR 129

SLAT CHAISE 133

NEST OF TABLES 139

LARGE STANDING PLANTER 142

JUNGLE GYM 147

GLOSSARY 156

INDEX 158

METRIC CHARTS 160

WORK SUPPORTS AND VISES

Whether you're a novice or an experienced do-it-yourselfer, the first task in building any project is choosing a method of making "little ones out of big ones"—that is, cutting the wood down to size.

Any cutting method you select should be safe, convenient, efficient and if possible, portable, and relatively inexpensive. By way of comparison, consider the Colonial craftsman who used the traditional system of holding and sawing that was brought over from Europe. His prize possession was a massive hardwood slab-top workbench with dogs, shoulder vise, tail vise, bench hooks, and hold-downs. With this setup, he could hold almost any shape of almost any size in almost any position. There is a distinct advantage when your work is gripped solidly, because this frees both of your hands. But such a rock-solid workbench takes up room, is hardly portable, and is expensive whether you buy or build it.

Our Colonial forebears followed the traditional methods of woodworking, in an age that valued handcrafting and that afforded people the

time to perfect it. But, we have an advantage that they lacked: mass-production that provides us with useful tools at reasonable prices.

Today any craftsman can make good use of our updated devices for supporting and holding work. These suit the speed, accuracy, and generally lower skill requirements of modern power tools.

The **saw horse** has been used in one form or another as a support, and in many cases as a tool holder, for a long, long time. Until recently, most carpenters built their own wooden horses, and some still do—for example, in residential construction. Inexpensive, lightweight, portable, folding metal horses are an alternative for the home-shop craftsman. These horses require a one-time-only assembly in your shop and they're topped off with a 2×4 rail, which may be used as a nailer.

The photograph at the bottom shows a pair of these horses, set up with some 2×4s on top. If the lumber has been laid there for trimming to length, the waste piece should extend *past* the horses and be sawn off *past* the horses.

A **temporary work table** can be

quickly set up by nailing lumber to the horses and tacking on a plywood sheet to form a work surface.

For crosscutting large panels, nail on the 2×4s to cover the span between the horses. Then, set up another group of 2×4s on top of and at right angles to the first ones. Place one 2×4 on each side of the proposed cut and one more at each end to complete the support of each panel as the cut is made. The panels on either side will not move or jump. Adjust the power-saw blade depth so that only the panel will be cut.

For ripping, only the 2×4s that span the horses are needed, but the same principle holds: provide close support on either side of the proposed cut and additional support at the ends of the panels, when they become separated.

Note that the procedures just covered are for rough cuts, made with the bad side of the plywood facing up. Guided cuts will be covered shortly. Read the safety section near the end of this introduction carefully.

Vises to hold wood are available in many forms. One is the multi-capability vise shown opposite, center right. The fixed jaw is L-shaped and may grasp the workpiece with either its horizontal or vertical leg. The movable straight jaw, along with its arm, can be quickly extracted and re-inserted at 90° to its first position to match either leg of the fixed L. The jaws have changeable hard and soft liners, grooved to handle cylindrical as well as flat stock. The maximum jaw opening is slightly more than 12 inches, and the movable jaw is articulated to handle wedge shapes. Rapid gross adjustment of the movable arm is achieved with a system of slots and a locking tooth; the fine adjustment range is controlled by a pair of hinge screws.

The base holds four dogs that fit in the jaw tops to grip irregular shapes. The vise may be rotated and locked in 45° increments on the base.

These metal saw horses are inexpensive, portable, and strong; they make a solid base for a temporary work table, and fold for storage.

With this vise mounted on one end of a work surface, long boards may be gripped for sawing. Clamp a pegged board vertically on the other end, hold one end of the board in the vise, and rest the other on a peg.

A pair of bench-top vises may also be used to hold long boards (bottom, right). These vises may be temporarily attached to the work surface by suction feet, supplied clamps, or screws or bolts, if you wish a more permanent arrangement. The bench-top vise shown here has articulating jaws—for handling wedge-shaped stock—plastic dogs, and holes for handling irregular shapes. It may be tilted up to a 45° angle in 15° increments off its base.

The aluminum jaw liners may be removed to expose the softer gripping surfaces behind, and there's a V groove in both the hard and soft jaws for holding cylindrical stock. Accessory items such as hold-down clamps and extra dogs are available.

The portable combination vise and worktable, shown at right, is the latest version of a basic design, with the advantages of several stages of development. It's self-supporting, with a 22×29-inch work surface when the tabletop jaws are fully opened. With the legs erected, the surface lies 32 inches off the ground; with the legs folded, the height drops to 24 inches.

There are several gripping modes. The rear vise jaw may be quickly set in one of three positions, providing maximum jaw openings of 9, 5½, and about 2 inches respectively. The fine gripping adjustment is made by turning two crank handles that advance the articulated front jaw.

By inserting dogs in both jaws, straight workpieces up to 16½ inches wide may be gripped on top; even wider pieces can be held using C clamps.

Another holding mode is unique; the entire front jaw may be lifted 90° and locked over the rear jaw. In this position, the movable jaw has a minimum opening of 0 inches and a maximum opening of 2 inches. This allows work to be slid flat and locked under the erect front jaw.

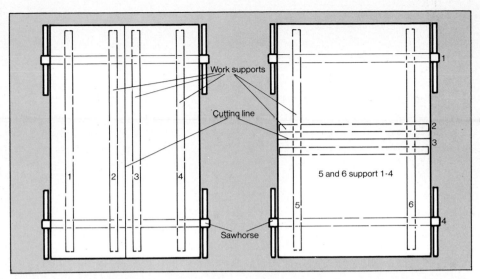

Panel ripping (left) needs only four supports placed parallel to the cut. To crosscut panels (right), place supports between horses, then four supports on top to hold the workpiece.

This combination vise and worktable provides an instant work surface, vise, tool-storage unit, and an overhead clamping device.

This vise has a convertible outer jaw, dogs, articulated jaws, interchangeable jaw liners, and 360° rotation.

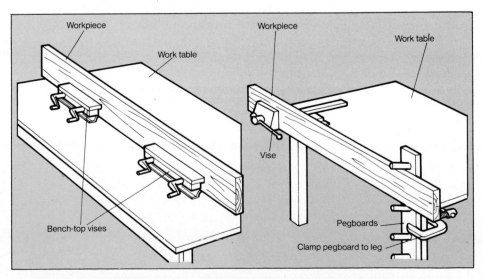

Long boards may be held by two bench-top vises or by a combination of a vise on one end of the workbench and a pegged board clamped at the opposite end.

SAWS, SAWING AIDS, AND GUIDES

Among stationary tools, the two most popular items are the radial and table saws. The basic functions of the radial saw are making cutoffs and shelf dadoes for casework; the table saw is used mainly for ripping. However, when either of these two saws is properly set up and accessorized, its abilities can be considerably extended, as has become increasingly apparent in the home-shop market since the end of World War II.

A **radial saw** on a stand by itself is of rather limited use. To trim or make a cutoff on a long board will not only be difficult and inefficient, it would be dangerous. But with long extension tables attached on either side of the tool, the job becomes simple. Set up a stop on one of these extensions, and you can saw any number of pieces to the same dimension.

A **table saw** can handle larger panels with greater ease by using a larger saw-table top, extension arms for the rip fence with an auxiliary supporting surface, and a large outfeed table that is about ¼ inch lower than the saw table itself.

In normal operation, the table saw miters with the sliding miter gauge set to the angle and the work pushed against the blade. The radial saw arm, in contrast, is set to the angle and the saw pulled across the workpiece, which rests against the fence.

Bevel cuts are made on the table saw by inclining the blade (some saws have a tilting tabletop, a considerably less desirable feature). On the radial saw, the motor and blade are inclined within the yoke.

Ripping is done on the table saw by setting the desired width between the blade face and rip fence and advancing the work. On the radial saw, the yoke (and blade) are rotated and locked at either the in-rip or out-rip position, the chute and anti-kickback pawls are adjusted to the workpiece, and the workpiece is advanced in the correct infeed direction.

Accessories common to both saws include special blades, hold-downs, dado cutters, molding heads and cutters, dust-collection systems, and shop-made jigs and fixtures, such as V miters and tenoning jigs. The table saw accepts a sliding universal jig, inserts for molding head and dadoes, a taper jig, miter gauge hold-down, and miter-gauge extensions. Accessories for the radial saw include molding-head guards, drill chuck, planer, and special tables.

A **bench-top band saw** is shown at bottom, right. It is a portable and relatively lightweight power tool that requires only a couple of square feet of storage space when not in use. In terms of function, this tool covers the range between a jig saw (or its hand equivalent, the bow saw) and the larger and considerably more expensive commercial stationary shop band saw.

The bench-top band saw's main task is cutting curves or irregular shapes, including notches. But it can also crosscut, miter-cut, and rip, with the aid of the supplied miter gauge, which fits in the table grooves. Although typical workpieces are less than 2 inches thick, you can cut pieces up to 4 inches thick (such as resawing tasks) and 10 inches wide; you are limited by the maximum vertical gap between the table and bottom of the upper guide bracket and the throat distance, that is, between the blade and the housing.

The band saw shown here has a 10 × 10-inch table that tilts up to 45° for beveling. The table is grooved to fit the miter gauge and has a machined recess for a blade insert that disperses the fibrous ripout waste as the blade teeth move downward past the workpiece.

Band saws use a blade in the form of a continuous loop. Straight cuts and mild curves require a blade ⅜ inch wide, while tighter curves demand progressively narrower blades,

The table saw will rip, crosscut, bevel, miter, taper, dado, mold, tenon, rabbet, slot, cove, disk-sand, and much more.

The radial saw will cutoff, rip, miter, dado, slot, mold, notch, bevel, rabbet, tenon with dado blades, drill, sand, and plane.

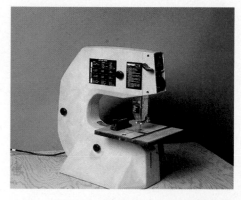

This bench-top band saw can rip, crosscut, bevel, resaw, cut freeforms, as well as sand by adding a belt adapter.

down to ⅛ inch wide. Blade widths run ⅛, ¼, and ⅜ inch and are designed to cut either wood, plastic or metal. In addition there's a sander/grinder belt and backup platen that can be substituted for the saw blade when needed.

The **jig saw** is the most common home-shop tool, second only to the drill—and with good reason. This tool and its accessories—such as the edge guide, trammel point, and special blades—can perform many tasks.

With a guide, the jig saw can cut straight lines. Curves can be made freehand. Here, as with the band saw, the tighter the radius, the narrower the blade, called a scroller blade. With the trammel and edge guide, you can cut perfect circles with ease. The platen or base can be tilted for bevel cutting; pocket cuts can be made with drilled starter holes at the corners or by plunge-cutting right through the workpiece, flattening the base on the work, and cutting away the internal waste.

Some jig saws have a rotating head above the blade holder, which can be unlocked for tight scrolling; others, such as the saw shown at right, have nine orbital positions to match the blade motion with the material and to maximize the speed.

Different blades are available to cut wood, plastic, or metal or for problem-material cutting. There are both fine- and coarse-toothed blades, as well as ultra-fine blades that can cut hardwood panel good side up. There are even special-purpose blades to cut roof shingles.

The **portable saw,** shown in use at top, right, is a no-nonsense tool that gets the job done. It has adjustments for depth of cut and bevel angle, like other portable saws, but that's where the similarity ends.

The worm-gear driven models are more expensive and heavier than the average saw. But their additional power, "side-winder" motor (the axis is 90° different from that of the average saw), industrial capacity, dual handles, extra-large adjustment locks, and better weight distribution make them worth their higher cost.

A portable worm-drive circular saw provides the ultimate in safe, controlled brute cutting force when used with a carbide blade.

This jig saw with an edge guide attached makes rip cuts easily. It also bevels, cuts perfect circles, and makes pocket cuts with ease.

You can load this protractor-based saw guide with a circular saw, as shown here, or with a router to crosscut or miter precisely and safely.

From the safety standpoint, the weight forward of the rear grip combines with the motor-shaft orientation to control kickback and reduce the saw reaction to a minimum in case you strike a nail, a knot, or anything else that impedes or binds the moving blade.

A quality portable saw will probably last a homeowner a lifetime, and it's one of those rare tools that's worth fixing in the unlikely event that repairs should ever be required.

Portable saws come in a variety of weights, power, blade sizes, and mechanical arrangements. Decide what you need before purchasing one.

SAWING GUIDES

If you need to make miters or cutoffs, either straight or beveled, on dimensioned lumber or similar workpieces, a radial saw with tables is the best tool for the job. But, if you don't happen to have one handy, here's a nifty alternative.

A **guide/work table** (page 11, bottom) is ready for use when you attach your portable saw to the carriage and place its plywood base on supports. It will handle workpieces up to $3\frac{3}{4} \times 17\frac{1}{2}$ inches, so there's no problem cutting a standard 2×12. There's a linear scale marked in inches on the fence and a degree-numbered scale on the protractor, with a fiducial mark on the clamp.

The saw carriage will also hold your router so that you can machine dadoes at angles from 0 to 45° in the crosscut mode or make a groove that runs with the grain if you lock the carriage to the rails and advance the workpiece along the fence.

A **rip-sawing guide** (upper right) is designed to help you rip properly supported plywood panel stock with your portable saw mounted on the carriage. The guide has a fence that rides along the straight edge of the workpiece. The saw carriage may be adjusted and locked to cut widths up to 24 inches, with either a straight or beveled blade adjustment. You may fit your jig saw or router to the carriage as well; with the router, for example, you can make dadoes, slots, and recesses for inlays.

The **aluminum guide** shown (bottom) comes in two sections: a single section can accommodate workpieces up to 4 feet long; two sections together handle pieces up to 8 feet long. It has its own clamps, whose heads fit into T slots in the extrusion. Dismantling or assembling the two 4-foot sections takes only a few seconds. When the guide is clamped in place on the workpiece, its low or flanged edge may be used for marking, scoring, and cutting with a utility knife. The flat edge or high side serves as a guide fence for portable saw, jig saw, or router.

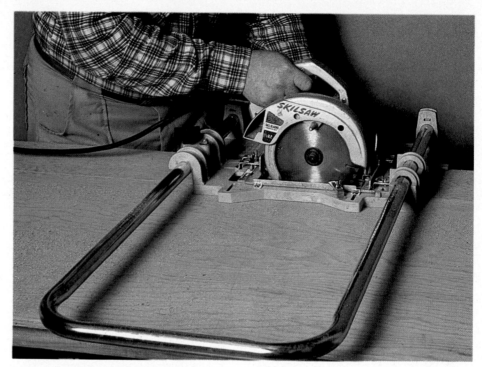

This guide will handle up to 24-inch cuts, armed with a portable saw, jig saw, or router. It's the perfect cutting aid for panel work.

You can mark, score, saw, or rout up to 8 feet with this guide, which breaks down into two 4-foot sections and has self-contained clamps.

FORMING, SHAPING, AND SMOOTHING

After sawing or blanking out component parts for a particular project, some additional work may be required (not including boring or joinery work). This work involves shaping, forming, and, to some extent, smoothing. Much of this work can be done quite rapidly using hand tools that are modified chisels or rasps.

The **spokeshave** is descended from the drawknife, a long, naked blade with end handles to pull or draw it toward the operator. The spokeshave has a narrow blade (typically less than 2 inches wide), mostly sheathed in a handled housing. There is a dual adjustment to increase or reduce the blade-edge exposure. The spokeshave can't remove stock as quickly as the drawknife, but it can be more accurately controlled.

The **block plane** is a small, adjustable low-angle plane that can be held in one hand. Its most popular use is probably scribing interior paneling for room corners. But it is also the perfect tool for breaking corners on wood projects, which means planing or sanding a tiny radius on edges that may prove dangerous or uncomfortable when handled. As you can readily see, both the block plane and the spokeshave are cleverly designed chisels.

Stanley's Surform® tools are a modern combination of the rasp and file. They are handles and blade holders of different shapes that support high-carbon tempered steel blades that have the appearance of expanded metal.

Surform® tools can do three jobs: (1) remove the maximum amount of waste—say, from the edge of a workpiece—when stroked along the edge at approximately a 45° angle; lesser angles will remove less stock; (2) smooth the edge if stroked parallel with it; (3) polish the edge when stroked at an angle slightly opposite the original angle.

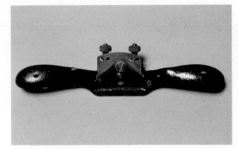

A spokeshave is the ideal tool for shaping concave, convex, or complex curves.

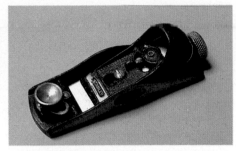

Block planes are hand tools used for scribing, breaking corners, and trimming.

The Surform® is both a rasp and a smooth file combined into one tool. Held at an angle to the work, it hogs; held parallel, it smooths.

The shaving-type former removes stock on the pull stroke.

The round-type former enlarges holes and shapes tight curves.

ROUTERS

Dollar for dollar, the router is probably the most useful and versatile tool that the home craftsman can buy. Not only will it cut slots, dadoes, rabbets, mortises, tenons, recesses, beads, coves, and otherwise decorate workpiece edges, but it will machine dovetail-drawer joinery, engrave freehand or pantographic letters and designs, emboss the front of cabinet doors and drawers, and trim plastic laminates. It can even be used as a light-duty shaper by mounting it, inverted, under a table with just the tool bit or portion of the tool bit exposed to the workpiece on the surface or edge.

The router tool bit is essentially a very high-speed rotating chisel that takes a very great number of little bites as it hogs out the waste. With routers, as with other power tools, there are two important factors: speed and feed. Speed is designed into the tool, but you must control the feed—that is, how quickly you move the tool through the work. Too slow a feed may burn the work and foul the bit. Too fast a speed will burn the bit and chop up the workpiece. You must always rout edges with the work to the *left* of the router, so to rout an outside edge, move the router counterclockwise.

The only adjustment you can make on the router itself is the plunge—that is, the depth that the tool bit goes into the work. The rule of thumb in routing is to make several passes, slowly increasing the tool bit's bite. Learning how to control the feed and adjust the plunge can only come from experience. It's a good idea to make test cuts on a piece of scrap wood.

Router bits have ¼-inch-diameter shanks (½ inch for industrial-grade models), and they are either high-speed steel or carbide-tipped. The best-quality bits are made with carbide tips and have replaceable roller-bearing guides.

The router, which is basically a high-speed chisel, cuts a dado accurately and quickly.

When mounted inverted under a worktable, the router becomes a light-duty shaper.

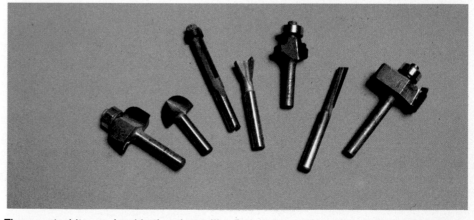
These router bits can do rabbeting, dovetailing, box coring, coving, ogee cutting, and trimming.

JOINTING AND SANDING

When working with hardwoods, it is necessary to start with one smooth, straight edge, which will ride against the rip fence on the saw. **The jointer** (at the top) converts rough edges into smooth ones in a jiffy. It can also do bevel jointing, face planing, and tapering.

Jointer blades are fixed on a rapidly spinning cutter head, which has a guard that snaps closed after the workpiece has passed. There's also a fence that can be angled over for bevel cuts or moved laterally to distribute the wear over the width of the entire cutter.

When cutting a workpiece with a saw, rip it just a touch oversize, say about 1/32 inch, and then run that edge through the jointer to remove the arc-shaped saw marks.

Sanding tools. Virtually all woodwork needs sanding. The basic idea of sanding is, first, to flatten the surface, and then, gradually, to make it smooth by using successively finer abrasives, each of which wipes out the grit marks of the previous one.

Two belt and two orbital sanders are shown at right. The first one (center, left) is a powerful machine that removes stock in a hurry, while at the same time flattening the surface and eliminating gross imperfections. Sand with the grain, down to a 60 grit.

The lighter-duty belt sander (center, right) is used to smooth out the sanding marks of the first one. Always sand with the grain, since it's difficult to remove cross-grain sanding marks. Use this tool down to 120 grit.

The half-sheet orbital pad sander (bottom, left) uses grits of aluminum oxide paper ranging from 40 to 150. It can be operated with either one or two hands. Move the tool over the work in overlapping arcs.

The quarter-sheet orbital pad sander (bottom, right) uses grits of aluminum oxide paper from 60 to 220 and is designed for one-handed use.

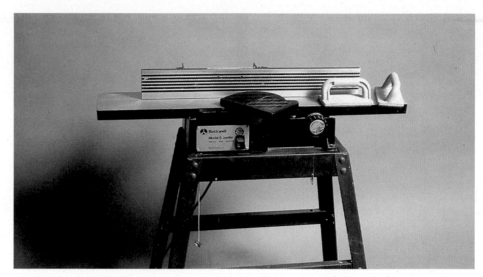

Jointers can taper, bevel, smooth, and flatten edges or faces of wood in one quick pass.

High power, auto-tracking, and a large 4-inch belt size characterize this belt sander.

This 3-inch belt sander provides moderate smoothing power.

This orbital 1/2-sheet pad sander can be used with one or two hands.

This 1/4-sheet orbital pad sander is used one-handed before applying the finish.

DRILLS, BITS, AND GUIDES

The directions for many of the projects in this book ask you to drill a hole that is perpendicular to the surface of the workpiece. Obviously, this can be done automatically with a drill press. However, if you don't have a drill press, use a drill guide to do the job correctly.

Older **drill guides** usually use a revolving drum—with different size holes—that is clamped over the work, with the drill inserted into the appropriate hole. Besides the limitations imposed by clamping and a number of bit types, this guide can produce only perpendicular holes.

Newer drill guides have centering dogs, variable-angle settings, depth stops, and V jaws for holding cylinders; they accept any spade bit or hole saw that fits through the base.

One is shown at the top, left, guiding a drill with a combination bit. Also shown is one style of combination bit made up of a hollow countersink and tapered twist bit. The two parts are integrated by tightening set screws with an Allen key.

A **bench-top drill press** (top, right) is light enough to travel and heavy enough to do the job. The head swivels 360° and the chuck accepts ½-inch shank drills. The head also carries a drill-storage index, variable-speed switch, chuck key-safety interlock, recommended speeds, work light, three-spoke quill crank, and knurled depth stops.

The metal table supporting the tool accepts drill-press vises; the distance from the center of the table hole to the post is 4½ inches, allowing you to drill at the center of a 9-inch circle on the table.

Also shown are some of the available drill bits and accessories. Plug cutters (bottom, left) should be used only on a drill press. Two sizes of plug cutters, the plugs they make, and the boring bits to make the matching holes in the workpiece are shown. Quality hole saws (bottom, right) have separate mandrels.

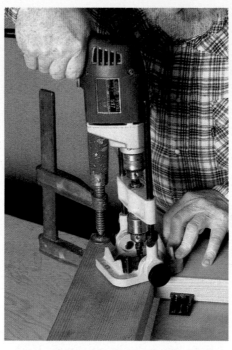

A drill guide will center holes and will control both the depth and the angle of drill entry.

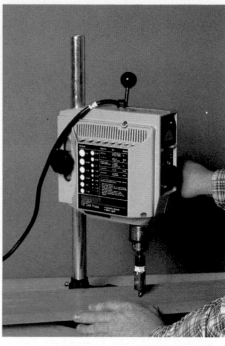

A portable bench-top press drills perpendicular holes and accepts many different bits.

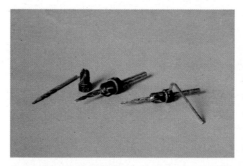

A combination drill has a tapered twist bit and locked countersink.

Three common bits for drill presses are spade, twist, and piloted boring.

Plug cutters cut wooden plugs that fit into holes cut by matched boring bits.

Larger holes may be cut out using a hole saw and mandrel chucked in a drill.

HARDWARE, PAINT, AND STAIN

Standard hardware is used in the projects throughout this book, except for a few special items, whose sources are listed in the project description.

Stainless steel screws are preferred for fastening those projects that may not receive a protective finish or do not have molding applied over screws. These screws may be obtained from industrial hardware suppliers. Where the screw finish is of secondary importance, hardened high-lead assembly screws are the choice; these may be obtained from industrial hardware suppliers, cabinetmakers' suppliers, or standard hardware or lumber suppliers.

Phillips head screws are preferred because their cross-head slots facilitate rapid installation, with either hand or power tools.

Most of the bolts specified are standard carriage types, but it's worth the slight extra cost to buy them galvanized. The hasps and hinges called for are found in standard hardware catalogues and therefore should be readily available.

It is a good practice to spray all hardware that will be used externally (not screws, nails, or bolts) with an exterior metal primer, and then with an exterior-finish metal paint.

Only one project, the Lighting Enclosures, requires electrical parts, all of which are standard items that can be purchased at any electrical supply store.

All projects or parts of projects that require painting should be painted first with an exterior primer and then an exterior-finish paint. Projects that are both stained and painted should have semi-transparent stain applied to the main T1–11 parts. Doors, molding, trim, and other parts are most easily painted separately, then installed and touched up later. Galvanized plumbing parts that require painting must be cleaned first with a vinegar and water solution.

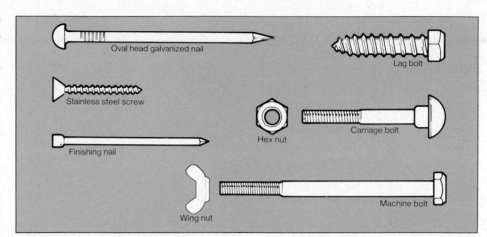

Assorted fastener hardware used to join wooden components together when assembling the projects in this book.

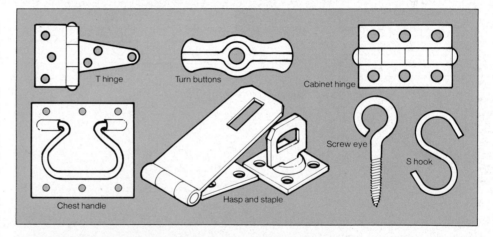

Standard hardware used in building the projects in this book. Spray these with a coat of metal primer, and then a finish coat for durability.

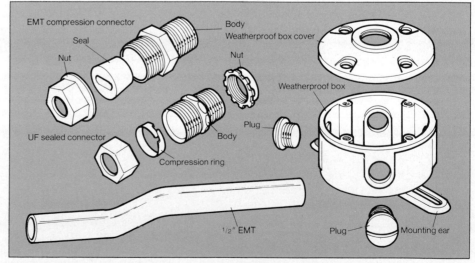

Metal, weatherproof, electrical parts used in the Lighting Enclosure project, to join the UF cable to the lighting fixtures.

SAFETY FIRST

When you're working in your shop, and especially when using power tools, there are certain precautions that you should *always* take, as well as certain things you should *never* do:

• *Always* be sure that you've got a safe electrical setup; be sure that no circuit is overloaded, and there is no danger of short-circuiting, especially in wet locations.

• *Always* read the labels on containers of paint, solvent, and other chemical products; observe ventilation, and all other warnings.

• *Always* read the tool manufacturer's instructions for using the tool, especially the warnings.

• *Always* use holders or pushers to work pieces shorter than 3 inches on a jointer. Avoid working short pieces if you can.

• *Always* remove the key from any drill chuck (portable or press) before starting up.

• *Always* pay deliberate attention to how a tool works so that you can avoid being injured. For example, always observe the proper infeed direction and correct use of the anti-kickback pawls and chute when ripping stock on a radial saw.

• *Always* make sure that any adjustment is locked before proceeding. For example, always check the rip fence on a table saw or the bevel adjustment on a portable saw before starting to work.

• *Always* prevent the workpiece from spinning on a drill (press or portable). It will tend to spin clockwise, the same as the drill rotation. Clamp and block the piece whenever necessary.

• *Always* wear a mask when sanding or handling chemicals.

• *Always* wear eye protection, especially when striking metal on metal; a chip can fly off—for example, when hammering a chisel.

• *Always* know the limitations of your tools. Don't try to force them to do what they weren't designed to do.

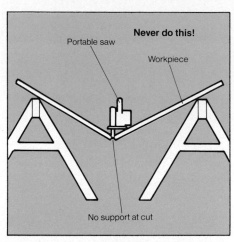

Kerf will close in unsupported area, jamming the blade, and causing kickback.

Eye protection must be used at all times when operating power tools.

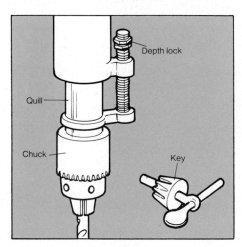

Always remove the chuck key before starting up a drill or drill press.

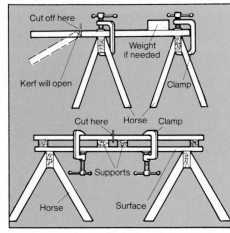

Use these safe methods when cutting off workpieces with portable saws.

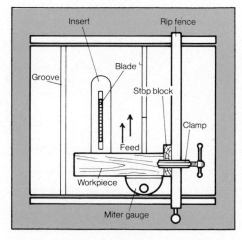

Use a stop block to prevent kickback when crosscutting short pieces.

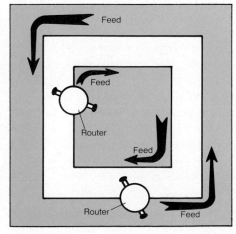

Always rout edges with work at left, feeding into the router bit from the right.

For example, don't force a thick piece of very dense wood such as maple through a consumer-grade table saw in one pass—use several shallow passes instead. Whenever possible, use carbide blades; they're cheaper in the long run—and safer.

• *Always* be aware that there is never time for your body's reflexes to save you from injury from a power tool in a dangerous situation; everything happens too fast. *Be alert!*

• *Always* keep your hands away from the business ends of blades, cutters, and bits. Use push sticks, jigs, and hold-downs instead of touching the workpiece.

• *Always* try to hold a portable saw with both hands so that you will know where your hands are.

• *Always* use a drill with an auxiliary handle to control the torque when large size bits are involved.

• *Never* work with power tools when you're tired or under the influence of alcohol or drugs.

• *Never* work with very small pieces of stock. Whenever possible, cut small pieces off larger pieces.

• *Never* change a blade or a bit unless the power cord is unplugged. Don't depend on the switch alone being off; you might accidentally hit it.

• *Never* work in insufficient light.

• *Never* work with loose clothing, hanging hair, open cuffs, or jewelry.

• *Never* work with dull tools. Have them sharpened, or learn how to do it yourself.

• *Never* use a power tool on a workpiece that is not firmly supported or clamped.

• *Never* saw a workpiece that spans a large distance between horses without close support on either side of the kerf; the piece can bend, closing the kerf and jamming the blade, causing saw kickback.

• *Never* support a workpiece with your leg or other part of your body if you intend to cut it with a portable or jig saw.

• *Never* carry sharp or pointed tools, such as utility knives, awls, or chisels in your pocket. If you want to carry tools, use a special-purpose tool belt with leather pockets and holders.

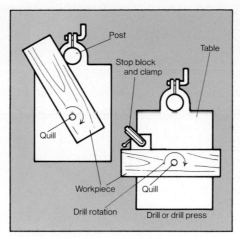

Always block small workpieces to prevent spinning while they are being drilled.

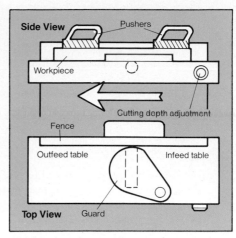

On jointers and planers, always leave guard in place, and use friction sole pushers.

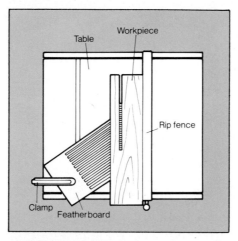

Use a featherboard to hold the workpiece against the rip fence.

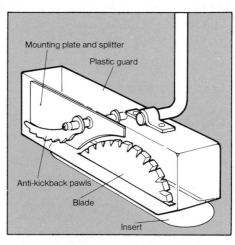

Always use the blade guard on a table saw when blade comes up through work.

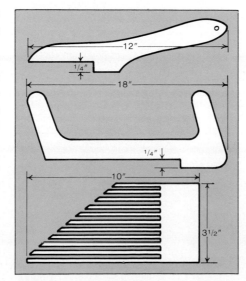

Make your own push sticks and featherboards, and use them for safety's sake.

Always keep the work area around power tools clear of all potential hazards.

UMBRELLA TABLE

No backyard area is really complete without an umbrella and an umbrella table. This redwood umbrella table has a smart-looking herringbone table-top pattern; it is strong, thanks to its triangular bracing with through-bolted supports, and it is large enough to hold any umbrella with ease.

In addition to these advantages, the table isn't difficult to build. A glance at the instructions shows that almost everything on the table is based on four-time symmetry. There are four cross members on top, four on the bottom, four legs, four diagonal braces, and a four-part symmetrical top.

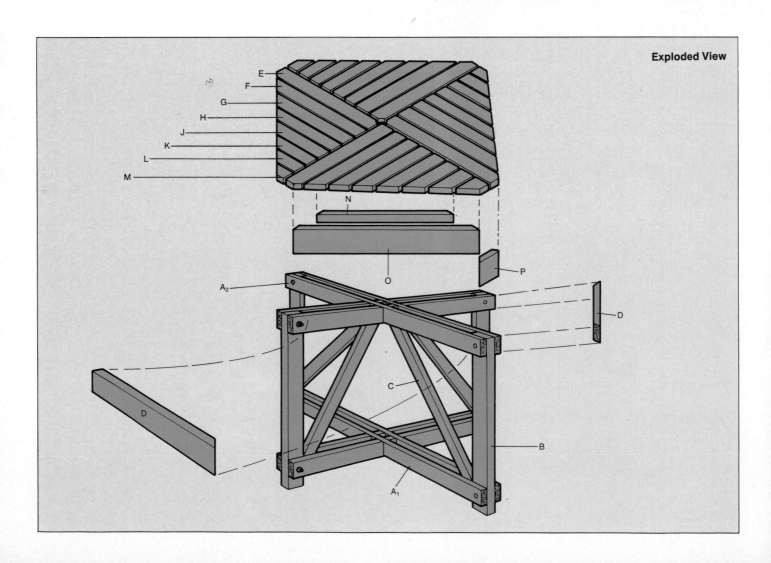

Exploded View

BILL OF MATERIALS

Qty	Size	Material
2	2×4×14′	Construction heart redwood
3	2×4×10′	Clear heart redwood
2	2×4×12′	Clear heart redwood
2	1×12×14′	Clear heart redwood
8	3/8×51/2″	Carriage bolts, nuts, washers
76	#8×11/2″	Flat head, Phillips head, stainless steel wood screws
	8d	Galvanized nails
	10d	Galvanized nails

PARTS LIST

All parts clear heart redwood, except A2

Part	Name	Qty	Description
A1	Cross member	4	11/2″×31/2″×60″
A2	Cross member	4	11/2″×31/2″×60″, ConHR
B	Legs	4	11/2″×31/2″×293/4″
C	Diagonal braces	4	11/2″×31/2″×345/8″
D	Spanner	4	11/2″×31/2″×351/2″
E	Board	4	3/4″×31/2″×32″
F	Board	4	3/4″×31/2″×30″
G	Board	4	3/4″×31/2″×26″

Part	Name	Qty	Description
H	Board	4	3/4″×31/2″×22″
J	Board	4	3/4″×31/2″×18″
K	Board	4	3/4″×31/2″×14″
L	Board	4	3/4″×31/2″×10″
M	Board	4	3/4″×31/2″×6″
N	Nailer	4	11/16″×11/16″×42″
O	Skirt trim	4	3/4″×41/4″×42″
P	Skirt trim	4	3/4″×41/4″×8″

Note: Pieces D, N, O, and P must be fitted. Pieces E–M will form a stepped edge that must be trimmed.

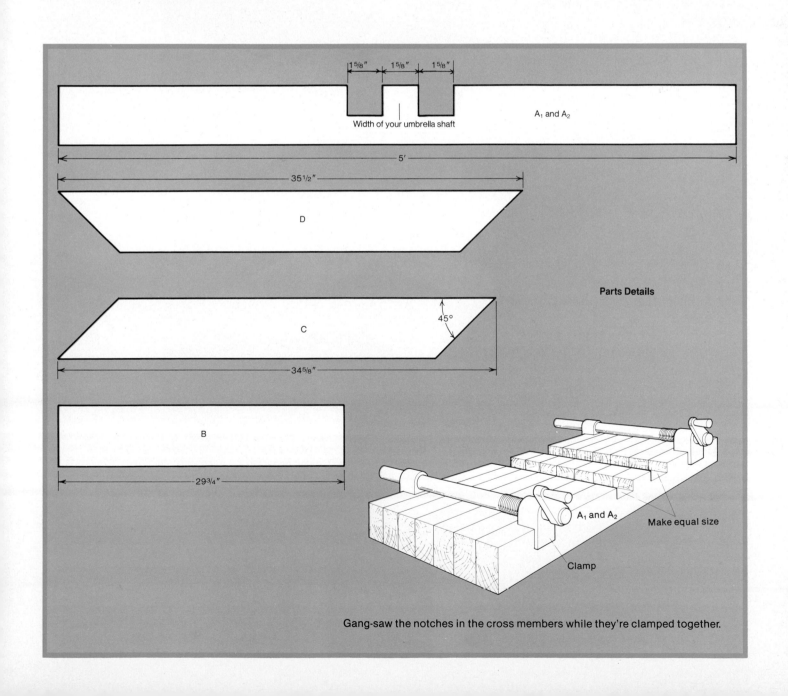

Parts Details

Gang-saw the notches in the cross members while they're clamped together.

STEP 1
CUTTING AND ASSEMBLING THE CROSS MEMBERS

Trim the cross members to length and saw their notches. To do this, use the gang-sawing method shown in the cutting diagram, either with a radial saw or with a portable saw and chisel. The upper cross, which will hardly be visible, may be made from construction heart redwood to economize a bit. Assemble the crosses by locking the notches (half-lap joints) and driving a 10d nail into each joint.

STEP 2
ASSEMBLING THE LEGS AND CROSSES

Set the upper cross on its back on a work surface, and place the leg tops between the four cross pair ends. Clamp the sandwich, and check for a right angle where the leg and cross members join, using a square. Then drill through the sandwich at all four positions, and install the bolts.

Set the structure on its legs and fit the lower cross to the legs, $3\frac{1}{2}$ inches off the ground (the width of a 2×4). Again, clamp the sandwiches together, drill, and bolt.

STEP 3
INSTALLING THE BRACES AND SPANNERS

Saw the 45° miters on the diagonal braces and insert all four of them between the two crosses. Make sure that the upper ends touch the inner part of the cross and the lower ends touch the inner edges of the legs. Check carefully with a carpenter's or rafter square to see if you're maintaining the right angles between the crosses and the legs before you clamp and drive in the 10d nails to lock the structure.

Make 45° bevels on both ends of the four spanners. The spanners provide a firm structure to support the outer ends of the tabletop boards later on, so when you install them, make sure that both ends are solidly nailed or screwed in place and that they are equidistant from the center of the cross. A good check is to see if

ASSEMBLING THE CROSS MEMBERS

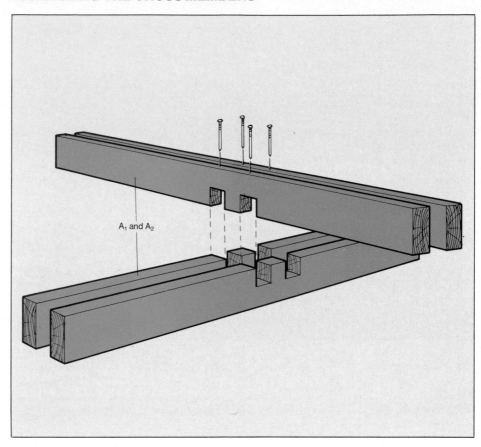

Test-fit the notches in the upper and lower cross members of each assembly, and check for square. If correct, nail members together through the joints.

ASSEMBLING THE LEGS AND CROSSES

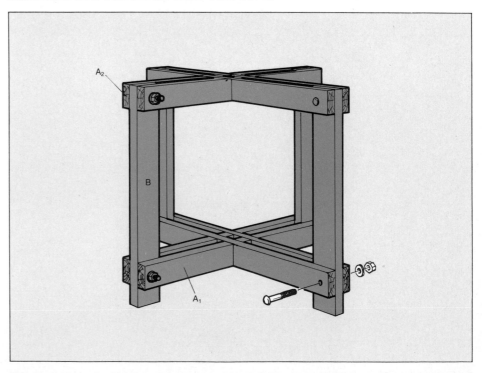

Place top cross assembly on table, clamp legs in place, drill, and bolt. Stand assembly over lower cross and raise lower cross to position. Clamp, drill, and bolt.

the four spanners form a true square when they're all in place. Also, make sure they're flush with the upper cross members.

STEP 4
CUTTING AND INSTALLING THE TOP BOARDS

A radial saw is the best tool to use to trim boards fresh from the lumberyard to the lengths required for the tabletop boards. However, this can be done with a portable saw and a fine-toothed blade operating with a guide, or by using a portable saw to cut the long boards into reasonable lengths and then finishing them on a table saw.

The table saw is the fastest and most accurate tool to use for ripping out 3½-inch-wide boards from a 1 × 12 (¾ × 11¼ inches actual size), already trimmed to the various lengths.

Installing the tabletop boards carefully will pay dividends in stability for years, so accuracy is the key to success here. The first board to be installed will be the longest one in whatever quadrant you choose. All boards will be spaced ¼ inch apart, gauged by a scrap piece of ¼-inch-thick plywood or similar material.

Aluminum or stainless steel nails are best for installing these boards. Set the nails with a punch; either putty or a small amount of redwood caulk can be used to plug the set holes. Finally, a quick sanding will render the work virtually invisible.

The first board's edge should be parallel to and ⅛ inch away from the theoretical centerline between the pairs of upper cross members. The inner end of the first board should be ⅛ inch away from the theoretical centerline of the adjacent pair of cross members. This may sound complicated, but look at the drawings carefully, and it will soon make sense. As you nail on the progressively shorter boards, make sure that the inner end of each one is exactly ⅛ inch from your theoretical centerline. An easy way to do this is to nail a guide completely across the area so the ends of the boards will butt against it.

INSTALLING THE BRACES AND SPANNERS

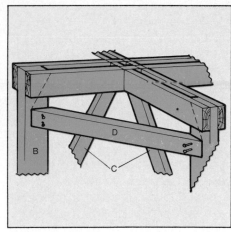

Diagonal braces keep the leg-cross assembly squared up. Insert braces between the cross members from the bottom outside to the top inside in all four positions.

Install the spanners with beveled ends in the four open areas of the upper cross as an outer support for the top boards.

INSTALLING THE TOP BOARDS

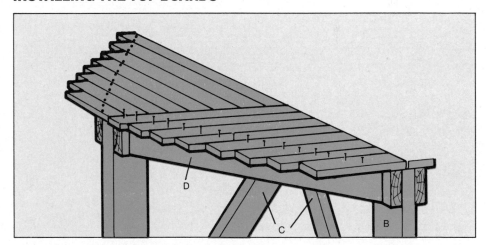

1. Install boards in four groups, 90° opposed. Space them ¼ inch apart and nail in place with aluminum or stainless steel nails (or stainless steel screws). Make sure that all nails are set or that all screws are countersunk.

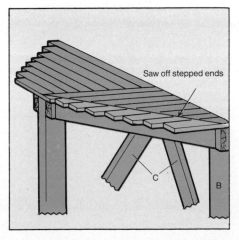

2. Snap a chalk line, as described in the text, and cut along this line with the aid of guide and fine-toothed saw.

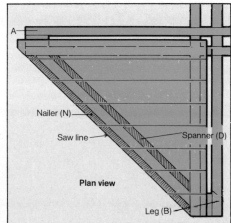

3. Add the nailer underneath the edge of the boards, and sand smooth. Also chamfer the top edge of the boards.

The outer ends of the boards will have a stepped appearance, which will be trimmed off later. When you start the second quadrant, remove the guide, and space out ¼ inch. That's where the first and longest board will go. When you've nailed all the boards in place, mark the two locations on the surface under which the outer corner of the end of the cross member is located for a particular quadrant. Snap a chalk line between these points. Saw along the line with the aid of a guide, removing the stepped ends and leaving a clean edge. Do this in all four quadrants.

STEP 5
INSTALLING THE NAILERS AND TRIM

Now, fit the nailer, with 45° miters at both ends, under the outer edges of the boards, flush with these edges and with the mitered ends tight against the cross members. Clamp these nailers in place. Drill holes through the boards into the nailers in a straight line, using a combination bit. Drive in the screws, and remove the clamps. Bevel-plane the board edge slightly for a smart appearance.

Fit up the long and short skirt trim, but remember that the end bevels are now 22½°. Clamp the wood in place, drill the holes, and drive in the screws. Be careful not to drill and drive in spaces where there already are other screws. With the skirts in place, you can appreciate the effect of the slight bevel you have just planed.

STEP 6
DRILLING THE CENTER HOLE

Saw a piece of 2 × 4 scrap into a square plug, and tap this up into the square hole at the center of the top cross. Then, load your drill with a holesaw; you'll probably need a 1½- or 1⅝-inch-diameter fit, depending on the umbrella being used. Center the holesaw and insert the ¼-inch-diameter pilot into the square plug. Drill the hole and drive out the plug. Set up your umbrella!

INSTALLING THE NAILERS AND TRIM

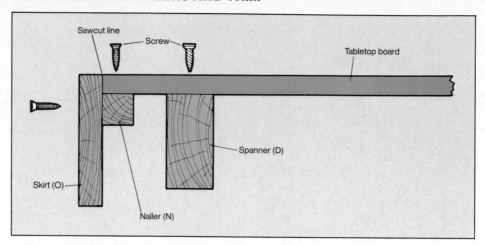

Cross-sectional view of tabletop edge shows the spanner supporting the boards and the nailer, just underneath the board edge and screwed to it. The skirt trim girdling the outside of the tabletop is screwed to the nailer, flush against the table boards.

DRILLING THE CENTER HOLE

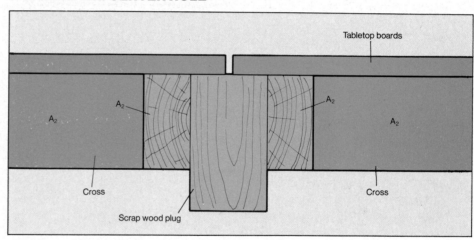

1. The hole formed at the cross centers receives your umbrella post. But, the tabletop boards now cover this hole in the top. The pilot of your hole saw needs an anchor, so tap a filler plug into the cross notch to pick up the pilot.

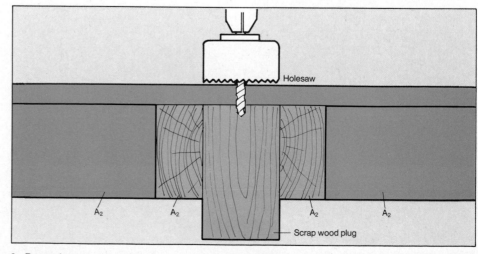

2. Press down on your drill, forcing the pilot through the ¼-inch space between all the boards at the center. Saw out a circular hole, and tap out the plug.

SLING CHAIR

There are a number of built-in advantages that make this little backyard sling chair both an interesting and a worthwhile project to tackle.

On the practical side, it helps to relieve the usual shortage of storage space for your outdoor furniture, barbecue, umbrellas, and related paraphernalia during the winter. Our chair has a knock-down design; four or five of them can fit in the space of one non-folding chair.

As for appearance, this chair makes a handsome addition to any yard, with its sculptured redwood frame and brightly colored canvas sling, which can be changed in less than a minute for a bit of variety.

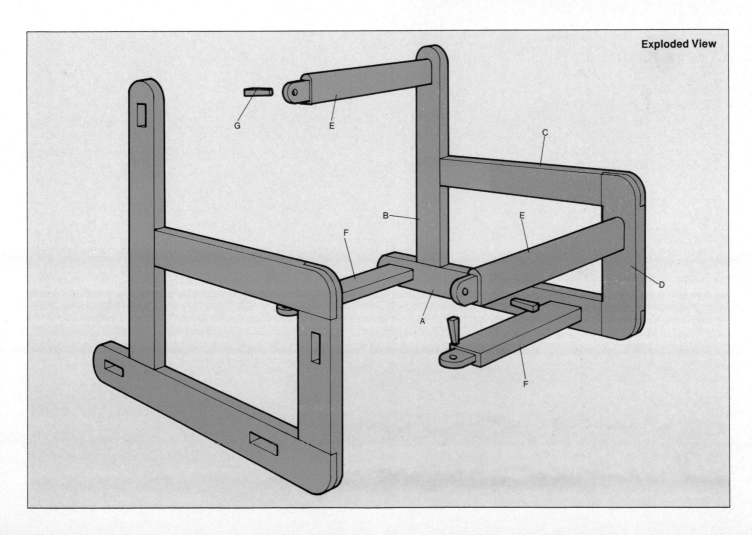

Exploded View

BILL OF MATERIALS

Qty	Size	Material
1	2×6×14′	Clear heart redwood
1	2×6×12′	Clear heart redwood
36	#8×1½″	Flat head, Phillips head, stainless steel wood screws
1	27×72″	Canvas

PARTS LIST

All parts clear heart redwood

Part	Name	Qty	Description
A	Base	2	1½″ × 5½″ × 29¾″
B	Back leg	2	1½″ × 5½″ × 32½″
C	Arms	2	1½″ × 5½″ × 24″
D	Front leg	2	1½″ × 5½″ × 25⅞″
E	Top stretcher	2	1½″ × 2½″ × 33″
F	Bottom stretcher	2	1½″ × 2½″ × 33″
G	Wedge	8	½″ × ⅞″ × 4½″

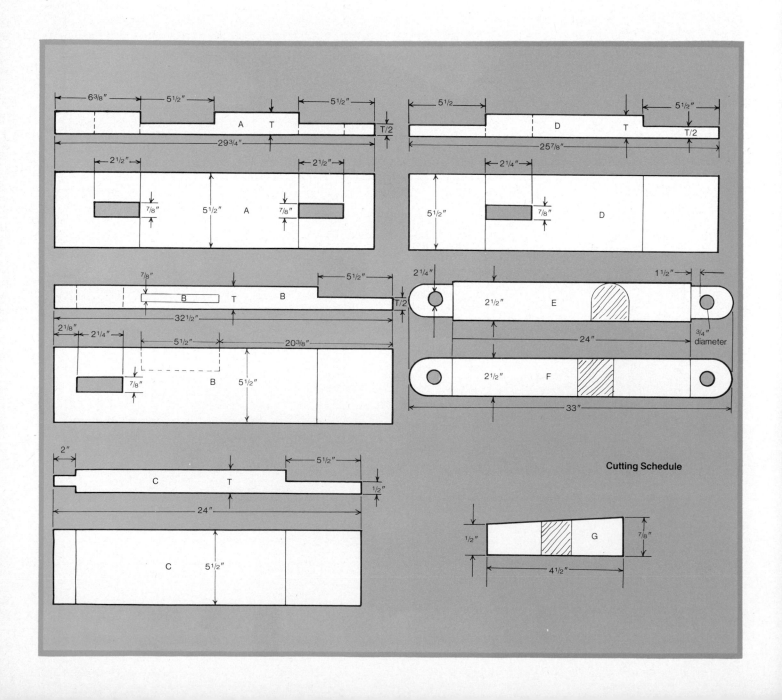

Cutting Schedule

Structurally, this sling chair uses two modular sides, held together by four stretchers. The tenoned ends of the stretchers are seated firmly in mortises cut into the sides and are locked into them by friction wedges, lightly tapped into holes drilled in the tenon protrusions.

The support sling provides a continuous seat and backrest. Two of the stretchers are enclosed in pockets that are stitched in the ends of this sling, thereby supporting it, while a third arm of the sling, under tension to the rear lower stretcher, provides stability.

STEP 1
CUTTING MORTISES AND TENONS IN THE SIDE PIECES

Once you've looked over the drawings, saw out the parts blanks, and prepare to machine or handcraft the half laps, mortises, and tenons; the method you use depends on personal taste and available shop facilities.

Each chair side requires one blind mortise-and-tenon joint and three half lap joints. Let's start with the mortise and tenon.

Generally it's easier to fit a tenon to a mortise, so complete the mortises first. Lay out the mortise with the aid of a combination square and folding or flexible rule. If you're making them by hand, drill a series of closely spaced, two-inch-deep holes within the rectangular marking. Any good drill guide will help you control the depth and ensure that the hole is perpendicular to the surface.

Before power tools became available, carpenters bored these holes with a bit and brace. If you've got a steady hand and a sharp eye, you might wish to give this method a try.

Either way, with most of the waste already removed from the mortise, select the widest chisel you have that will fit along the length or width. Hold the tool vertically with the edge on the outline, the bevel side facing inward, and shear down the walls in one motion for each position, clearing away the remaining wood. Clean the bottom of the mortise with a

CUTTING THE BLIND MORTISES

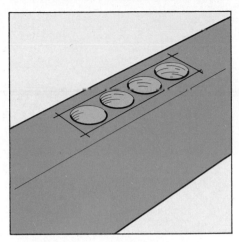

1. Drill a line of holes within the mortise layout to remove the majority of the waste wood.

2. Chisel down the inside walls of mortise, removing waste wood and smoothing. Flat of chisel should face outward.

CUTTING THE STRETCHER TENONS

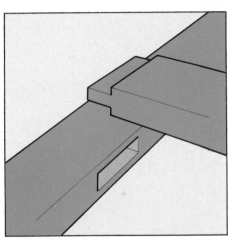

1. Two-shouldered arm tenon fits into the blind mortise of back leg.

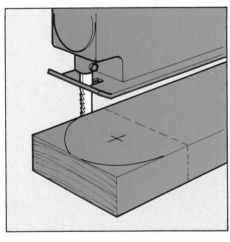

2. Lay tenon on end, including hole center and shoulder stop line. Jig saw the profile to shape, and sand smooth.

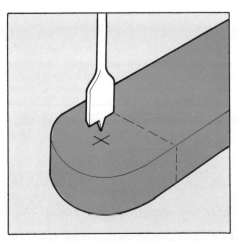

3. Drill the center hole now; any splintering or roughness due to drilling will be removed in the next step.

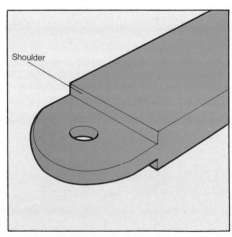

4. Remove the waste with a back saw, with the workpiece held in a vise or with a table saw, radial saw, or router and jig.

chisel that is slightly narrower than the mortise's width.

Those who own drill presses with mortising attachments have the option to machine the mortises completely. But, if you lack a full-size hollow chisel and its bit (as would probably be the case with large mortises), just make overlapping cuts with the size you have.

Mark the two tenon shoulders (only two stop marks are needed) and the thickness on the end and edges.

If you're going to make the tenons by hand, score the shoulder and edge stop lines with a sharp knife to break the grain. Then, with the workpiece held horizontally in a vise or miter box, make the crosscut with a fine-toothed back or fret saw. Clamp the piece vertically, and saw away the waste on both sides, leaving the completed tenon.

Tenons may be cut easily on a radial or table saw with dado blades, or with a universal jig and single blade on a table saw. Depth of cut must be adjusted in all cases to leave a 3/4-inch-thick tenon.

If you're using dado blades on a radial saw, hold the workpiece against the fence with the arm at 0°; on a table saw, hold it against the miter gauge set at 0°.

When using a table saw and jig, hold the piece against the miter gauge, set at 0°, and make the stop cuts. Then, clamp the piece vertically in the jig, and make the second cut to remove the waste.

The half laps must be marked on both pieces that will form the joint and then be machined on a radial or table saw using a dado set. The description of the slat chair project explains the general method, but for this project the radial saw arm and table saw miter gauge will be set at 0°.

STEP 2
ASSEMBLING THE SIDES

After a trial fit of all chair side pieces, complete their assembly with screws, but keep the corners clear of screws. With a compass, mark radii at all the corners of the

ASSEMBLING THE SIDES

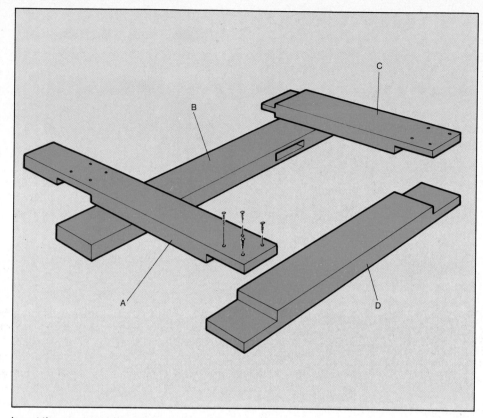

Insert the arm tenon into the back-leg blind mortise. Place all the half lap joints in position. Drill holes, and drive screws to assemble. Keep corners clear.

ROUTING THE EDGES

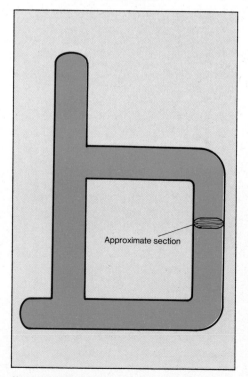

Jig saw all curves at corners, and sand smooth. With a router and rounding-over bit, shape all edges, inside and outside.

TEST-FITTING THE WEDGES

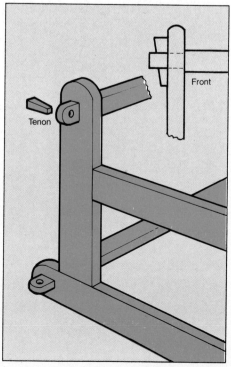

Insert the radiused and pierced stretcher tenons into the through-mortises in the sides; check the fit, including wedges.

side pieces, and finish them off with band or jig saw and belt sander.

STEP 3
MAKING STRETCHER MORTISES AND TENONS

Mark out and cut the mortises in the side assemblies that will receive the stretcher tenons. Here, the mortises are not blind but completely pierce the sides. Therefore, to avoid splintering, provide scrap backups tight against the second sides of the mortises.

Make the tenons using the same method you used for the side pieces. But, after marking the tenon and wedge holes, drill the holes first, and then cut the tenon itself. Note that the front and rear top stretcher are contoured on their top surfaces and that the tops of the tenons reduced 1/4 inch to compensate.

STEP 4
ROUTING THE EDGES

Assemble the sides and stretchers with the wedges as a trial fit. If all's well, disassemble the sling chair and set the sides on a work surface. Then, finish all side edges, both inside and out, with a router equipped with a 3/8-inch-radius rounding-over bit with roller guide (as in the Slat Chair project base). Then, sand all surfaces smooth.

STEP 5
MAKING AND INSTALLING THE SLING

Assemble the chair and measure the fit of the sling with muslin; include the end pockets and the tail that picks up the rear lower stretcher in a pocket. Buy bright-colored canvas for the sling. Double and seam the edges, and sew in the stretcher pockets. Add the tail with its pocket. Then, assemble the stretchers to one side of the chair, slip on the sling, and add the second side. Tap the wedges home with a soft-faced hammer.

ASSEMBLING THE CHAIR

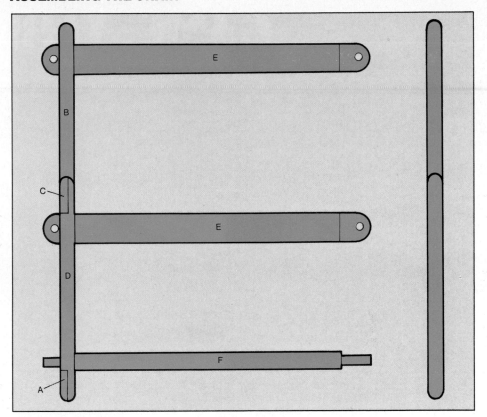

With wedges removed, one or both sides may be removed by pulling straight out. This method is used to install or remove the sling for cleaning or repair.

MAKING THE SLING

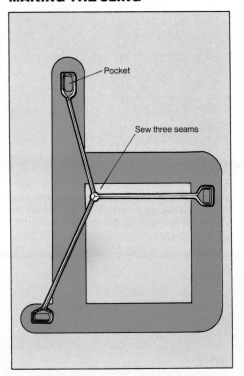 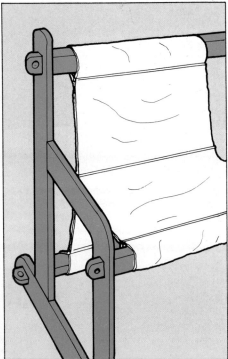

1. The main part of the sling goes from the rear to front stretcher, while the tail goes to the rear to hold the shape.

2. This chair is designed for a 6-footer. To lower the seat, lower the front stretcher an inch or two.

GAME TABLE

Both kids and grownups will enjoy this all-wood gaming table. It's designed for both indoor and outdoor use, and it's lightweight yet stable. The game-board insert can be flipped over for instant conversion from backgammon to checkers or chess.

The tabletop is equipped with four chip pockets, one for each seated player. These make it appropriate for most board games, as well as card games and mah jongg.

The basic building material is redwood, which is used for the feet, legs, supporting structure, and game-board support. The game board itself is made from a particle-board core that is veneered on all surfaces. The veneers on the top and bottom surfaces are chess and backgammon marquetry arrays with a mitered mahogany border and a matching edge. The entire game board has several coats of protective urethane varnish.

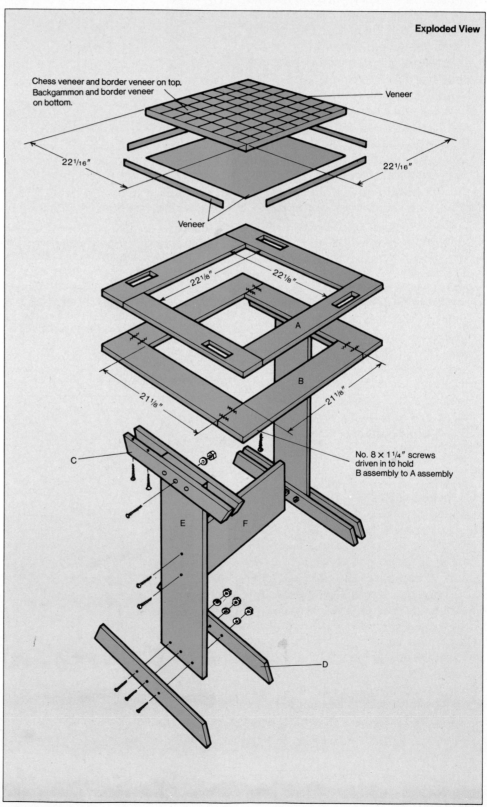

Exploded View

Chess veneer and border veneer on top. Backgammon and border veneer on bottom.

Veneer

22 1/16"

22 1/16"

Veneer

22 1/8"

22 1/8"

A

B

21 1/8"

21 1/8"

C

E

F

No. 8 × 1 1/4" screws driven in to hold B assembly to A assembly

D

BILL OF MATERIALS

Qty	Size	Material
1	5/4 × 12 × 10'	Clear heart redwood
1	1 × 12 × 10'	Clear heart redwood
1	3/4 × 22 × 22"	Particle board
1	18 × 18"	Checkerboard 78C3W assembled veneer*
1	20 × 20"	Backgammon 47BG20 assembled veneer*
1	pint	Veneer cement*
12	5/16 × 31/2"	Carriage bolts, nuts, washers
16	#10 × 3"	Flat head, Phillips head, stainless steel wood screws

Qty	Size	Material
60	#8 × 11/4"	Flat head, Phillips head, stainless steel wood screws
8	1/2 × 5"	Steel corrugated fasteners
1	pint	Urethane varnish

*Available from Constantine, 2050 Eastchester Road, Bronx, NY 10461. Tel: 1-800-223-8087.

PARTS LIST

All parts clear heart redwood, except G

Part	Name	Qty	Description
A	Upper top piece	4	3/4" × 5" × 271/8"
B	Lower top piece	4	3/4" × 51/2" × 265/8"
C	Beam	4	11/16" × 211/16" × 24"
D	Feet	4	11/16" × 211/16" × 32"
E	Leg	2	11/16" × 81/2" × 29"
F	Stretcher	1	11/16" × 51/2" × 2313/16"
G	Core	1	3/4" × 22" × 22", particle board

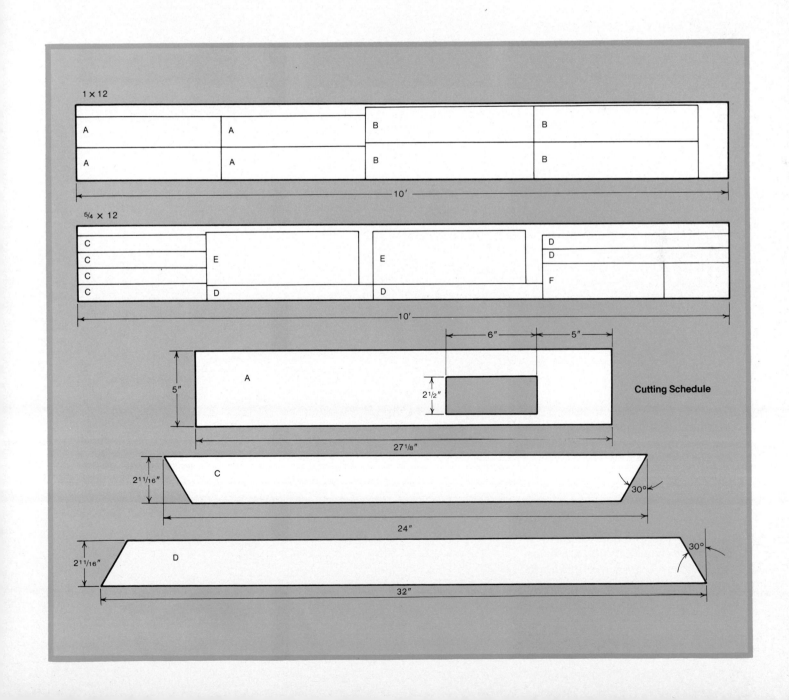

Cutting Schedule

MAKING THE GAME BOARD

It will probably take you about as long to make the game board as it will to make the rest of the table. First, saw the particle board to size. If the veneer is somewhat lumpy, follow the supplier's instructions for flattening it out before use.

Mark the outline for the chess marquetry array on one side of the board, for the backgammon array on the other. Then, tape the border pieces in position, with each one overlaying its neighbor. Double cut the 45° corner miters, as you would when making wall-covering matches. Make sure to identify each piece and its matching board location.

The veneer supplier furnishes a work sheet that explains the whole procedure. He also supplies veneer cement and saws. Here are a few additional tips that you may find useful.

The veneer is attached with contact cement, which is applied to both the core and the back of the veneer. The cement must be allowed to dry until a brown paper bag (Kraft paper) can be slid across the surface without grabbing. The veneer sticks where you put it, so get it right the first time. You can prevent mistakes by slipping a waxed paper separator between the core and the veneer as you move them into position.

Note that the game arrays are held together by thin paper and glue. The contact cement is applied to the other side. After the arrays have been cemented to the core and dried, the paper attached to the finish side must be removed carefully by applying a mist of water, followed by scraping; a repeat performance may be necessary.

Veneer the edge first, the game array second, and the border last. After the veneer pieces are laid down, they must be set by striking a small, flat, wooden block randomly over the surface. Trim the edges carefully with a razor blade, sharp utility knife, or sanding block. When everything is set, cleaned, sanded, and wiped with a tack cloth, apply the varnish.

MAKING THE CHIP POCKETS

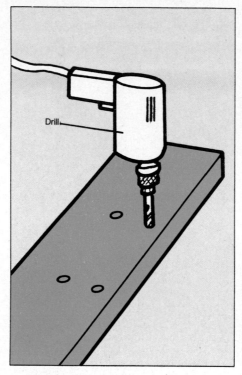

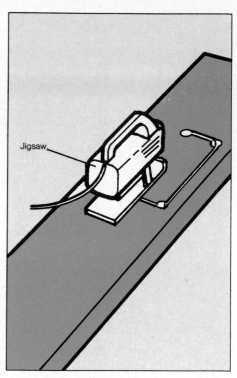

1. Drill the jig-saw starting holes in all four corners of the chip pocket layout on the four A pieces.

2. Place the workpiece so that the good face is down. Insert the jig-saw blade into a hole, and saw out the pocket.

ASSEMBLING THE TABLETOP

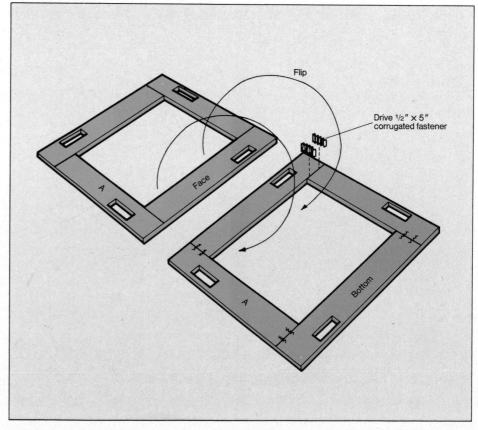

Flip the four A pieces so that their good sides face down. Drive in four pairs of fasteners. Do the same to the top sides of the B pieces for temporary assembly.

MAKING THE TABLE

Most of the woodwork is straight-forward and will pose no problems; however, the following shop notes may be helpful.

The tabletop is a laminate consisting of an upper and lower section. The upper section pieces have chip-pocket cutouts, which are made with drill and jigsaw. The lower section provides the base for these pockets and includes a small four-sided ledge that supports the game board.

Identify the table parts as you cut them out. Note that both upper and lower sections are temporarily assembled with corrugated fasteners. This keeps all parts together until the two sections can be screw-assembled with the overlapping joints.

When you are ready to drill through and bolt up the sandwich formed by beams and legs at the upper end, or feet and legs at the lower end, clamp all the parts together to freeze them in proper position. Use a carpenter's or rafter square to ensure a right angle at these assembly points.

Make sure to be careful when you drill and screw through the beams into the laminated table support. Avoid the chip pockets and be careful to use depth control on your drill to avoid piercing the A section.

PREPARING BEAMS, LEGS, AND TOP FOR ASSEMBLY

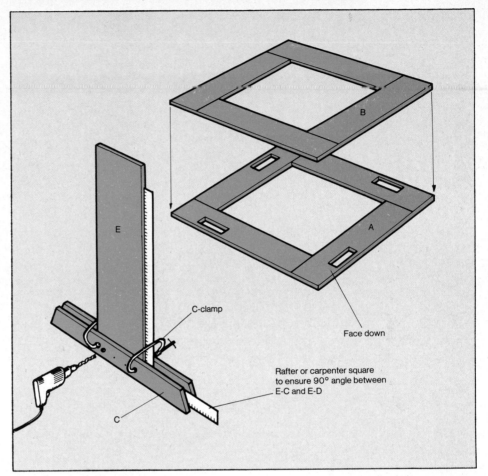

Place lower top assembly over upper top assembly, and screw together. Avoid hitting chip pockets. Square and clamp legs into sandwiches with both beams and feet, for accuracy, before drilling the assembly bolt holes.

SCREWING TOP TO BEAMS

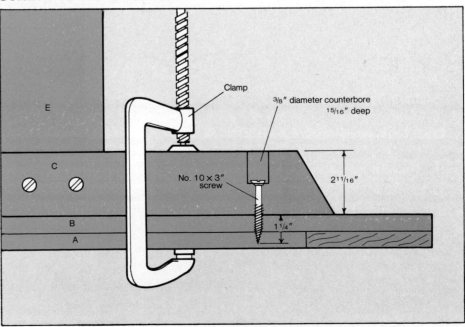

Clamp leg and tabletop assembly together. Drill and counterbore screw holes where they'll miss pockets and shallow enough so that the screws won't pierce the top.

PERIMETER BENCH

If you are looking for an outdoor bench that combines good looks, easy construction, reasonable cost, comfort, and utility, why not try your carpentry skills on this project?

Sounds like too much to expect from a small project? Not really! Ten 2×4s and a length of 2×6 are the major components needed to build this contoured seat bench.

As the name implies, the perimeter bench's natural habitat is the borders of backyard decks, but a simple change in its supports will adapt it for in-ground mounting. Judging from our experience, three or four benches can be built over a weekend.

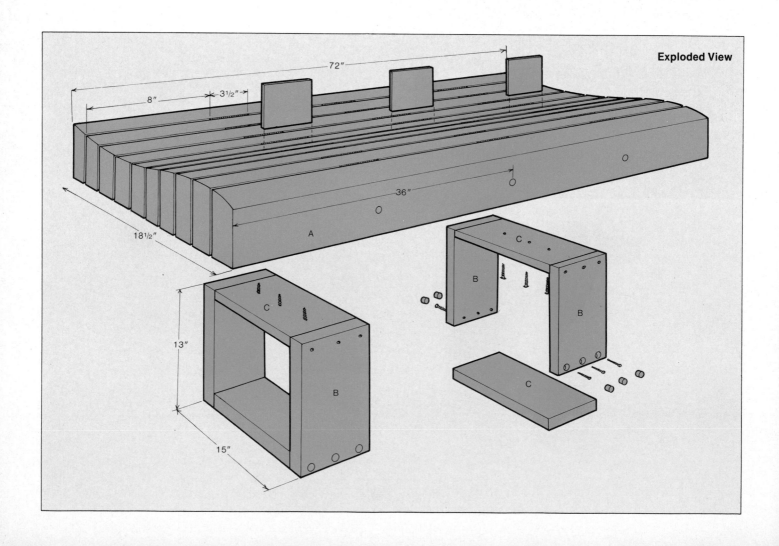

Exploded View

72"

8"

3½"

18½"

36"

A

13"

15"

B

C

BILL OF MATERIALS

Qty	Size	Material
1	2×6×10'	Clear heart redwood
2	2×4×14'	Clear heart redwood
4	2×4×12'	Clear heart redwood
60	#10×3"	Flat head, Phillips head, stainless steel wood screws
	2d	Galvanized, oval head nails
1	1/2×12"	Maple dowel (or plugs)*

PARTS LIST

All parts clear heart redwood

Part	Name	Qty	Description
A	Slat**	10	1½" × 3½" × 72"
B	Leg	4	1½" × 5½" × 13"
C	Brace	4	1½" × 5½" × 12"

* You can also make plugs from redwood with a plug cutter.
** The slats are beveled and assembled according to the numbered profile drawing.

CUTTING AND ASSEMBLING SLATS

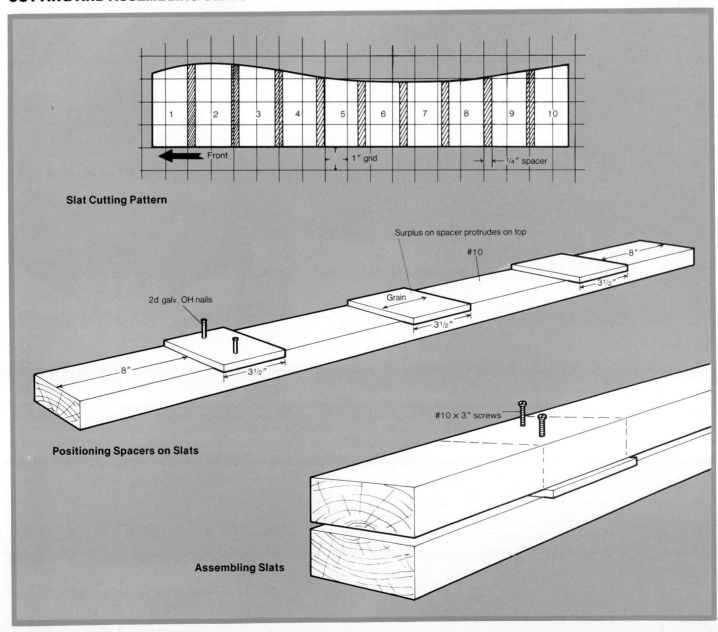

Slat Cutting Pattern

Front

1" grid

1/4" spacer

Surplus on spacer protrudes on top

#10

8"

3½"

Grain

3½"

2d galv. OH nails

8"

3½"

Positioning Spacers on Slats

#10 × 3" screws

Assembling Slats

STEP 1
CUTTING THE SLATS

Begin work on the bench by trimming to length ten redwood 2×4s. Now, check the drawing that shows the bench's 2×4 slats in cross-section. Note that #1, #3, and #10 are the same shape and that #4 and #9 are the same. Also, #5 is the same as #8, and #6 is the same as #7. Only #2 is full thickness.

Therefore, first identify one slat as #2, and set it aside. Then make paper or cardboard patterns of the remaining four slat shapes, and set up the blade height, blade angle, and fence distance on your table saw to accommodate the first of these.

If you've chosen the #1–3–10 pattern first, simply rip the same bevel angle on all three slats, and mark them for identification. Then take your next pattern, say the #4–9 pattern, and set the saw up for it. Bevel two slats and identify them. Repeat this for the #5–8 and #6–7 patterns.

STEP 2
CUTTING THE SPACERS

You should have a pair of 2-foot-long pieces of 2×4 left over from the 14-footers. From these you need to saw out twenty-seven spacers, each 3½ inches square and ¼ inch thick.

It takes a larger-diameter saw than available in most home shops to rip through the 3½-inch width of a 2×4 in one pass. However, this may be done in two passes with the average 10-inch home-shop saw.

With the fence set to cut a ¼-inch thickness, adjust the blade height to 2¼ inches. Clamp a featherboard hold-down to the table to keep the workpiece against the fence, and perform the first pass, using a push-stick or similar scrapwood aid to advance the workpiece.

Flip the workpiece end for end, and make the second pass. The ¼-inch-thick piece will eject toward the infeed end of the saw table. Occasionally, this ejection may be rapid, so stand clear of it. Repeat the procedure twice more on this 2×4 (for a total of three ¼-inch-thick slabs) and two times on the second 24-inch-long 2×4.

COUNTERBORING AND PLUGGING SCREW HOLES

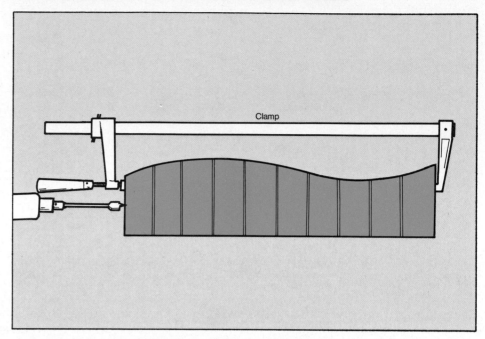

1. The screws that hold the first and tenth slats must be hidden under wood plugs, which fit into counterbores drilled on the same centers as the screw holes.

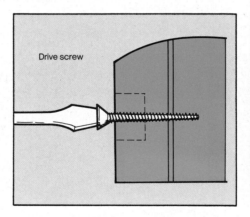

2. After counterboring and drilling, drive the screw. The diameters of the dowel and the boring bit must be the same.

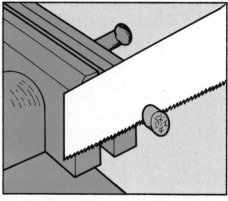

3. To cut a plug, clamp the dowel in a vise between pieces of scrap wood, and saw off a suitable length.

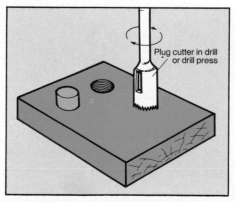

An alternate method for making a plug is to cut it from a piece of wood using a plug-cutter bit, driven by a drill or drill press.

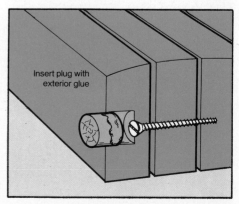

4. Apply glue to the hole. Then rotate the plug as you press it in to distribute the glue. When the glue is dry, saw the plug off close to the surface, and sand.

By doing this, you'll retain some workpiece stock to the left of the blade for control. Next, take the five slabs, and sand them lightly to remove the saw overlap marks. Then crosscut the twenty-seven spacers from these slabs. There should be three extra spacers, plus some scrap.

STEP 3
STARTING THE BENCH ASSEMBLY

Arrange the identified slats in proper order. Now, mark the locations of the spacers on the side of the #2 slat that faces #1. Fasten the three spacers to the face of #2 slat at these locations, flush with the bottom and with the spacer grain running lengthwise. Attach each spacer with a pair of 2d galvanized oval head nails, at diagonally opposite corners.

Mark the outer face of #1 slat for two screws at each spacer location. These screws will fasten #1 to #2 permanently. To hide the screwheads: (1) counter bore holes 1/2-inch diameter × 1/4-inch deep at the screw locations; (2) combination-drill for #10 × 3-inch screws; (3) align the slats and drive the screws; (4) install plugs over the screws with waterproof glue; (5) saw or sand off excess plugs and sand smooth.

STEP 4
FINISHING THE ASSEMBLY

Mark the spacer locations on the #3-slat side of slat #2. Tack on the spacers flush with the bottom. Align the combined #1 and #2 slats plus #3 on a flat surface, and clamp the pack together. Then, on the #4-slat side of #3, mark the #10 screw locations, combination-drill them, and drive the screws in flush. Slats #1, 2 and 3 are permanently attached.

On the #4-slat side of #3, mark the locations of and tack-nail the spacers, covering the screws. Align and clamp slat #4 to the pack, and repeat the procedure. When you get to the tenth slat, repeat the plugging technique to hide the screws.

Install the legs and braces. Trim the spacers flush with the seating surface, and sand the surface.

TRIMMING SPACERS AND SANDING

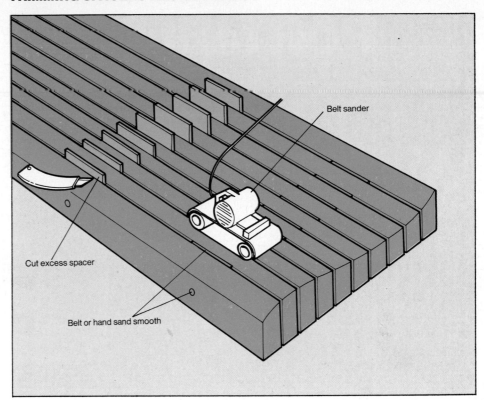

Use a utility knife to cut the excess spacer material, with the grain and as close as possible to the slats. Then sand the spacers flush with the top surface with a light-duty belt sander. If necessary, sand with fine paper.

ASSEMBLING LEGS AND BRACES

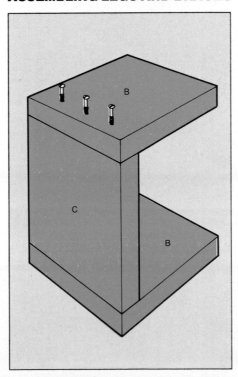

Assemble two legs with one brace between them in a C shape, using pre-drilled holes and screws.

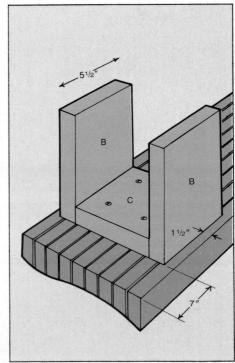

Invert the bench and place the C assembly on top of it. Pre-drill holes, and drive screws to mount the assembly. Attach the lower brace to the legs.

PORTABLE BAR UNIT

When summer comes, it's time for outdoor living, and the focus of family activity shifts from the family room to the backyard deck or patio. Cooking moves out to the barbecue or grille, and your bar or wine cellar can be as close as this portable bar cabinet.

The cabinet is castered to move about easily on any hard, flat surface, and its generously sized 32- × 48-inch top should handle any load your guests impose. The cabinet itself is the size of a 32-inch-wide base kitchen cabinet, and it has a bottom and a middle shelf for storage. The top has bottle storage; the door backs, space for glasses.

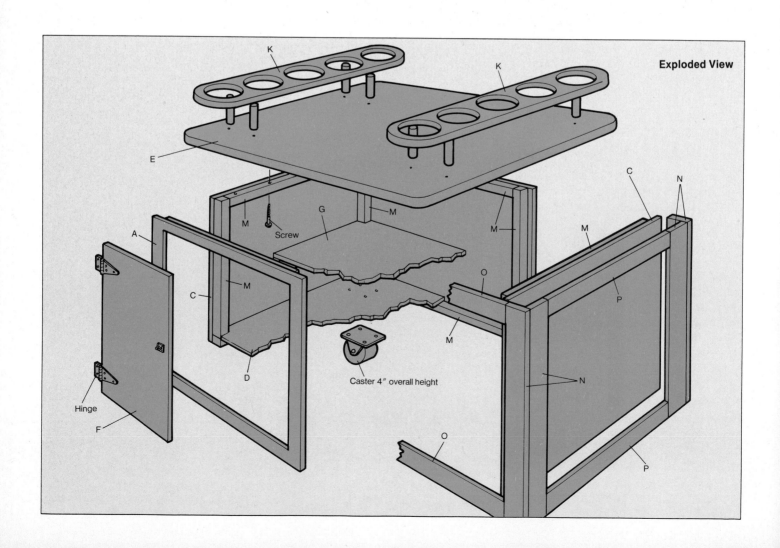

Exploded View

Screw

Caster 4" overall height

Hinge

BILL OF MATERIALS

Qty	Size	Material
1	$5/8 \times 4 \times 8'$	T1–11 plywood
1	$3/4 \times 4 \times 8'$	A-C plywood
1	$5/4 \times 12 \times 6'$	Spruce
1	$1 \times 6 \times 16'$	Clear white pine
1	$1 \times 8 \times 10'$	Clear heart redwood (CIHR)
2	$1 \times 36''$	Maple dowel
2	Pkgs. 4"	Tee hinge (Stanley #V908)
1	Pkg. 3½"	Hasp (Stanley #CD917)
2	4" O.A. ht.	Fixed casters
2	4" O.A. ht.	Swivel casters
16	$1/4 \times 1\,1/4''$	Carriage bolts, nuts, washers
16	$\#8 \times 1\,1/2''$	Flat head, Phillips head, stainless steel, wood screws
160	$\#8 \times 1\,1/2''$	Flat head, Phillips head, hardened assembly screws

PARTS LIST

Part Name		Qty	Description
A	Front	1	$5/8'' \times 31\,3/4'' \times 31\,7/8''$, T1–11 plywood
B	Back	1	$5/8'' \times 31\,3/4'' \times 31\,7/8''$, T1–11 plywood
C	Sides	2	$5/8'' \times 24'' \times 31\,7/8''$, T1–11 plywood
D	Bottom	1	$3/4'' \times 24'' \times 30\,1/2''$, A-C plywood
E	Top	1	$3/4'' \times 32'' \times 48''$, A-C plywood
F	Door	2	$3/4'' \times 14'' \times 28\,3/4''$, A-C plywood
G	Shelf	1	$3/4'' \times 20'' \times 30\,1/2''$, A-C plywood
H	Shelf support	2	$3/4'' \times 2\,1/2'' \times 18''$, A-C plywood
I	Glass holder top	2	$3/4'' \times 4\,1/4'' \times 12\,1/2,$ CIHR
J	Glass holder bottom	2	$3/4'' \times 4\,1/4'' \times 12\,1/2''$, CIHR
K	Bottle holder	2	$3/4'' \times 7\,1/4'' \times 32''$, CIHR
L	Bottle holder standoff	8	$1'' \times 5\,1/2''$, maple dowel
M	Nailers	1	$1\,1/16'' \times 1\,1/16'' \times 30'$, spruce
N	Vertical trim	8	$3/4'' \times 2\,1/2'' \times 31\,7/8''$, pine
O	Horizontal long trim	4	$3/4'' \times 1\,1/4'' \times 28\,1/2''$, pine
P	Horizontal short trim	4	$3/4'' \times 1\,1/4'' \times 20''$, pine

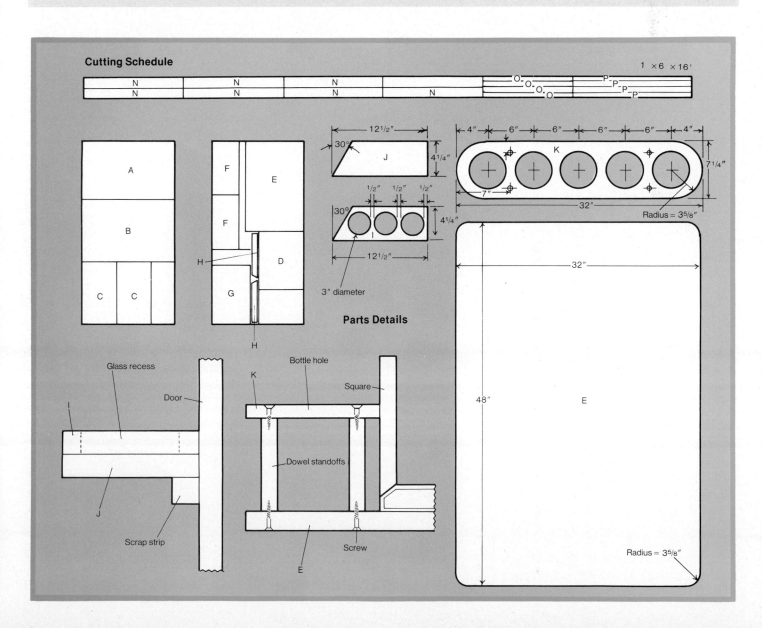

Cutting Schedule

$1 \times 6 \times 16'$

Parts Details

12½" 30° J 4¼"

½" ½" ½" 30° I 4¼" 12½"

3" diameter

4" 6" 6" 6" 6" 4" K 7¼" 7" 32" Radius = 3⅝"

32" 48" E Radius = 3⅝"

Glass recess Door I J Scrap strip

Bottle hole K Square Dowel standoffs Screw E

STEP 1
PREPARING MAJOR CABINET PARTS

The basic cabinet uses T1–11 paneling for the front, back, and sides, A-C paneling for the bottom, shelf, and doors, plus spruce corner nailers as reenforcements. First, saw out the plywood parts according to the parts list and detail drawings. The nailers are best fitted on the spot in their individual locations.

Set up the blade-to-fence distance for the first two of the four pocket cuts required to remove the door-opening waste in the front. Lower the blade, position the workpiece, face up, and start the saw. Then carefully raise the blade through the workpiece, and advance the workpiece. Repeat this procedure on the opposite side, which has the same dimension. Then set up the saw for the last two pocket cuts, and perform them.

The doors are simple rectangles that require no further work at this time; the top should be cut with a 3⅝-inch radius at all four corners to match the radii of the bottle holders, which will be discussed later.

The shelf rectangle requires two notches at the rear to clear the vertical nailers, while the bottom must be notched at all four corners.

STEP 2
STARTING THE ASSEMBLY

Cut to length four vertical corner nailers. Place each side, face up, over two of them, and fasten them together with screws. There is no need to pre-drill holes, since the wood is soft and the screws will be covered by trim later. Now, cut to length four pieces of horizontal nailer—to fit between the vertical nailers at the top and bottom—and install them.

The front and back panels may now be screwed to the vertical nailers of the side assemblies, with their side edges flush with the side surfaces. Next, cut to fit and install both top and bottom nailers inside the front and back panels, butting them against the vertical nailers.

Drill holes through all top nailers so that screws can be driven through them later to attach the top. Then,

CUTTING THE FRONT

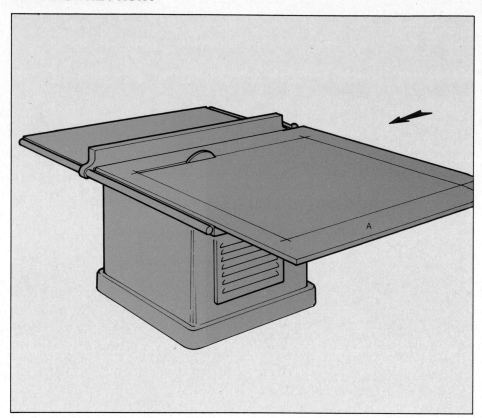

Set the fence distance to match width of rail or stile. Lower the blade. Position the front on the saw table. Carefully raise the blade up through the front and advance it.

ATTACHING NAILERS

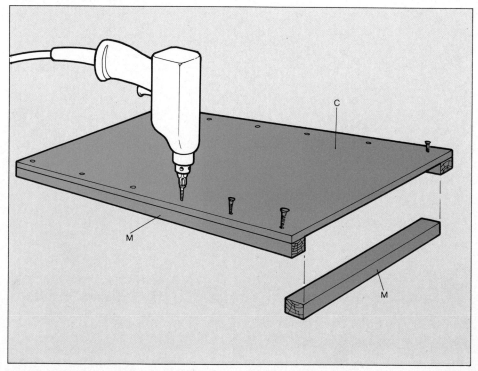

Nailers connect the sides, front, back, and bottom. To attach these nailers, drive screws through the edges of the panels into them. Trim will hide exterior screws.

cock the bottom, place it inside the cabinet on top of the bottom nailers, and screw it down.

Invert the cabinet. Lay out the mounting holes for the casters, providing clearance for the swivel casters to rotate. Drill the holes, mount the casters, and set the cabinet upright. Add the shelf supports, but not the shelf. This will make it easier to install the top later. Stain the cabinet.

STEP 3
INSTALLING TRIM AND PAINTING

Saw out the trim pieces slightly longer than needed. Make up the corners (vertical trim). Then fit all the horizontal trim between them. Paint all trim, doors, shelf, top and bottom.

STEP 4
MAKING BOTTLE AND GLASS HOLDERS

While the paint is drying, cut out the blanks for the bottle holders and the glass holders. All four glass holder blanks must be mitered 30° at one end. Next, lay out 3-inch diameter holes, spaced 1/2 inch apart on the two top pieces and starting 1/2 inch from the butt end. These holes are best made with a hole saw, mounted in a drill press with the workpiece clamped down over scrap on the press table. If you don't have a drill press, clamp the workpiece down tightly on the top of a large, flat scrap wood surface. This will prevent a rough edge as the hole saw exits and will also keep the workpiece from spinning.

Since most hole saws have 1/4-inch-diameter pilot bits, use your drill guide to drill 1/4-inch-diameter pilot holes at your layout centers. Then switch to the hole saw; if you guide it carefully, the hole saw's pilot bit will follow the pre-drilled pilot hole most of the way to provide an opening.

Next, lay out the 4-inch-diameter holes and radii on the bottle-holder blanks. The same procedure is used to make these holes as for the glass-holder holes. When the drilling is complete, cut the corner radii with a band or jig saw, and sand the edges smooth. Also, sand the hole edges on both the bottle and glass holders.

ASSEMBLING THE CABINET

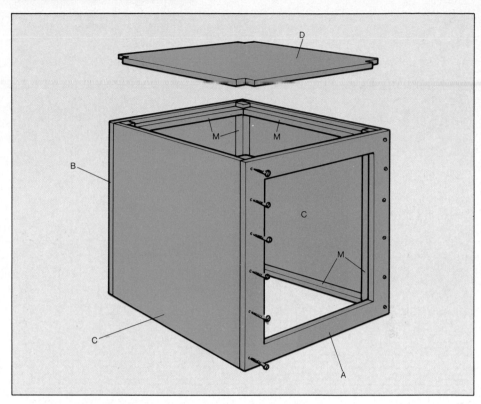

Start the nailers on the sides. Then add the front and back to these by driving screws into the corner nailers. Next, install the top and bottom nailers inside the front and back. Now saw the corner clearance notches in the bottom, position it, and install it.

INSTALLING THE CASTERS

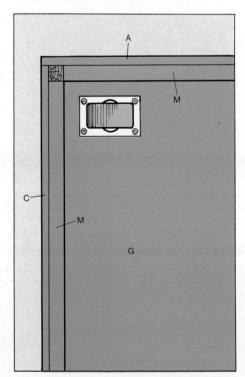

Invert the cabinet. Position the casters near the corners, but make sure that the swivel casters have swing clearance.

INSTALLING TRIM

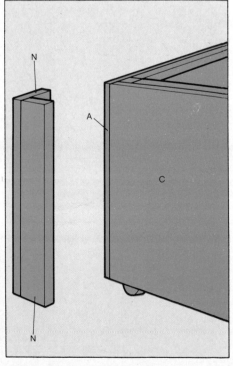

Corner trim is pre-assembled and then nailed over corners, hiding screws. Top and bottom trims fit between these.

Now, drill the four holes in the bottle holders for the standoff screw attachments, using a combination bit and a drill guide. Trim the dowel standoffs to length squarely. Punchmark a center pilot on one end of each standoff, and attach them to the bottom surfaces of the bottle holders with screws, driven in from above and countersink. Set the bottle holders aside for now.

Attach the glass-holder tops to the bottom and these in turn to a scrap redwood nailer. Set these assemblies aside for now.

STEP 5
FINAL ASSEMBLY

Place the top in position on the cabinet, and drive screws up through the holes in the top nailers into the bottom surface of the top. Now, position the bottle-holder assemblies on the top surface with the aid of a square. Draw a light pencil line around the base of each standoff on the top surface. Remove the bottle holders and drill 1/8-inch-diameter screw pilot holes. Then press the bottle holders down firmly on the top surface, and back-drill upward through the pilot holes into the standoffs, using a combination bit. Fasten the bottle holders with screws.

Lock down the shelf to the supports. Note that the doors are inset with respect to the trim but overlaid with respect to the T1–11 front. Therefore, the trim, especially the corners, must be nailed in place before the doors can be mounted. These nails must be set and the holes plugged with filler or putty before touching up.

All metal hardware not already painted should be primed and finish-painted with an exterior-use product such as Rustoleum. Screw the hinges to the door fronts, allowing equal vertical distances from the door tops and bottoms. Mount the door, equalizing the gaps as much as possible. Screw the glass holders to the door backs with clearance for opening and closing, and add the hasp and staple to complete the job.

ASSEMBLING THE BOTTLE HOLDER

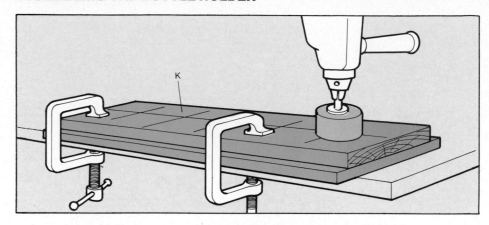

1. Lay out the pattern for the holes on the bottle-holder blank. Then, clamp the blank down firmly, either to a drill-press table or to a work surface. Chuck the hole saw in the drill press or in a 1/2-inch drill with auxiliary handle, and carefully work the hole saw through.

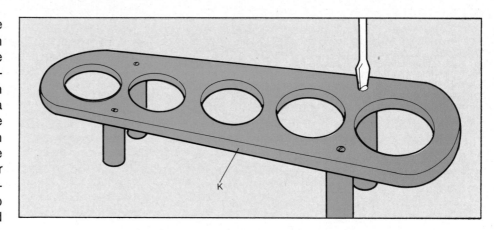

2. Drill center pilots in the standoffs and combination holes in the holder. Drive screws through the holder into standoffs.

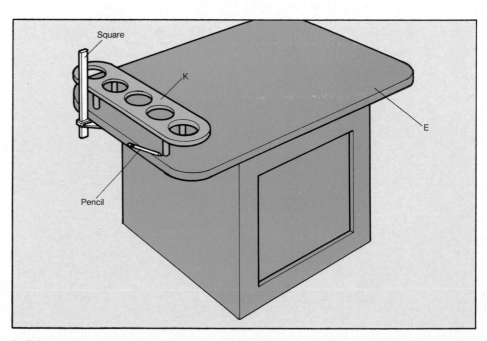

3. Drive screws up through the top nailers into cabinet top. Put bottle holders on top ends with combination square. Outline standoffs, remove holders, and drill screw holes through center of circles. Replace standoffs over holes, clamp holders, and drive screws up into standoffs.

BIRDHOUSE

Almost everyone is an amateur birdwatcher to some degree, and you can have command performances with this charming Tudor-style birdhouse in your backyard.

Before you build it, however, spend a few moments at the local Audubon Society or a reference library to learn a few particulars about birdhouses. Different birds require different-size entrance holes, different house heights above ground, locations, areas, house volumes, and distances from hole to floor. Since ours is an average birdhouse, you may want to modify it to attract a particular type of bird.

All birdhouses must be made secure from predators; they all require periodic cleaning.

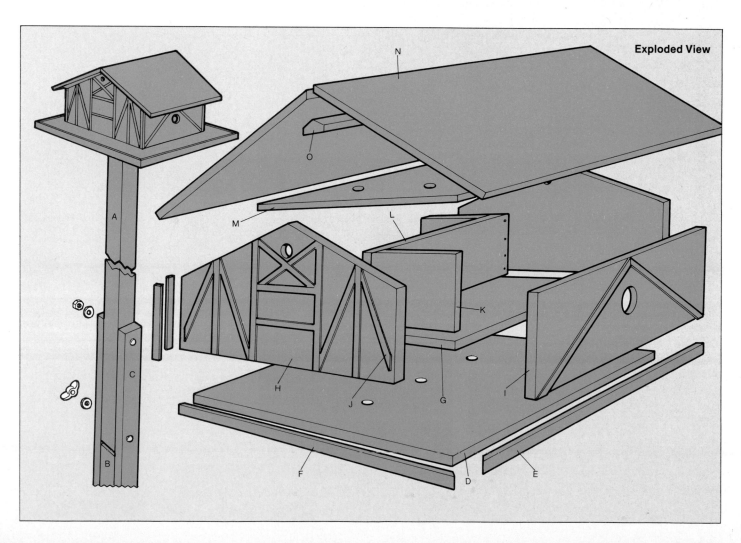

Exploded View

BILL OF MATERIALS

Qty	Size	Material
1	4 × 4 × 10′	Pressure-treated lumber (P/T)
1	2 × 4 × 10′	Pressure-treated lumber
1	1/2 × 2 × 4′	A-C plywood
1	3/4 × 2 × 4′	A-C plywood
1	1/4 × 10″ × 13″	A-C plywood
1	1 × 2 × 6′	White pine
1	2 × 4 × 1′	Douglas fir
1	18 × 20″	Aluminum flashing
2	3/8 × 6 1/2″	Carriage bolts, washers
1	3/8	Hex nut
1	3/8	Wing nut
	10d	Oval head nails
	3d or 4d	Oval head nails
		Stain for post, roof, bars
		Paint for walls

PARTS LIST

Part	Name	Qty	Description
A	Upper post	1	3 1/2″ × 3 1/2″ × 7′, P/T
B	Lower post	1	3 1/2″ × 3 1/2″ × 3′, P/T
C	Post shoulders	2	1 1/2″ × 3 1/2″ × 5′, P/T
D	Sub-base	1	3/4″ × 17″ × 20″, A-C plywood
E	Sub-base short trim	2	1/4″ × 3/4″ × 18″, pine
F	Sub-base long trim	2	1/4″ × 3/4″ × 21″, pine
G	Base	1	3/4″ × 10″ × 13″, plywood
H	Front, back	2	1/2″ × 14″ × 10″, A-C plywood
I	Side	2	1/2″ × 10″ × 6 1/4″, A-C plywood
J	Brown bar trim	18′	1/8″ × 3/8″, pine
K	Divider short wall	2	1/2″ × 6 1/4″ × 5″, A-C plywood
L	Divider	1	1/2″ × 10″ × 5″, A-C plywood
M	Ceiling	1	1/4″ × 10″ × 13″, A-C plywood
N	Roof half	2	1/2″ × 9 3/4″ × 17″, A-C plywood
O	Roof joiner	1	1″ × 1 1/2″ × 10″, pine

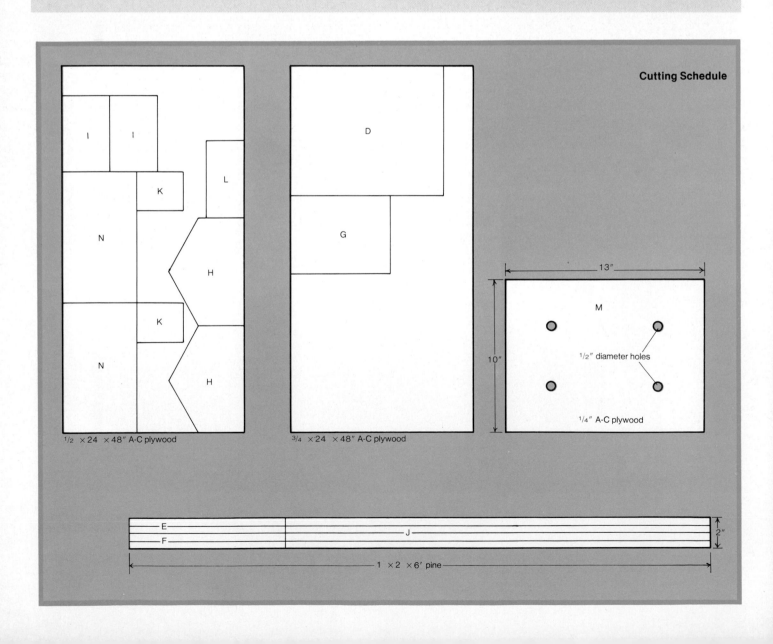

Cutting Schedule

1/2 × 24 × 48″ A-C plywood

3/4 × 24 × 48″ A-C plywood

13″

10″

M

1/2″ diameter holes

1/4″ A-C plywood

2″

1 × 2 × 6′ pine

Our birdhouse offers protection from predators by being mounted off the ground and by having the bottom surfaced with sheet metal, which affords no claw grip to small critters. The removable roof and the folding post make periodic cleaning easy. Best of all, you probably have most of the materials lying around your shop, with the possible exception of the 4 × 4.

STEP 1
MAKING AND INSTALLING THE POST

Start by cutting the 10-foot 4 × 4 into two pieces, one 7 feet long and the other 3 feet. Also, cut the 10-foot 2 × 4 in half. Then nail the two 5-foot long 2 × 4s to the 3-foot section of 4 × 4, forming a sandwich, with everything flush at one end.

Next, clamp the 7-foot piece of 4 × 4 between the 2 × 4s of the lower section, leaving a 3/4-inch gap between the two pieces of 4 × 4. Then drill two 3/8-inch-diameter holes completely through the clamped sandwich at points 3 inches and 20 1/4 inches above the gap. Put one carriage bolt with a washer and hex nut in the top hole, and the other carriage bolt with washer and wing nut in the lower hole.

Excavate a 42-inch-deep hole at the location you have chosen for your birdhouse. Then drop in 6 to 8 inches of 5/8-inch stone. Place the lower section of the post in the hole on top of the stone, and backfill the hole, while keeping the post plumb on two adjacent faces. You may backfill the hole with concrete or tightly packed dirt; concrete provides longer-lasting support.

The concrete will cure sufficiently in a couple of days, so if you want to stain the post, simply remove the bolt with the wing nut, and bend the post over to a convenient height for brushing.

STEP 2
PREPARING THE PARTS

Saw out all plywood parts, and bevel cut the top edges of both sides and the top edges of the roof halves.

Now, with the blade still set at the

CUTTING THE SIDES

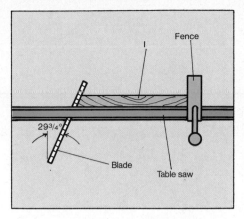

Set the blade at the bevel angle, adjust the fence distance, and advance each side through with one edge against the fence.

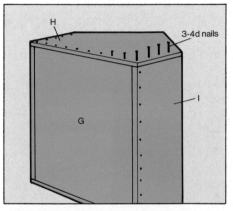

2. Place the front over the base and side edges. Nail together. Invert the assembly, and nail the back to it.

CUTTING THE ROOF

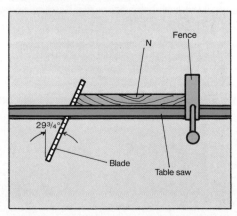

Cut the roof pieces on the saw in the same manner you used to saw the sides.

ASSEMBLING THE HOUSE

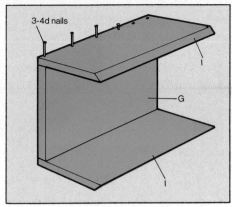

1. Align one side with the base edge, and nail the two together. Invert them, and nail on second side in the same manner.

ASSEMBLING THE DIVIDER

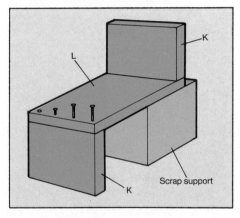

Place the divider over one of the short walls, and nail the two together. Invert the assembly, and nail on the second wall.

CUTTING THE "SHINGLES"

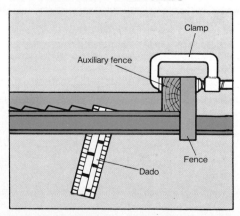

With wood auxiliary fence clamped, set the angle on dado blades. After each pass, move the fence one "shingle" course.

correct bevel angle, set the fence on your table saw so that you can lay the short piece of 2×4 flat on the table with one edge against the fence, and cut the bevel angle for the roof joiner. After cutting one bevel, lay the 2×4 down on the opposite face, and cut the second bevel.

Return the bevel angle of the blade to zero. Mark the 2×4 so that the distance between the cusp where the bevels meet and the flat at the bottom will be 1 inch. Then set the fence accordingly. With the cusp to the left of the blade (as viewed from the infeed end) and the uncut edge of the 2×4 against the fence, advance the 2×4 to separate the roof joiner from the rest of the 2×4.

Strip up the bar trim and the subbase long and short trim. Then switch over to a dado blade (pack or wobble) for a cut about ½ inch wide. Set the dado at a bevel angle of 5 to 7° and a cutting height of about ⅛ inch at the high point. Then attach a wood auxiliary fence to the metal fence, and you're ready to machine cut the "shingle courses."

Move the first roof half into position, face down over the table, oriented so that the rake of the "shingles" will be correct. If you want to play it safe, run a scrap piece through first to orient your thinking to the way the dado blade alters the workpiece.

With the fence set accordingly, advance the workpiece through the first pass, then the other workpiece (the second roof half) through its first pass. Adjust the fence to allow machining of the second course, and advance the workpieces through. Continue this sequence—adjusting the fence, advancing the first roof half, advancing the second roof half—until the "shingle" courses are complete.

STEP 3
ASSEMBLING THE HOUSE

Begin to put the birdhouse together by joining the base to the sides using 3d or 4d oval head, galvanized nails. Next, add the front and back by nailing them into the base and sides. The assembly should now

CUTTING THE ROOF JOINER

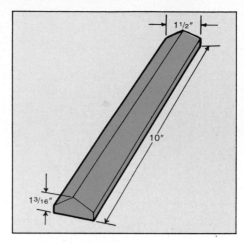

1. The roof joiner, when completed, looks like a long house when viewed from the gable end.

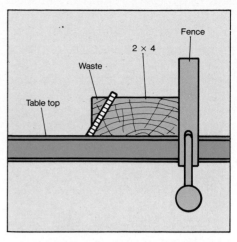

2. Set the blade at the bevel angle, and adjust the fence. Make first pass (above), flip 2×4, and make the second pass at same setting.

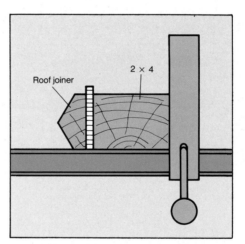

3. Set the blade straight up, and adjust the fence to separate the roof-joiner section (drawing top, left). Pass the 2×4 through.

ASSEMBLING THE ROOF

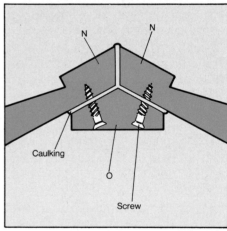

Caulk roof edges and top of joiner. Drive screws through the joiner into both roof halves from below.

ASSEMBLING THE POST

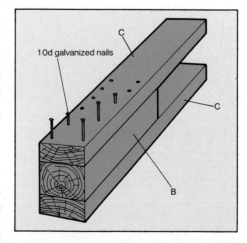

1. Cut the 10-foot length of 4×4 into a 3-foot and a 7-foot section. Nail the 2×4s to the 3-foot section of 4×4 to form a sandwich.

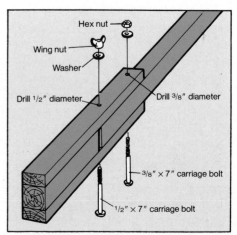

2. Insert the 7-foot length of 4×4 with a small end-to-end gap. Drill holes and install bolts, one with wing nut.

resemble a rectangle with gabled ends, open at the top.

Since this is a "two-family" house and needs a dividing wall, assemble the two short walls to the main dividing wall to form a stylized Z, when seen in plan view.

Make up the roof assembly by attaching the two roof halves to the roof joiner with screws, driven from below. You might wish to caulk this joint as you assemble it.

Drill the entrance holes in the sides, and the ventilation holes in the peaks of the front and back as well as the ceiling. On hot days, the warm air rises through the ceiling and out the vent holes, while fresh return air comes in through the entrance holes.

Now, fit the long and short trims to the sub-base by miter-cutting the corners, and nail these pieces in place. Place the sub-base on its face, and attach a full skin of aluminum flashing to the bottom surface with small nails or staples. This prevents small animal claws from gripping the sub-base from the post.

Stain the bar trim, roof, and sub-base, but paint the house front, back, and sides—first with exterior primer and then with exterior finish. When the stain has dried, apply a coat or two of exterior flat- or satin-finish varnish. When everything is dry, fit and attach the bars to the colored sides, front and back walls of the house with staples or small brass nails.

With the post folded but supported in a horizontal position, attach the sub-base to it with screws. The house may then be attached to the sub-base by screws driven in from the inside of the base.

Next, place the divider assembly in the house and fasten it to the front and back with small screws or nails, driven through the divider's short walls. Now, place the ceiling in the house. It will rest on the divider assembly. Next, fit the roof to the house; it should stay in place in part due to the friction-fit of the roof joiner ends against the inner faces of the front and back walls. Finally, erect the post, and replace the bolt and wing nut.

ASSEMBLING THE BASE

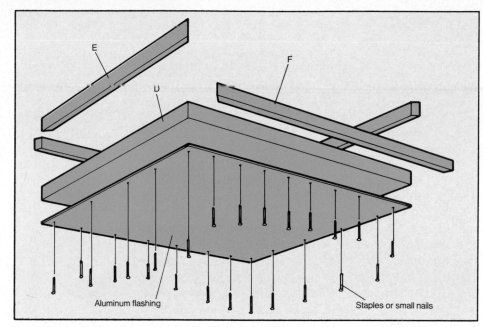

Fit the mitered ends of both long and short trims and nail them to the sub-base edge. Cut a piece of aluminum flashing to size, and tack or staple it to the bottom.

ATTACHING BASE TO POST

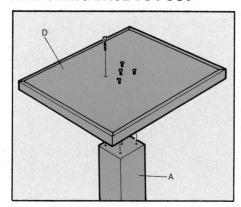

Center the sub-base assembly over the top end of the 7-foot 4×4, and secure it in place with five or six screws.

CUTTING HOLES

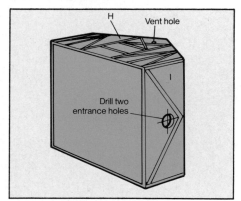

Back up the bird entrance and ventilation holes in the sides, front, and back of house, and drill them through.

ATTACHING HOUSE TO BASE

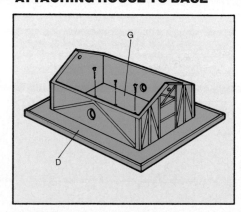

Center the house over the sub-base, and drive screws through the base into the sub-base, flush with floor.

INSTALLING DIVIDER AND CEILING

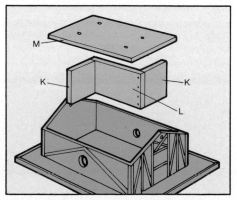

Push the divider assembly down into the house. It will be a snug fit. Then add the ventilated ceiling on top of divider.

GARBAGE STORAGE

If you build one of these trim-looking garbage storage units, you'll never have to take up garage space with garbage cans again. The cabinet will easily hold a pair of galvanized metal 20-gallon cans, as well as a supply of plastic bags and ties.

During the week while you're accumulating garbage, keep the front doors of the unit shut, and open the lid to load the cans from the top. There's no need to worry about animals breaking in: all the cabinet doors can be locked. The hinged top is held by chains in the open position, so you can remove the can lids and hang them on the holders in the top.

When it's garbage day, roll the cabinet to the sidewalk, remove the cans through the front doors, and roll the cabinet back.

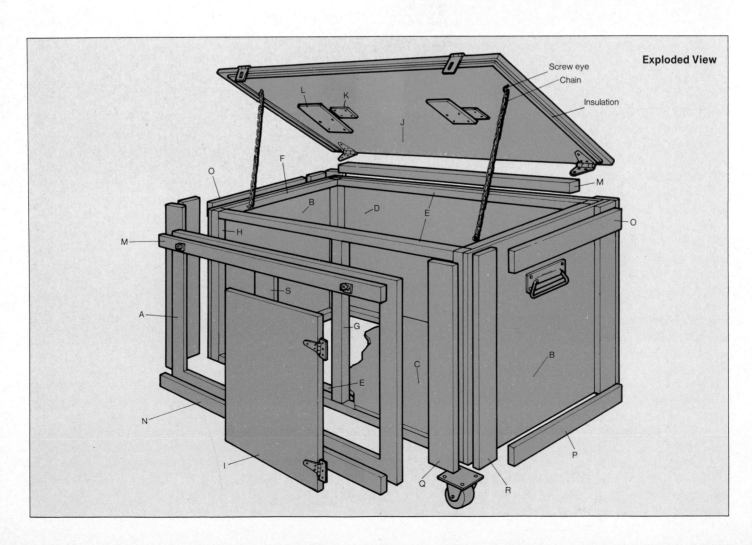

Exploded View

Screw eye
Chain
Insulation

BILL OF MATERIALS

Qty	Size	Material	Qty	Size	Material	Qty	Size	Material
2	$5/8 \times 4 \times 8'$	T1-11 panel	1	6' length	Light chain	1	pkg.	Stanley SP1316-3 $1/4 \times$
1	$3/4 \times 4 \times 8'$	A-C plywood	1	pkg.	Stanley 8450-108 medium			$1^3/4"$ Self-adhesive foam
1	$2 \times 4 \times 12'$	Douglas fir			screweyes	2	4" O.A.	Fixed casters
1	$2 \times 4 \times 8'$	Douglas fir	1	pkg.	Stanley 8470-1 S hooks		height	
1	$1 \times 6 \times 12'$	White pine	2	pkg.	Stanley CD1205-3-$1/2$	2	4" O.A.	Swivel casters
2	$1 \times 6 \times 8'$	White pine			Chest handle		height	
2	pkg.	Stanley V908-4 tee hinges	150	#8 $\times 1^3/4"$	Flat head, Phillips head,	16	$1/4 \times 1^1/4"$	Carriage bolts, nuts,
1	pkg.	Stanley V902-4 strap			"Twinfast" or "Zapper"			washers
		hinges			screws			Exterior stain
4	pkg.	Stanley CD917-3-$1/2$	6d		Oval head galvanized			Exterior primer
		Click-lock hasps			nails			Exterior trim paint

PARTS LIST

Part	Name	Qty	Description	Part	Name	Qty	Description	Part	Name	Qty	Description
A	Front	1	$5/8" \times 48^1/2" \times 35"$, T1-11	G	Backer	1	$1^1/2" \times 2^3/8" \times 31^1/4"$, fir	O	Top trim, short	2	$3/4" \times 2^1/2" \times 22"$, pine
B	End	2	$5/8" \times 20^{13}/16" \times 35"$, T1-11	H	Corner nailer	4	$1^1/2" \times 1^1/2" \times 35"$, fir	P	Bottom trim, short	2	$3/4" \times 2" \times 22"$, pine
C	Floor	1	$3/4" \times 20^{13}/16" \times 47^5/16"$, A-C ply	I	Door	2	$3/4" \times 21" \times 30"$, A-C ply	Q	Corner trim, wide	4	$3/4" \times 2^1/2" \times 35"$, pine
D	Back	1	$5/8" \times 48^1/2" \times 35"$, T1-11	J	Top	1	$3/4" \times 24" \times 51"$, A-C ply	R	Corner trim, narrow	4	$3/4" \times 1^3/4" \times 35"$, pine
E	Cleat, long	4	$1^1/2" \times 1^1/2" \times 44^5/16"$, fir	K	Spacer	2	$5/8" \times 3" \times 6"$, T1-11	S	Center trim	1	$3/4" \times 2^3/8" \times 30^1/2"$, pine
F	Cleat, short	4	$1^1/2" \times 1^1/2" \times 17^{13}/16"$, fir	L	Lid holder	2	$5/8" \times 3" \times 9"$, T1-11				
				M	Top trim, long	2	$3/4" \times 2^1/2" \times 46"$, pine				
				N	Bottom trim, long	2	$3/4" \times 2" \times 46"$, pine				

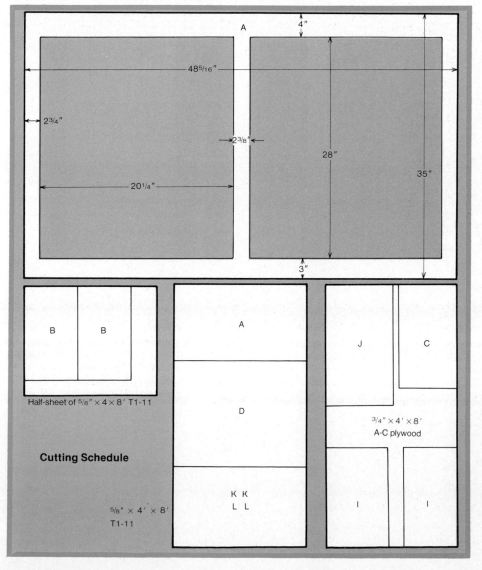

Cutting Schedule

Half-sheet of $5/8" \times 4 \times 8'$ T1-11

$5/8" \times 4' \times 8'$ T1-11

$3/4" \times 4' \times 8'$ A-C plywood

ASSEMBLING THE CABINET

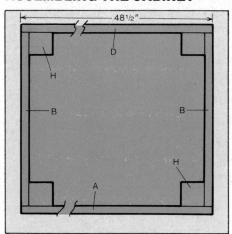

Plan view shows attachment of front, back, and corner nailers to ends.

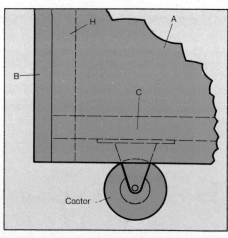

Phantom view shows back, end, corner nailer, cleat, and fixed caster.

STEP 1
PREPARING THE MAIN CABINET PARTS

The cabinet is paneled on all four sides with T1–11 plywood, reinforced at all internal corner joints and edges with 2×2s (1½×1½ inches). A ¾-inch plywood floor, screwed to the lower reinforcement cleats, serves as a base for the casters. Doors, lid, trim, and hardware are essentially add-ons to the basic cabinet.

Before starting, look over the main drawing, as well as the Parts List, Materials List, and Details. Note that after the pieces shown in the cutting schedule have been sawn out, pocket cuts must be made in the front for the door openings. This is best accomplished with a table saw but can be done with a portable saw and guide, if necessary.

The cleats are ripped from 2×4 stock and trimmed to length as needed. A-C plywood is used for the floor, lid, and doors; all trim is made from white pine.

STEP 2
ASSEMBLING THE CABINET

Start by screw-fastening the four vertical cleats to the corners of the front, back, and ends. Then, add the lower, horizontal cleats. The floor, which rests on these cleats, must be notched at the corners to clear the vertical corner cleats before it is installed. Install the floor, and then invert the cabinet. Lay out and drill the mounting holes for the casters, allowing clearance for the swing of the swivel caster. Attach them with the ¼-inch-diameter carriage bolts. With this job completed, you'll be able to set the cabinet on its feet, and the remaining work will not require any heavy lifting.

Add the upper horizontal cleats, which fit inside the top edges of the front, back, and ends. Also, add the backer, which provides support behind the front's center stile.

STEP 3
PAINTING AND STAINING

This is the time to stain all the T1–11 cabinet panels. Never attempt to complete the dry assembly and then

CABINET ASSEMBLY DETAILS

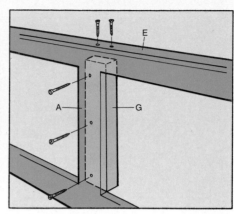

Hold the base and swing the caster in an arc to make sure that the swivel casters clear the cleats at the corners.

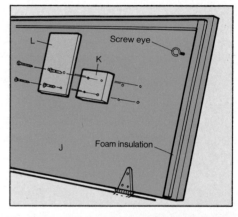

The 1½-inch-thick backer acts to stiffen the center stile; it is attached to both top and bottom cleats.

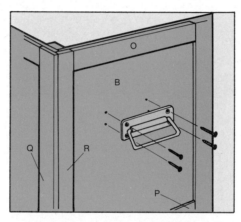

Each end has a chest handle to pull the rolling cabinet. Adjust its height to suit your own.

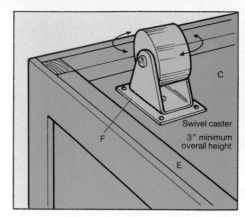

The inside of the top is fitted with two lid holders and two spacers. These free your hands when filling garbage cans.

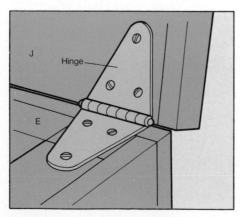

Strap hinges are mounted to both upper cleats at the corners on both ends of the cabinet and to the underside of the top.

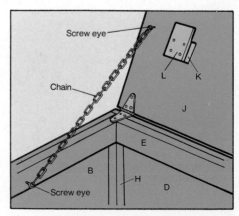

When open, the top leans back out of the way, and thus it can't hit you. Chains and screw-eyes constrain the top.

paint and stain the project, unless you wish to make everything the same color. Besides, stain works very well with the T1–11 panels, while paint is the best finish for the pine trim.

Apply urethane to the entire inside of the cabinet, and set it aside to dry. Prime the doors, lid, and trim with an exterior oil or alkyd, and let them dry. When they are dry, apply at least one coat of exterior latex paint.

The hardware should be protected with a metal primer and, when dry, may be given a finish coat. Metal paints, such as Rustoleum, are available in spray cans for convenience.

STEP 4
ADDING THE TRIM

We found that the easiest place to start trimming was at the corners, by pre-assembling the wide and narrow pieces before attaching them to the cabinet. When installed, they will hide the corner assembly screws that join the panels to the cleats. Some minor fitting may be necessary when you add the upper and lower horizontal trim and the vertical center trim, but there's no problem. You'll want to do a bit of touch-up painting at the end, anyway. All nails used to mount the trim should be set, and the resulting holes filled with linseed oil putty.

STEP 5
INSTALLING DOORS, LID, AND HARDWARE

Mount the hinges to the doors first, allowing equal distance from both top and bottom edges. Set the cabinet on its back over a rug or blanket, and place the doors in a balanced position. Drive the hinge-to-cabinet mounting screws. Add hasps and set the cabinet upright.

Align and mount the hinges on the lid first; then mount them on the cabinet top. Support the lid until you have installed the chains, eyes, and S hooks.

Mount the lid holders, lid latches, and chest latches. Finish up by attaching the foam insulation to the lid bottom and letting it set up with the lid shut tight.

INSTALLING THE HASPS

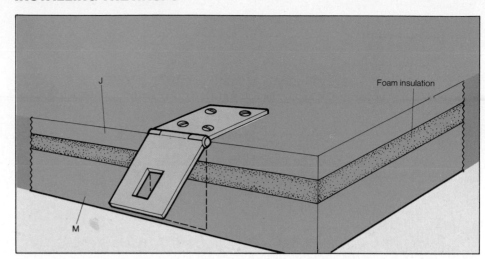

Before aligning the safety hasps that hold the top closed, install the foam insulation on the underside of the top. This insulation prevents slamming of the top, allows for the strap hinges' thickness, and keeps out small rodents.

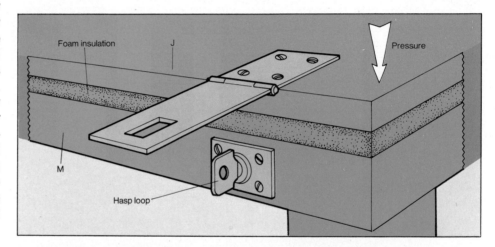

Apply weight or downward pressure on the top to compress the insulation, and then position the special locking staple so that compression will be maintained when the staple is in use. The staple may be rotated 90° to a detent to lock the hasp.

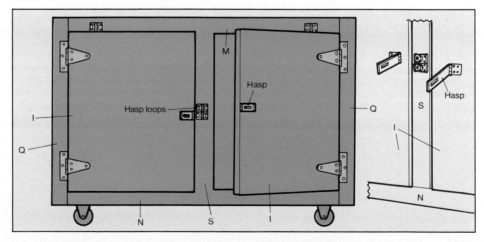

A front view shows the top hasp staples, the doors and hinges, and the door hasp staples mounted on the center stile. When the door hasps (shown at right) are mounted on the doors, they must be staggered vertically to align with the locking staples on the stile.

PORTABLE POTTING UNIT

Folks with green thumbs and the urge to grow or propagate plants and flowers will appreciate this portable potting bench. It's constructed of redwood and plywood, with large redwood wheels and a fold-up tractor handle attached to a very wide steerable front axle base.

Closed storage is provided by a pair of large cabinets on the redwood base. Between them is open storage. The optional tiled working area on top is easily cleaned and fenced on three sides. The bench is perfect for potting work and moves easily from shed or garage to yard and garden.

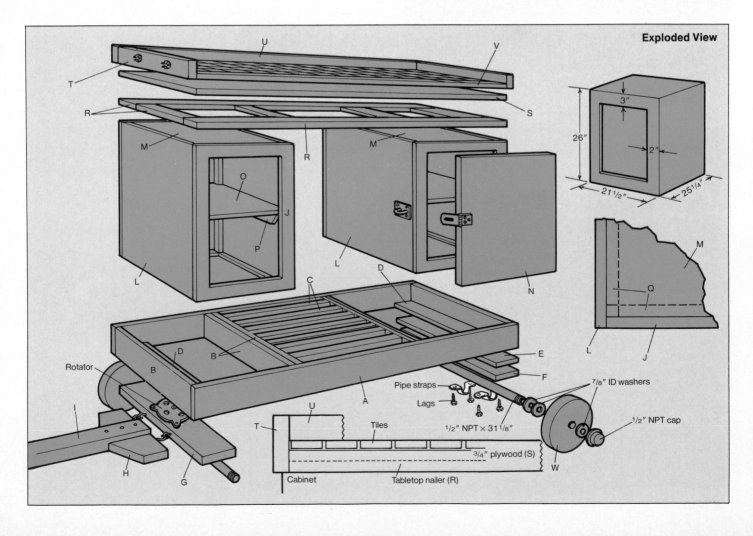

Exploded View

BILL OF MATERIALS

Qty	Size	Material
3	3/4 × 4 × 8'	A-C plywood
1	2 × 10 × 10'	Construction heart redwood (ConHR)
3	2 × 6 × 12'	Construction heart redwood
1	2 × 6 × 6'	Construction heart redwood
1	2 × 4 × 6'	Construction heart redwood
1	8/4 × 2 × 4'	Oak*
1	5/4 × 4 × 1'	Oak*
1	5/4 × 8 × 12'	Pressure-treated lumber (P/T)
1	1 × 6 × 10'	Clear heart redwood (CIHR)

Qty	Size	Material
1	7 1/2"	Rotator #91K8**
2	Pkgs. 4"	Tee hinge (Stanley #V908)
2	Pkg. 3 1/2"	Hasp (Stanley #CD917)
100	#12 × 3"	Flat head, Phillips head, stainless steel, wood screws
350	#8 × 1 1/2"	Flat head, Phillips head, hardened assembly screws
3	5/16 × 2 1/2"	Carriage bolts, washers, nuts
6	1/4 × 2"	Hex head machine bolts, washers, nuts
2	1/4 × 1 1/2"	Lag bolts, washers
2		Spring-loaded, screw-in tool clips

Qty	Size	Material
4		Screweyes (Stanley #8450-106)
12	7/8 I.D.	Washers
8	1/2" n.p.t.	Pipe straps
16	1/4 × 1 1/4"	Lag bolts, washers
4	1/2" n.p.t.	Caps
1	1/2" n.p.t.	Pipe nipple, 31 1/8" long, threaded both ends
1	1/2" n.p.t.	Pipe nipple, 40 7/8" long, threaded both ends
45	4 × 8"	American Olean Quarry Natural tiles
1	unit	L & M Surco Surpoxy 111 epoxy mortar
5	pounds	L & M Surco tan grout Stain Primer paint, finish paint

PARTS LIST

Part	Name	Qty	Description
A	Long rail	2	1 1/2" × 5 1/2" × 63", ConHR
B	Short rail	6	1 1/2" × 5 1/2" × 23 1/8", ConHR
C	Grille bars	7	1 1/2" × 5 1/2" × 14 7/8", ConHR
D	Axle support	2	1 1/2" × 5 1/2" × 23 1/8", ConHR
E	Spacer	1	3/4" × 7 1/2" × 26 1/4", ConHR
F	Fixed axle base	1	1 1/2" × 7 1/2" × 26 1/4", ConHR
G	Swivel axle base	1	1 1/2" × 7 1/2" × 36", ConHR
H	Handle base	1	1 1/16" × 4" × 10 1/2", oak
I	Handle	1	1 1/2" × 1 1/2" × 41", oak

Part	Name	Qty	Description
J	Cabinet front	2	3/4" × 21 1/2" × 26", A-C plywood
K	Cabinet back	2	3/4" × 21 1/2" × 26", A-C plywood
L	Cabinet side	4	3/4" × 23 3/4" × 26", A-C plywood
M	Cabinet top/bottom	4	3/4" × 20" × 23 3/4", A-C plywood
N	Door	2	3/4" × 21 1/2" × 23 1/2", A-C plywood
O	Shelf	2	3/4" × 18" × 20", A-C plywood
P	Shelf support	4	3/4" × 16" × 2 1/2", A-C plywood
Q	Nailers	1	1 1/16" × 1 1/16" × 48', (P/T)

Part	Name	Qty	Description
R	Table top nailer	1	1 1/16" × 1 1/2" × 18', (P/T)
S	Table top	1	3/4" × 24 9/16" × 60 3/8", A-C plywood
T	Side fence	2	1 1/2" × 5 1/2" × 26 1/4", ConHR
U	Back fence	1	3/4" × 5 1/2" × 63 1/2", CIHR
V	Front fence	1	1 1/2" × 5 1/2" × 60 1/4", ConHR
W	Wheels	4	1 1/2" × 9", ConHR

*Try to get these scrap size pieces from a local furniture or cabinet shop.
**Available at Constantine, 2050 Eastchester Road, Bronx, NY 10461. Tel: 1-800-223-8087

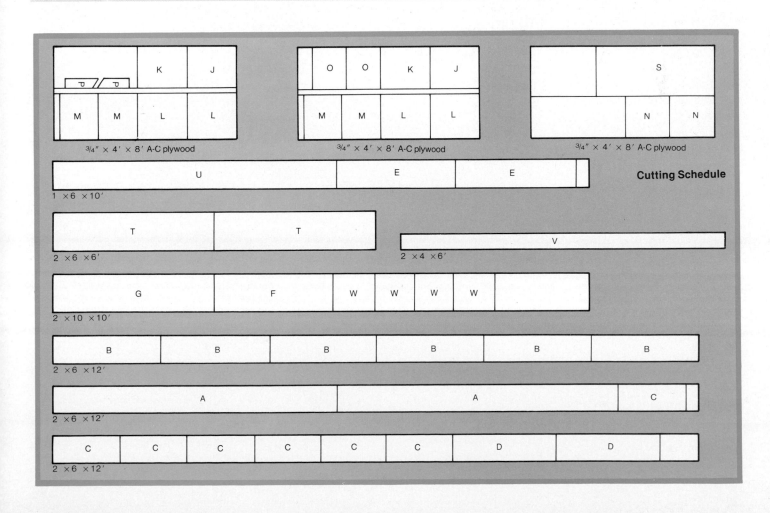

¾" × 4' × 8' A-C plywood   ¾" × 4' × 8' A-C plywood   ¾" × 4' × 8' A-C plywood

Cutting Schedule

1 × 6 × 10'

2 × 6 × 6'   2 × 4 × 6'

2 × 10 × 10'

2 × 6 × 12'

2 × 6 × 12'

2 × 6 × 12'

As the bench is assembled, it not only grows in size but also gets quite a bit heavier and more difficult to move. Therefore, it's a good idea to attach the wheels and axles to the base early on.

STEP 1
BUILDING THE BASE

From redwood, saw out the long and short rails, grille bars, axle supports, spacer, fixed axle base, and swivel axle base. Assemble the box frame by screwing together the long and short rails.

Then, make up a subassembly from the grille bars and a pair of short rails. Add the doubled short rails, and center the completed assembly in the box frame. Drive screws through the box frame's long-rail faces into the eight short-rail ends of the grille assembly.

Now, add the axle supports, which are nested in the ends and flush with the bottom of the base. Drive screws into these supports from all three available sides (the two long rails and one short rail on each end). Next, add the spacer to the base, attaching it to both the axle support and the surrounding rails. This spacer represents the thickness of the rotator on the steerable end. Then install the fixed axle base, driving screws right through the spacer into the rails and axle support. Make sure to check for 90° corners with a carpenter's or rafter square at all stages.

STEP 2
MAKING THE WHEELS

Draw circles on redwood with compasses, and cut out the rough wheels with a band or jig saw. Drill a pilot hole through the circle centers, and mount the wheels, one at a time, on a scrap board with a nail driven through the hole. Position this board so that the wheel may be hand-rotated against a belt or disk sander, and sand the circumference smooth. The circumference edges are most easily shaped using a router, set up inverted as a shaper, mounted in a table available commercially for this purpose. Load a roller-bearing-guided rounding-over bit in the router

ASSEMBLING THE BASE AND GRILLE

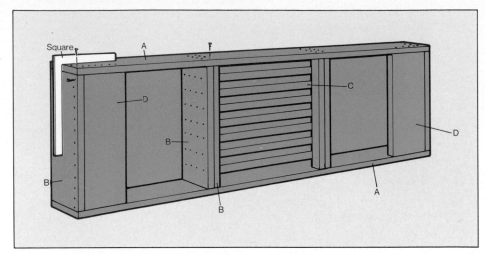

Assemble the rails by driving long screws through holes drilled with a combination bit. Assemble the grille bars with the inner rails, and then add them to the main base-rail structure. Check for square corners throughout the entire operation.

MOUNTING THE AXLE BASES AND ROTATOR

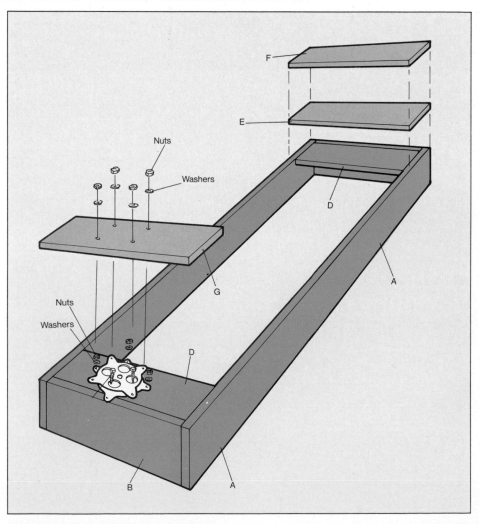

The axle supports fit in the end areas between the long and short rails. Screw them in place on three sides. The spacer in the rear makes up for the thickness of the rotator at the front. The fixed and swivel axle bases are installed next.

and adjust the tool-bit height for the desired cut. Place the wheel flat on the table, and rotate it in a counter-clockwise direction against the tool bit. Be sure to use eye protection. Drill 7/8-inch-diameter axle holes at the wheel centers.

STEP 3
INSTALLING WHEELS, AXLES, ROTATOR, AND HANDLE

The pipe nipples are cut to the correct length at the plumbing supply store. Therefore, all you need to do is to assemble the wheel, caps, nipples, and washers in the order shown in the drawing and to tighten up the caps. The shorter axle assembly is for the rear, or fixed, axle, while the longer one is for the front, or steer-able, axle.

Lay out two centerlines on the swivel axle base, one parallel with the long axis and one parallel with the short axis. Then center the rota-tor over the swivel axle base so that the ears line up with these axes, and trace the mounting holes on them. Drill 1/4-inch-diameter holes at these locations.

Invert the base, and place the rota-tor on both the front short rail and the axle support. Center it between the long rails, with two ears of the bot-tom plate over the front short rail and the other two ears over the axle sup-port. Then mount the rotator to the base, using lag bolts for the front rail and carriage bolts for the support.

Mark a hole center on the axle sup-port (on the base) directly under one of the free ears of the rotator's top plate (which will be fastened to the swivel axle base). This mark should be made near the middle of the axle support for convenience. Drill a 3/4-inch-diameter hole through the axle support at this mark. Now, you can insert carriage bolts, one at a time, through this hole, into the ear hole on the top plate, and then into the 1/4-inch-diameter holes of the swivel axle base. Lock plate and base to-gether with washers and nuts.

Mount the axle assemblies to their respective bases with pipe straps and lag bolts. The handle and handle-base assembly are attached

MAKING THE CABINETS

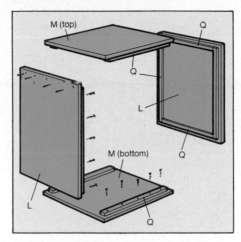

1. Each cabinet has twelve reinforcement nailers, one for each edge joint. The sides overlap the tops.

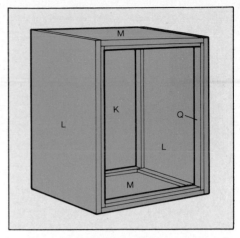

2. Add the pocket-cut front and the solid back over the open box cabinet structures, driving screws into the nailers.

SHAPING AND MOUNTING THE WHEELS

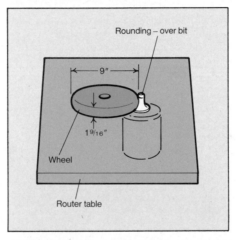

1. The wheels have been sawn and sanded. Form the rounded edges with a table-mounted router, using a rounding-over bit with a roller guide.

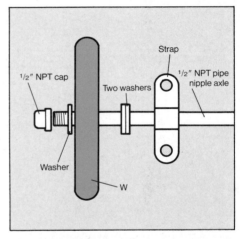

2. Drill axle holes in wheels. Then assemble them on pipe with washers, caps, and pipe straps. Mount assembly to base.

MOUNTING THE CABINETS ON THE BASE

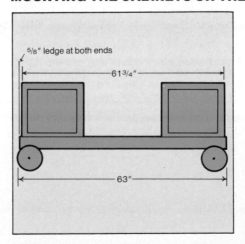

1. Mount painted cabinets on base-rail assembly with screws at precise locations so that top will fit exactly later on.

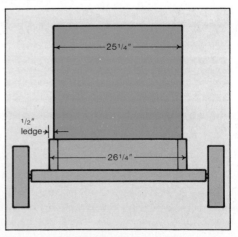

2. Note spread of swivel axle to permit tight turns. Note ledges formed at junctions of cab-inet and base assembly.

to the swivel axle base with pairs of screweyes, as shown. To facilitate this, temporarily open the eyes on the handle base, pick up the screweyes from the swivel base, and close the opened eyes, using pliers.

STEP 4
BUILDING THE CABINETS

Saw out all plywood parts for the cabinets, including backs, fronts, sides, tops, bottoms, doors, shelves, and shelf supports. Also, saw out all cabinet nailer (1¹/₁₆-inch square) stock. Pocket-cut the door opening in the cabinet fronts, as shown in the Portable Bar project.

Note that the sides overlap the top and bottom and that the front and back overlap both sides as well as the top and bottom. Fit the nailers, screw them to the appropriate panels, and assemble the cabinets by screwing through the panels into the nailers. Drive these screws slightly below the surface, plug the holes with filler or putty, and sand all edges smooth. Apply exterior primer, and then exterior finish paint to all cabinet, shelf, and door surfaces.

STEP 5
MOUNTING CABINETS TO BASE

The cabinets are screwed to the base near each end. They are positioned to leave a ¹/₂-inch ledge at both front and back and a ⁵/₈-inch ledge at each end.

STEP 6
ASSEMBLING TABLETOP NAILER AND TABLETOP

Trim the six pieces of tabletop nailer to size, and screw them to the tops of the cabinets. Make sure that the cabinets are installed on the base squarely and that the nailers are square as well. This is necessary for a good fit of the tabletop, which is the next piece to be added.

When installing the tabletop, make sure to allow an ¹¹/₁₆-inch ledge at each end and at the front, with no ledge at the rear. You could now simply add another plywood layer to the tabletop and paint it, but the suggested tile top adds a real touch of class.

ASSEMBLING THE TOP

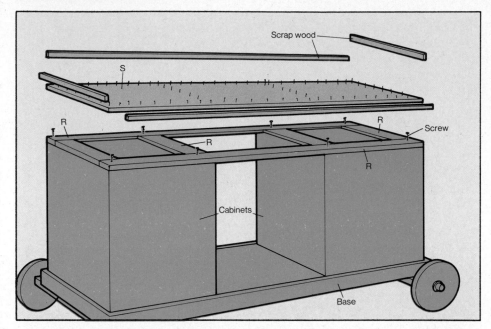

Install the network of nailers over the tops of the cabinets. Keep the proper ledge dimensions where nailers and cabinets join. Then screw the plywood top in position on the nailers, flush at the edges. Add scrap border for tile work, which will be done later.

MAKING THE HANDLE AND HANDLE BASE

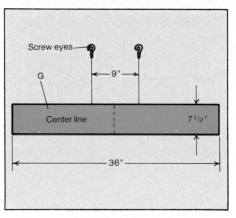
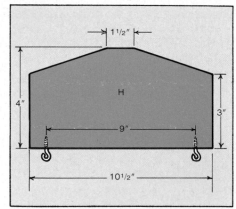

1. The handle attaches to the front edge of the swivel-axle base with heavy-duty screweyes. Mark the edge, and install them.

2. Make the hardwood base, and install its screweyes. Open them with pliers. Drill assembly holes in base and handle.

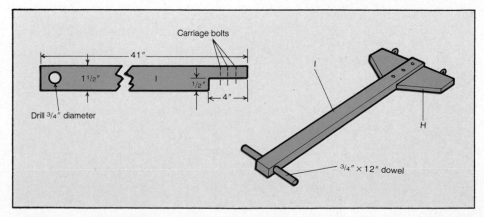

3. Drill the dowel hole in the top of the hardwood handle, install, and lock the dowel. Bolt the base to the rabbeted hardwood handle. Connect the screweyes, and close them. Later, the handle will be folded up and the dowel snapped into holders.

STEP 7
INSTALLING THE TILE TOP

Nail a temporary scrap wood border around the top, using the ledge on the three sides where it exists. The size of the top will accommodate the 45 4-×8-inch American Olean Quarry Natural flat tiles, with no cutting, in a 3 × 15 array. They are set with epoxy mortar. The tools you'll need are a ¼-inch square-notched trowel for spreading the mortar, a flat scrap wood board and hammer to beat in the tiles, a grout float, and some burlap rags.

Make up the mortar by first mixing the resin with the hardener and then adding the powder, according to the instructions. Spread the mortar on the plywood top with a sweeping motion and with the trowel angled to control the cusp depth at ³/₁₆–¹/₄ inch. Epoxy mortar has a limited working life, so set out the tiles quickly, beat them in to lock them in place, and level the tile surface, using a scrap board and hammer randomly. Now, sight down the joints, and straighten up any crooked lines. Also, remove any excess mortar.

STEP 8
FINAL ASSEMBLY

While the epoxy is curing, screw in the shelf supports, and add the shelves. Hang the doors, and install the hasps and staples.

STEP 9
GROUTING AND FINISHING UP

Twenty-four hours after setting the tiles, mix up grout to a creamy, thick consistency, and spread it around with the float, forcing it into the open tile joints. Allow a few minutes for setting. Then remove the surface residue with burlap rags. This requires firm pressure and perhaps a second or third polishing with damp and then dry rags.

Remove the scrap wood border around the tile, and clean the ledge. Nail the fence parts to the top, and screw the fence parts to each other. Set the nails, and plug the holes. Then carefully run a narrow bead of caulk around the tiles and fence joint.

MIXING AND APPLYING THE EPOXY

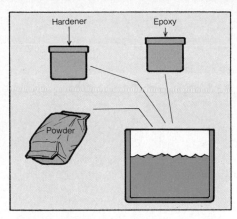

1. Epoxy mortar has three ingredients: epoxy resin, hardener, and powder. Mix the first two together; then add the third. This mixture has a limited working time.

2. Apply the mortar, which should be fairly stiff, in long, sweeping arcs with a ¼-inch notched trowel.

BEATING IN THE TILES

Move a scrap board over the field in random directions, and strike it with a hammer to set and flatten the tiles.

APPLYING THE GROUT

Work the grout, at the consistency of thick cream, into the empty joints between the tiles with a rubber-bottom float.

CLEANING THE TILES

After the grout has partially dried, polish the tile surface with burlap to remove any residue.

REMOVING THE SCRAP EDGE

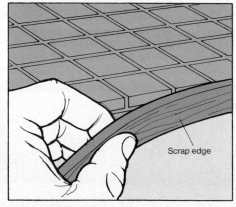

When the grout has set, remove the scrap border, install the redwood fence, and caulk the joint between fence and tiles.

DOGHOUSE

Man's best friend deserves a home of his own to shelter from the elements. This doghouse has a base of pressure-treated lumber to prevent water or insect damage, plus a multi-layered floor with a built-in, expanded polystyrene slab that provides protection from the cold.

The construction is mainly exterior A-C plywood, pressure-treated lumber, and galvanized nails. The removable roof is built much like the one on your own house, except that it lacks rafters. It has sheathing, covered by impregnated felt, which in turn is covered by asphalt shingles with a 5-inch weather exposure. It's a well-made house designed along traditional lines.

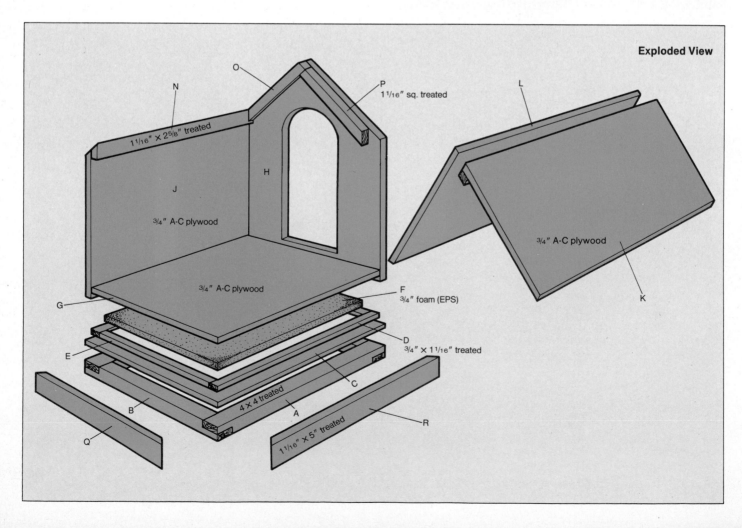

Exploded View

N

O

P
1¹¹/₁₆″ sq. treated

L

1¹¹/₁₆″ × 2⁵/₈″ treated

H

J

¾″ A-C plywood

¾″ A-C plywood

¾″ A-C plywood

F
¾″ foam (EPS)

G

K

D
¾″ × 1¹¹/₁₆″ treated

E

C

B

4 × 4 treated

A

R

Q

1¹¹/₁₆″ × 5″ treated

BILL OF MATERIALS

Qty	Size	Material
2	3/4 × 4 × 8'	A-C Plywood
1	4 × 4 × 12'	Pressure-treated wood (P/T)
1	5/4 × 6 × 12'	Pressure-treated wood
1	5/4 × 6 × 8'	Pressure-treated wood
1	Bundle	3/4" Expanded polystyrene foam (EPS)
	6d nails	Oval head, galvanized
50	#8 × 1 1/2"	Flat head, Phillips head, Twinfast or Zapper Screws
1	Quart	Exterior primer paint
1	Quart	Exterior finish paint
1	Bundle	Roof shingles
1	3 × 9'	Piece #15 saturated felt
	3/8"	Staples
	3/4"	Roof nails, galvanized

PARTS LIST

Part	Name	Qty	Description	Part	Name	Qty	Description
A	Long base support	2	3 1/2" × 3 1/2" × 37", P/T	J	Side	2	3/4" × 35 1/2" × 23 3/4", A-C ply
B	Short base support	2	3 1/2" × 3 1/2" × 24", P/T	K	Roof half, narrow	1	3/4" × 20" × 43", A-C ply
C	Base	1	3/4" × 24" × 37", A-C ply	L	Roof half, wide	1	3/4" × 20 3/4" × 43", A-C ply
D	Nailer, long	2	3/4" × 1 1/16" × 35 1/2", P/T	M	Roof nailer	1	1 1/16" × 1 1/16" × 48", P/T
E	Nailer, short	2	3/4" × 1 1/16" × 20 3/8", P/T	N	Side reinforcement	2	1 1/16" × 2 5/8" × 33 1/2", P/T
F	Insulation	1	3/4" × 20 3/8" × 33 3/8", EPS foam	O	End reinforcement, short	2	1 1/16" × 1 1/16" × 16", P/T
G	Shelf	1	3/4" × 22 1/2" × 35 1/2", A-C ply	P	End reinforcement, long	2	1 1/16" × 1 1/16" × 17", P/T
H	Front	1	3/4" × 24" × 35", A-C ply	Q	Skirt, short	2	1 1/16" × 5" × 26 1/8", P/T
I	Back	1	3/4" × 24" × 35", A-C ply	R	Skirt, long	2	1 1/16" × 5" × 39 1/8", P/T

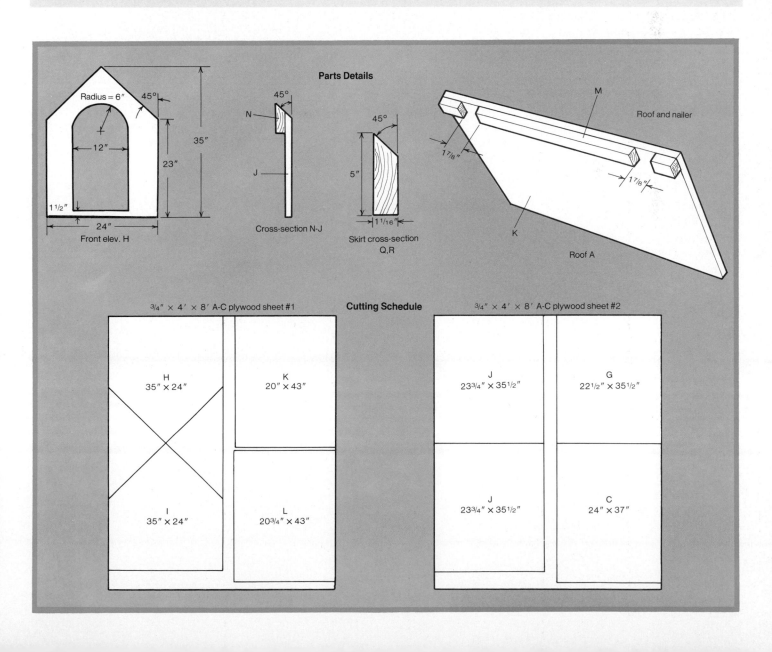

Parts Details

Front elev. H

Radius = 6"
45°
12"
23"
35"
1 1/2"
24"

Cross-section N-J

45°
N
J

Skirt cross-section Q,R

45°
5"
1 1/16"

Roof and nailer

M
1 7/8"
1 7/8"
K
Roof A

Cutting Schedule

3/4" × 4' × 8' A-C plywood sheet #1

H
35" × 24"

K
20" × 43"

I
35" × 24"

L
20 3/4" × 43"

3/4" × 4' × 8' A-C plywood sheet #2

J
23 3/4" × 35 1/2"

G
22 1/2" × 35 1/2"

J
23 3/4" × 35 1/2"

C
24" × 37"

STEP 1
MAKING THE BASE

Saw out all wood and plywood parts as specified in the cutting schedule and parts details. Make the half laps in the ends of all 4 × 4 base support parts. A radial saw is the easiest tool to use, but if you don't have one, mark the laps, crosscut them with a portable saw, and then chisel the waste away. Be sure to test fit the corners as you remove the waste from these joints to avoid damage and the necessity of making new ones.

As you assemble the short and long base-support pieces, ensure a true rectangle by holding a carpenter's or rafter square against a corner.

Nail the plywood base to the base support to lock your rectangle automatically and permanently. The edges of the plywood will be flush with the edges of the 4 × 4s.

Draw the outline of the nailers on the plywood surface; note that there should be a 3/4-inch ledge or rabbet formed all around the nailer rectangle. This ledge or rabbet will nest the plywood walls of the house later.

With a utility knife, cut the EPS to fit snugly within the nailer rectangle. (Incidentally, try to buy extruded EPS, rather than the cast type. The extruded type is 20 to 25 percent more effective in preventing heat transfer.) Then, nail the bottom shelf over the EPS and into the nailers and plywood below them. This shelf's edges will be flush with the nailer's outer edges as well.

STEP 2
MAKING THE FRONT AND BACK

Angles on the gable portion of the front and back may be cut on a radial saw or a table saw or with a jigsaw or portable saw. If you use a portable saw, mark and cut the bad side. Use a plywood blade if possible, and press masking tape over the cutting line to control or eliminate most of the splintering. Fine-toothed blades are available for use on a jigsaw, which will let you mark and cut on the good side of the plywood.

To lay out the opening in the front, measure and draw all the straight

MAKING THE BASE SUPPORT

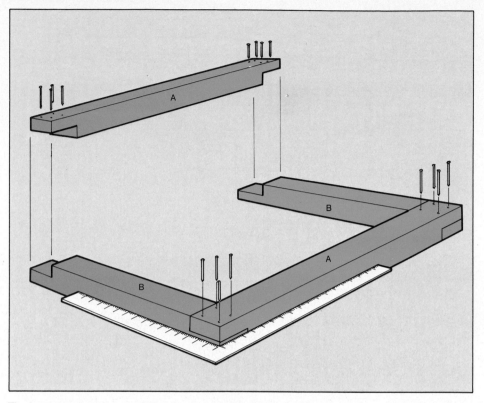

The base supports are made of 4 × 4 pressure-treated lumber, so they are suitable for ground contact. After machining the half laps at the ends, assemble all supports at the corners, using galvanized 10d or 12d nails. Be sure to maintain a true rectangle.

ASSEMBLING THE BASE

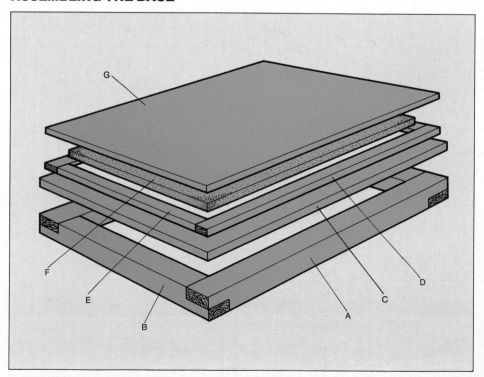

The sandwiched pieces that attach to the base supports are the plywood base, the nailer rectangle, the expanded polystyrene insulation, and the plywood bottom shelf.

lines, the bottom, the sides, and the vertical centerline. Draw the 6-inch radius at the top of the opening by placing the point of a compass on the vertical centerline, 14 inches from bottom, and swinging a semicircular arc. Cut out the opening with a jigsaw.

STEP 3
MAKING THE SIDES

Bevel the top edge of each side; saw out, trim off, and bevel both side reinforcements. Then, saw and trim both the long and short reinforcements. Screw these to the inside edge of both front and back and place them so they are flush with the top edges of the plywood. They strengthen the gable tops of the front and back and may also serve as nailers to which the roof may be attached permanently, in case you don't want a removable roof for ease of cleaning.

The side reinforcements are screwed to the inner top edges of the sides and positioned so that the bevels on both side and reinforcement form a continuous line. When this is done, seat the sides on the side ledges, with their ends flush with the end ledges, and nail them in place.

STEP 4
ASSEMBLING THE WALLS AND BASE

Next, trial-fit the front and back. They should: (1) sit on the end ledges; and (2) just cover the ends of the sides. Furthermore, the long and short reinforcements should fit just inside the side reinforcements. If the fit is correct, nail through the face of the front and back into the ends of the sides. If you have an active and powerful dog, you can strengthen the house by adding nailers to the four vertical internal corners and screwing through the front, back, and sides into them. Cut out the skirts, bevel their top edges, miter the corners, and nail them in place.

STEP 5
MAKING THE ROOF

Note that one roof side is wider than the other because the wider

ATTACHING FRONT AND BACK REINFORCEMENTS

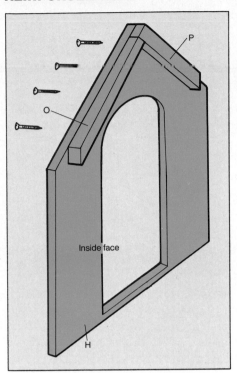

The reinforcements that are screwed to the front and back may serve either as stiffeners or as nailers for a permanent roof.

ATTACHING SIDE REINFORCEMENTS

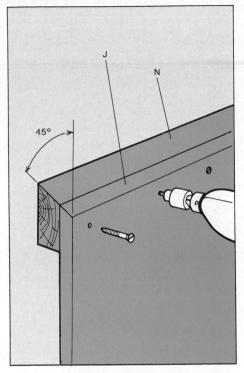

Bevel the side reinforcements to 45° angles at the top, and screw them to the inner side faces at the top.

ATTACHING THE SIDES

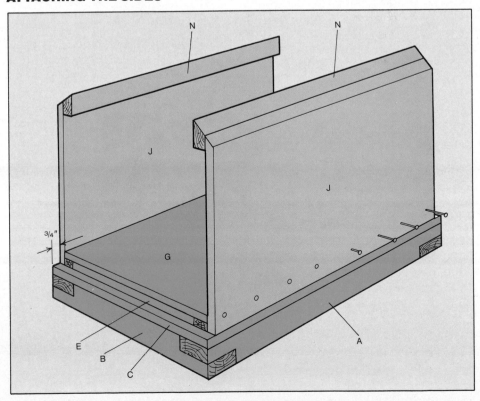

Rest the bottom edges of the sides on the side ledges, formed at the joint of the nailer and base. Position the sides flush at front and back, and nail them in.

roof side fits over the edge of the shorter side. Cut out the three roof nailers that join the two roof halves together. When the roof is in place, the longer piece will fit between the front and back nailers. Spaces at each end of the longer piece accommodate the front and back and their nailers; the roof nailer then continues out to both ends. Screw both roof sides to their nailers to make the roof assembly, and place it over the front and back for fit.

Now, staple saturated #15 felt to the roof, starting at the lowest part and going from front to back. Do the same on the opposite half. When you set the next higher piece of felt in place, overlap the piece below by 2 inches. Trim the felt off clean at the edges with a utility knife.

STEP 6
LAYING THE ROOFING

Note that three tab-butt asphalt shingles are typically 1×3 feet with slots or keys every foot. To avoid these gaps at the roof bottom, place the first or lowest row of shingles so that their tabs and slots face upward, with the granule surface facing outward. Allow a 3/4-inch overhang both at the ends and off the side of the roof, and nail the shingles in place as shown on shingle wrapper. This forms the starter course.

Next, nail the first exterior row on top of the starter course, but with the butts and slots facing downwards. Measure up 5 inches, and snap a chalk line from end to end. Nail on the second course with the butts touching this line, but lay the first shingle in that row 6 inches to the right or left to stagger the joints. Continue this procedure from both sides right up to the ridge. Use a utility knife to cut the shingles.

To make the caps over the ridge, if none are provided, cut each shingle into three equal pieces, fold these over the ridge, and nail in place, allowing 5 inches exposure. The nails for the first cap are hidden by the second cap, and so on.

Remove the roof; sand and paint the project, except the floor.

ATTACHING THE FRONT AND BACK

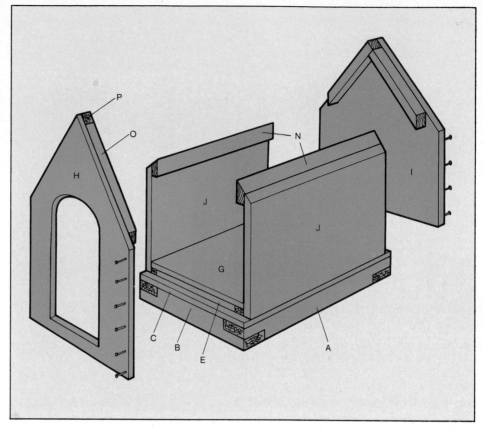

Trim the nailer ends of the front and back to fit between the side reinforcements. Then install front and back on the appropriate ledges.

ASSEMBLING THE ROOF NAILERS

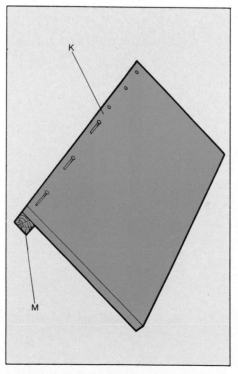

Center a 33¼-inch length of roof nailer on the top edge of the small roof half, and nail the two pieces together. Nail the second half.

LAYING THE ROOFING

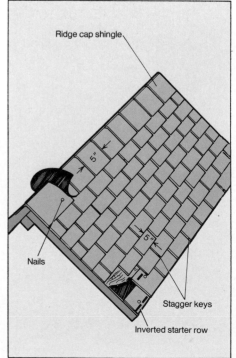

Staple felt to the roof. Nail on an inverted starter course at the bottom; additional courses with 5-inch exposure. Cap the ridge.

BARBECUE CART

Backyard barbecues with family and friends can be great fun, especially if you have the logistics under control. The purpose of our rolling barbecue cart is thus to provide organization and storage of all necessary items, both before and after the food is cooked. During the barbecue, it may be left open, providing a convenient 18 square feet of tabletop surface.

The top may be left closed for small gatherings or swung fully open to reveal space for the butcher block and a recess with a three-part acrylic server for hot or cold dishes, whose temperature is controlled by a water bath beneath.

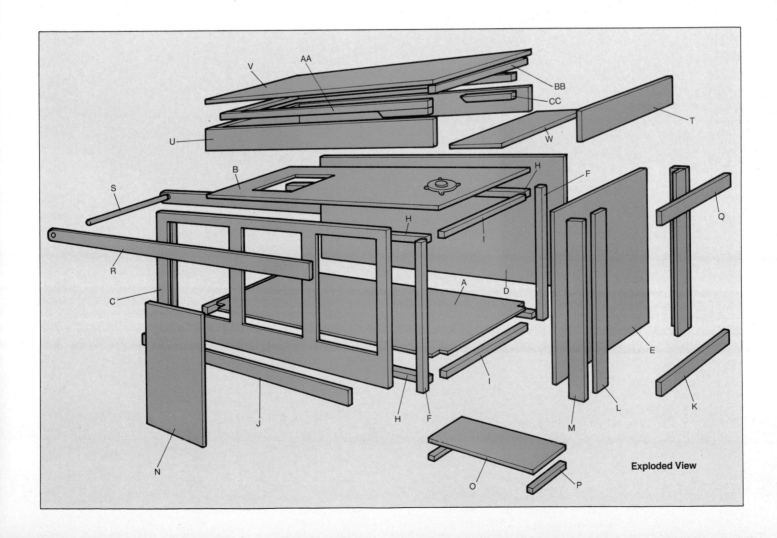

Exploded View

BILL OF MATERIALS

Qty	Size	Material
1	5/8 × 4 × 8'	T1–11 panel
2	3/4 × 4 × 8'	A-C plywood
1	2 × 10 × 2'	Construction heart redwood (ConHR)
1	2 × 4 × 6'	Douglas fir
1	5/4 × 8 × 8'	Spruce
1	4/4 × 10 × 6'	Red oak
3	1 × 3 × 14'	White pine
1	1 × 36"	Maple dowel
1	1/2" n.p.t.	Galvanized pipe, threaded at both ends
2	1/2" n.p.t.	Galvanized caps
4	1/2"	Pipe clamps
8	#12 × 1"	Truss head screws
6	1" inside diameter	Washers
6		Self-closing hinges (overlay door type)
225	#8 × 1 3/4"	Flat head, Phillips head, hardened assembly screws
1		Heavy-duty swivel (lazy Susan) N. 91K8
8	#12 × 1"	Pan or truss head screws
2	5/16 × 2 1/2"	Carriage bolts, nuts, washers
1 pkg.		Stanley CD4 turn buttons
		Stain
		Exterior primer
		Exterior trim paint

PARTS LIST

Part Name		Qty	Description
A	Bottom	1	3/4" × 20 13/16" × 47 5/16", A-C ply
B	Top	1	3/4" × 24" × 50 1/2", A-C ply
C	Front	1	5/8" × 30" × 48 1/2" T1–11 panel
D	Back	1	5/8" × 30" × 48 1/2" T1–11 panel
E	End	2	5/8" × 30" × 20 13/16" T1–11 panel
F	Corner nailer	2	1 1/2" × 1 1/2" × 30", fir
G	Corner nailer/leg	2	1 1/2" × 1 1/2" × 34 3/4", fir
H	Long cleat	4	1 1/16" × 1 1/16" × 44 1/4", spruce
I	Short cleat	4	1 1/16" × 1 1/16" × 17 7/8", spruce
J	Bottom trim (long)	2	3/4" × 2 1/2" × 50", pine
K	Bottom trim (short)	2	3/4" × 2 1/2" × 22", pine
L	Corner trim (narrow)	4	3/4" × 1 3/4" × 25", pine
M	Corner trim (wide)	4	3/4" × 2 1/2" × 25", pine
N	Door	2	3/4" × 12 3/4" × 22", A-C ply
O	Shelf	1	3/4" × 12" × 47 5/16", A-C ply

Part Name		Qty	Description
P	Shelf cleat	2	3/4" × 2 1/2" × 11 1/2", A-C ply
Q	Top trim (short)	2	13/16" × 2 1/2" × 22", oak
R	Top trim/ handle	2	13/16" × 2 1/2" × 60", oak
S	Handle	1	1" diameter × 23 5/8, dowel
T	Swing-top end	2	3/4" × 3 3/4" × 22 1/2", A-C ply
U	Swing-top side	2	3/4" × 3 3/4" × 50 1/2", A-C ply
V	Swing-top deck	1	3/4" × 24" × 50 1/2", A-C ply
W	Rotator support	1	3/4" × 10" × 22 1/2", A-C ply
X	Swing-top leg	2	1 1/16" × 1 1/16" × 37 1/2", spruce
Y	Top leg brace	1	3/4" × 4" × 22 3/8", A-C ply
Z	Bottom leg brace	1	3/4" × 4" × 22 3/8", A-C ply
AA	Long swing-top nailer	2	1 1/16" × 1 1/16" × 49", spruce
BB	Short swing-top nailer	2	1 1/16" × 1 1/16" × 20 3/8", spruce
CC	Rotator support spacer	2	1/2" × 1 1/16" × 10", spruce
DD	Wheels	2	1 1/2" × 9" diameter, Con H R

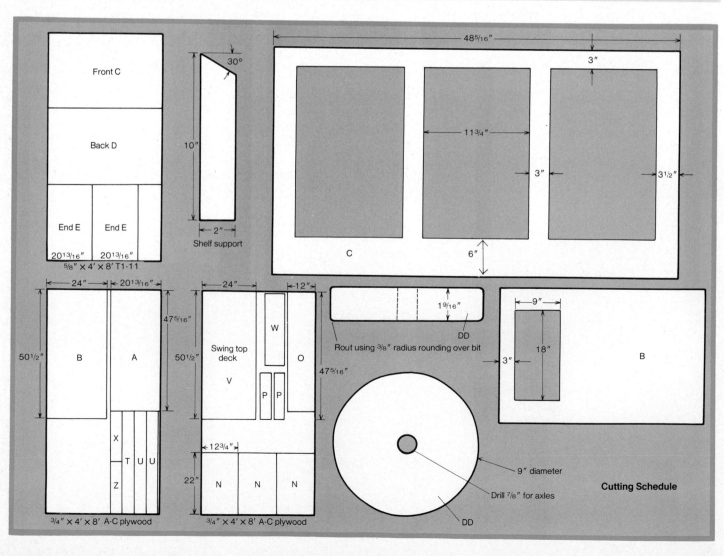

Cutting Schedule

STEP 1
PREPARING THE MAJOR PARTS

Saw out all cabinet panel parts, including front, back, ends, top, and bottom. Then do the same for the swing top.

Make the three pocket cuts in the cabinet front, plus the one required in the top, to fit the hot/cold server that you purchase. Note that these dimensions may very well differ from ours. All of these pocket cuts are done most quickly and safely on a table saw, with the workpieces face up.

Next, cut out the corner nailers and nailer/legs from 2 × 4 (1½- × 3½-inch) stock, as well as the remaining horizontal nailers from 5/4 (1 1/16 inches) stock required for the main cabinet. In order to get this project under control early on, make up the axle units, and then cut out and prepare the redwood wheels.

STEP 2
MAKING THE WHEELS

To complete the wheels, drill an ⅛-inch through hole at the compass center mark. This will serve as a temporary axle hole for a nail, driven into a scrap plywood board. The outline of the wheel should overhang this board. Then, clamp the board next to a disk or stationary belt sander so that the wheel circumference may be sanded smooth as the wheel is rotated past the sander.

Next, mount your router inverted, as a shaper, and load it with a roller-guided rounding-over bit. Carefully rotate the edges of the wheel past the spinning bit to obtain the desired contour. Finally, drill the permanent ⅞-inch diameter holes for the ½-inch n.p.t. (national pipe thread) axles, and assemble the axle, washers, wheels and caps, ready to roll.

STEP 3
STARTING THE ASSEMBLY

The most efficient way to proceed with the cabinet is to make the basic assembly and stain the vertical panels. Then, while the stain dries, cut out, sand, and prime all the pine trim and the top.

Do the same for the oak trim and handles, but give these a couple of

CUTTING AND ASSEMBLING THE CABINET

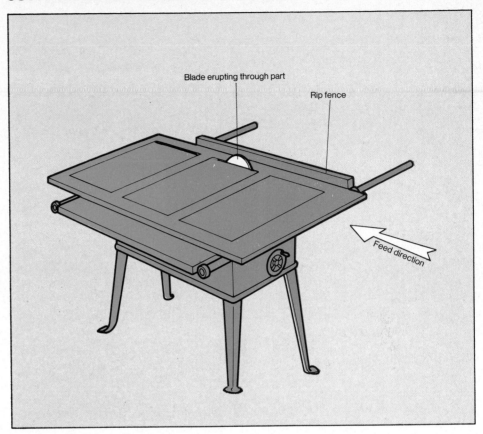

1. With fence adjusted and piece in place, raise blade, and advance the piece.

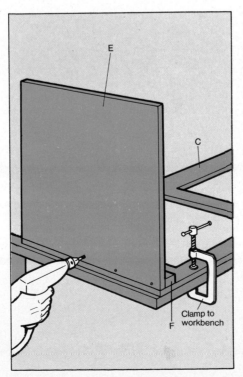

2. With corner nailer attached to the front, place the end into the rabbet formed at the corner. Drive the assembly screws home.

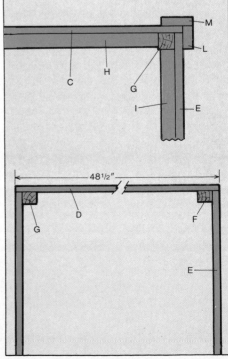

3. Top drawing shows assembly of front, end, nailer, cleats, and trim. Bottom drawing shows back, end, and nailers.

coats of exterior urethane varnish, not paint. Once the primer has dried on the trim and top, apply exterior latex trim paint to them. The panels, trims, top and handles are finished separately because it would be a tough job to apply the different finishes if these pieces were assembled.

The vertical T1–11 panels will be screwed to the nailing reinforcements at the internal corners and edges. You won't need to pre-drill the screw holes; they'll be hidden by trim.

But, you'll have to pre-drill the screw holes using a combination bit when you install the oak parts later on, because only special hardened screws can be driven through a hardwood such as oak without a clearance hole. Also, countersinks are needed because the screwheads will be visible after assembly.

STEP 4
CONTINUING THE BASIC ASSEMBLY

Start by screwing the corner nailers or leg nailers to the ends of both the back and front. Note that both the front and the back overlap the ends, so be sure to leave 5/8-inch space between the nailers and the edges of the front and back to nest the edges of the ends.

Then, clamp the front face down to a work surface, and add on the ends by driving screws through them into the nailer, at locations not already occupied by the first screws.

Set the back face down on the work surface, and place the assembly of front and two ends on it. Drive the screws home to join all four surfaces. Add the bottom horizontal cleats, which support the plywood bottom, and the upper horizontal cleats, which will be fastened to the underside of the top. Drill screw holes in these upper cleats for the top mounting screws.

Notch the corners of the bottom to clear the corner nailers, and screw it in place. Then invert the whole assembly and mount the wheel-and-axle assembly to the bottom nailers with pipe clamps. The cabinet can be righted and set on its legs and

ASSEMBLING THE CABINET (CONTINUED)

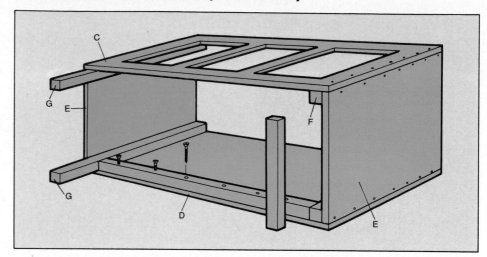

4. Looking up into the bottom of the cabinet, you can see the front, back, and ends attached at the corners to the legs and nailers. The lower cleats, which butt against these legs and nailers, serve to stiffen the front, back, and ends.

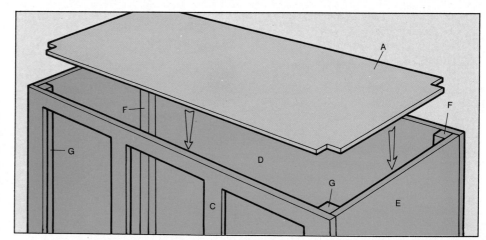

5. The bottom corners must be notched to clear the legs and nailers. The bottom is then placed in the cabinet, on top of the lower cleats, and screwed to them. This integrates the entire structure and locks it into a true rectangular shape.

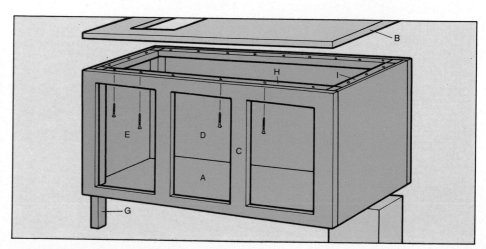

6. Drill holes through the horizontal cleats at the tops of the front, back, and ends. Then place the top in position on the cabinet. Weight the top down, or clamp it, and drive screws up from the bottom through the cleat holes into the top.

wheels. At this time, finish up the staining and painting.

STEP 5
INSTALLING THE TRIM, SHELF, AND TOP

Clamp the two oak top trim/ handles together with a piece of backup scrap to prevent splintering when the bit exits. Then, with the aid of a guide, drill the 1-inch diameter holes for the dowel handle.

Install these handles, as well as the remaining horizontal oak trim, with the screws. Next, nail on the lower horizontal pine trim. Finally, pre-assemble the two parts of each vertical corner trim, fit them between the upper and lower trims, and nail them in place. Note that the edge of the wide piece covers the edge of the narrow piece, giving the effect of equally wide corner pieces when in place. Set the nails, plug the holes, and touch up the paint.

Mark off the locations for the shelf supports on the inner faces of the ends, and install the supports with screws. Place the shelf on these supports, and screw them together. You may also wish to include a center support for the shelf. This can be merely a rap cleat, screwed to the inner face of the back.

Now, set the top in place on the cabinet, allowing equal overhang at the edges. Then drive screws up through the four cleats into the bottom surface of the top, locking it down.

Cut an oak scrap piece about $1/8 \times 3/4 \times 24$ inches, and screw or nail it to the top, about an inch from and parallel to the end with the pocket-cut hole. Wax the surface of this rubbing strip, which will touch the bottom edges of the swing top when it is rotated.

Don't mount the doors now; they'll only get in the way when you work on the swing top and the rotator.

STEP 6
MAKING THE SWING TOP

Screw the swing-top ends and sides together. Then, fit in the four nailers, and assemble the ends and sides to them with screws. Now,

INSTALLING THE TRIM

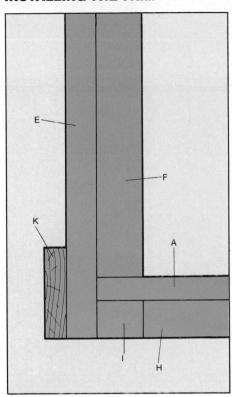

1. This view shows how the bottom, corner nailer, bottom cleat, end, and bottom-end trim fit together.

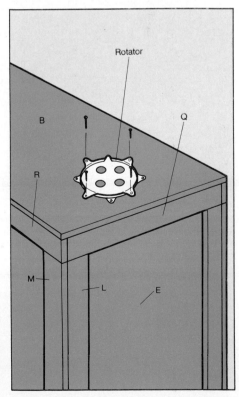

2. A view of the exterior corner shows the bottom, horizontal trim, and two-piece corner trim in place on two adjacent faces.

DRILLING THE HANDLE

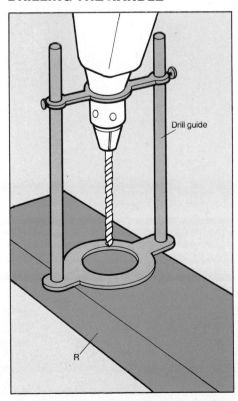

Use a drill attached to a guide to ensure a 90° angle between the hole axis and the handle surface.

INSTALLING THE ROTATOR

Screw the bottom rotator plate to the top. Offset the top plate, and drill a large hole in the top to install other screws.

screw the swing-top deck to the nailers. All screws whose heads are exposed should be countersunk and plugged prior to painting.

The rotator sits directly on the cabinet top and is attached to the swing top with a plywood support and its spacers. These spacers, which are placed between the rotator support and the nailers, are gauged to control the height of the bottom edges of the swing top above the cabinet top.

The swing-top end opposite the rotator will be supported in the closed position by the oak rubbing strip. So set this all up for a dry run with everything in place but not installed. Make sure that a constant 1/8-inch gap exists between the swing top and the cabinet top. This step is essential, especially if you have a rotator other than the one suggested.

If the spacer thickness is all right, screw the spacers to the nailers and the rotator support to the nailers through the spacers.

STEP 7
INSTALLING THE ROTATOR

First, lay out the location of the rotator on the cabinet top, on the right end (above the wheels). Center it from front to back and along a line 5³/₄ inches from the right end. This will center the rotator on the swing top support.

Next, punch-mark the four holes in the top, corresponding to those in the ears of the lower rotator plate. Then drive home the four #12 pan or truss head screws.

Now, with the lower rotator plate fixed to the cabinet top, turn the upper plate either clockwise or counterclockwise. The object here is to cause the upper plate holes *NOT* to align with the lower plate holes (where the screws are). The friction between the plates should then hold the upper plate in the position you have placed it.

Punch-mark the top in the center of the upper plate holes. Then drill completely through the top using a 1/2- to 5/8-inch diameter bit. You might want to back the top up with scrap wood to avoid splintering when the drill bit exits.

ASSEMBLING THE SWING TOP

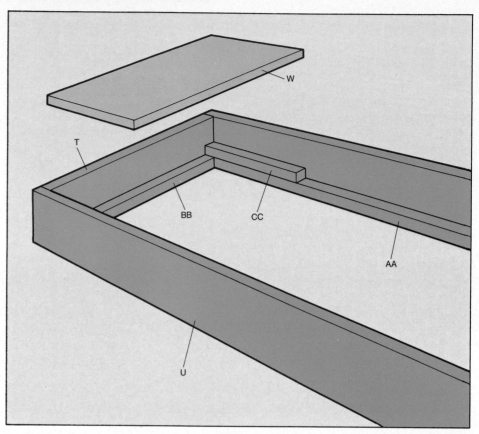

The thickness of the support spacers between the swing-top nailers and the rotator support matches the thickness of the rotator on the opposite end.

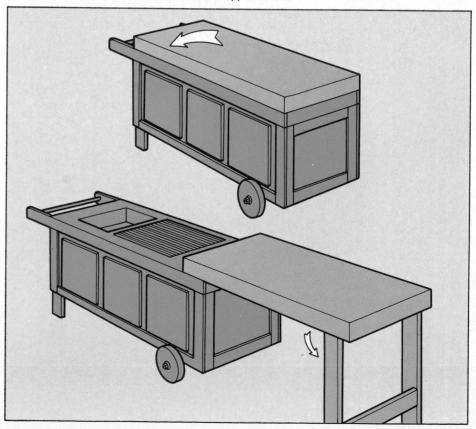

When the swing top is in the open position, the surface space is almost doubled, allowing room for a butcher block. Turn buttons lock the swing top closed.

The swing top should be primed, finish-painted, and thoroughly dry before you go further. Now, without moving the upper plate of the rotator, place the swing top squarely on top of the cabinet. It will actually rest on the rubbing strip and the upper rotator plate. Place a small rug or similar protective layer and then some heavy weights (or another pair of hands) on the top to hold it down firmly.

Then duck down inside the cabinet's right side-door opening, and look up. You'll see the holes just drilled through from above. Insert a punch into each of the four holes in turn, center it, and make a punch mark on the underside of the rotator support. Do not move anything.

Start a #12 pan or truss head screw in each of these holes and drive them home; don't move the top at all during this operation. If all's well, the work on the rotator is complete. If your doors have been painted and their hinge metal-primed and finished, mount the hinges on the doors and the doors on the front, covering the openings.

STEP 8
FINISHING UP

The swing top may be kept in the closed position, completely over the cabinet, whether in use or not. The turn buttons in the locked position will ensure this. In this mode, the leg assembly is folded up inside.

However, when the swing top is in the open position, the left end must be supported by the leg assembly in the down position. Thus, the leg assembly is hinged with carriage bolts at the swing-top's left end, opposite the rotator.

Screw the leg braces to the legs at the locations shown. Drill the holes in the swing-top sides. Match up those in the leg tops and check the radius of the leg tops. As these dimensions are quite critical, you might want to try them out with a short, scrap substitute on one side, just to be sure. In any event, make sure that the total width of the leg brace is not too wide to fit within the confines of the swing top. Check the legs in both up and down positions.

TOP ASSEMBLY DETAILS

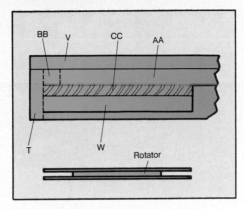

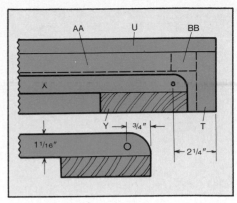

Cross-sectional view showing swing top, swing-top nailers, rotator support, and support spacer with rotator below.

Cross-section of swing top shows leg and upper brace in folded position. Round off brace end, and position bolt hole as shown.

MOUNTING THE WHEELS

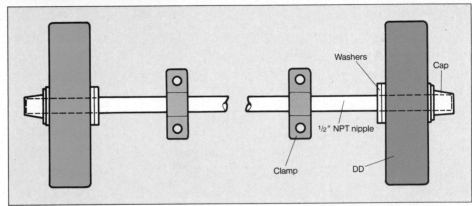

The cart is supported on one end by wooden wheels, mounted on a plumbing-pipe axle, retained by caps, and spaced by washers. The entire assembly is clamp-mounted to the bottom cleats. The cart becomes mobile when the handle is lifted at the fixed leg end.

ASSEMBLING THE LEG BRACE

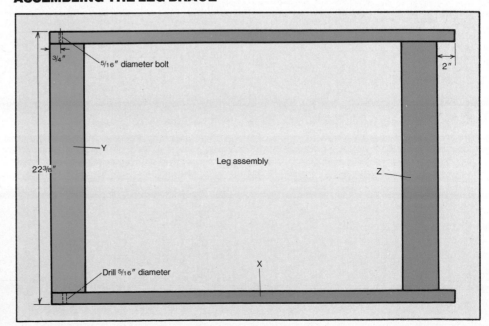

In the open position, the outboard end is supported by a set of legs and braces that fold up into the swing top for storage when it's not in use.

LIGHTING ENCLOSURE

Most homes have walks, decks, patios, gardens, or recreational areas that would welcome the charm and illumination of attractive lighting. Of course, commercial fixtures are available, but for the most part, these are metal and in basic tier or mushroom shapes.

This lighting project is a redwood enclosure, open at the bottom and louvered at the front. Access for any maintenance is easy from both below and front through removable louver assemblies.

The electrical set-up is built with weatherproof boxes, EMT raceway with connectors, and light fixtures that have a 100-watt capacity and are vaportight.

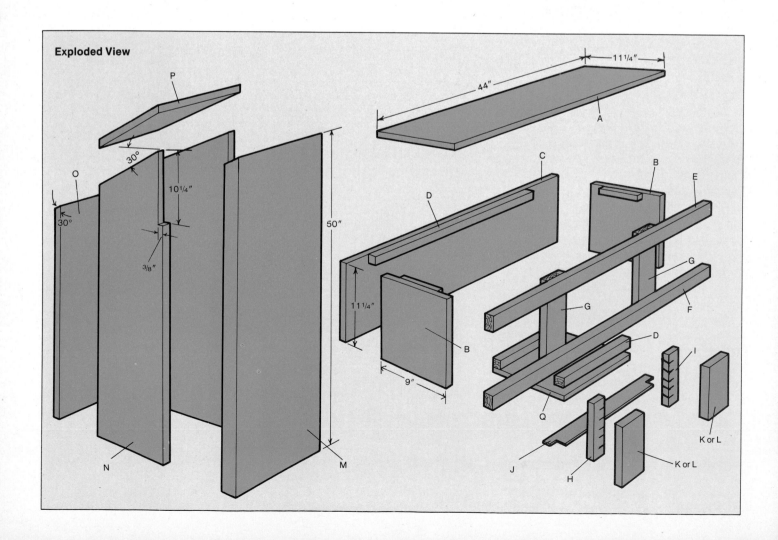

Exploded View

BILL OF MATERIALS

Qty	Size	Material	Qty	Size	Material	Qty	Size	Material
1	2×6×8′	Clear heart redwood	4	½″	EMT compression connectors	1	½″	90° metal sweep
1	5/4×12×8′	Clear heart redwood				2	½″	Bushing
1	1×12×12′	Clear heart redwood	1	½″	UF sealed connector	1	#10–32	Green ground screw
1	1×12×6′	Clear heart redwood	1	4′ length	EMT conduit	4		Wire nuts
2	100 Watt	Vaportight surface fixture, glass globe, cast guard (Stonco VCXL11GC or equivalent)	1	4′ length	14 gauge UF cable	80	#8 × 1½″	Flat head, Phillips head, stainless steel wood screws
			1	4′ length	14 gauge THWN conductor, black			
			1	4′ length	14 gauge THWN conductor, white	8	#12 × ¾″	Pan head screws
1	4″	Vaportight round box						Cuprinol #10 (in-ground wood preservative)

PARTS LIST

All parts clear heart redwood

Part	Name	Qty	Description	Part	Name	Qty	Description	Part	Name	Qty	Description
A	Top	1	¾″ × 11¼″ × 44″	H	Left-hand louver carrier	3	1¹/₁₆″ × 1¹/₁₆″ × 5¾″	L	Outer louver stiles	2	¾″ × 2¼″ × 5¾″
B	End	2	1¹/₁₆″ × 9″ × 11¼″	I	Right-hand louver carrier	3	1¹/₁₆″ × 1¹/₁₆″ × 5¾″	M	Post front	1	1½″ × 5½″ × 50″
C	Back	1	¾″ × 11¼″ × 44″	J	Louvers	15	¼″ × 1½″ × 10½″	N	Post sides	2	¾″ × 5½″ × 50″
D	Cleats	1	1¹/₁₆″ × 1¹/₁₆″ × 10′	K	Center louver stiles	4	¾″ × 2½″ × 5¾″	O	Post back	1	1¹/₁₆″ × 5½″ × 47½″
E	Top rail	1	¾″ × 2¹¹/₁₆″ × 44″					P	Post top	1	¾″ × 8½″ × 7″
F	Bottom rail	1	¾″ × 2¹¹/₁₆″ × 44″					Q	Bottom brace	1	¾″ × 10″ × 9″
G	Divider	2	¾″ × 2¾″ × 10³/₁₆″								

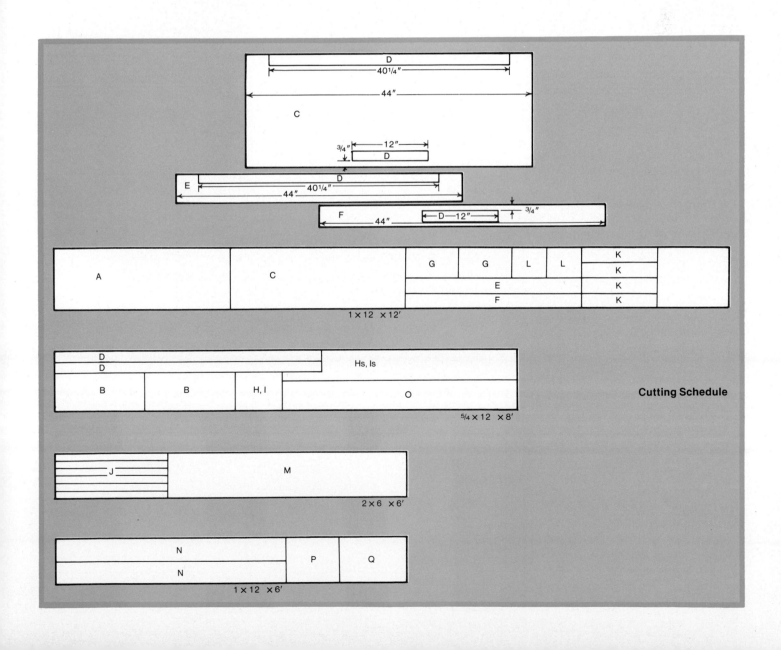

Cutting Schedule

The light enclosure is basically a long box that is open at the bottom, louvered at the front, and supported by a thick, hollow post. All electrical connections are made in weatherproof boxes within the long box, while the post houses the UF (underground feeder) cable, which supplies power from a GFI breaker at the house electrical panel.

After gathering all the wood, hardware, and electrical supplies in your shop, study the drawings and explanations carefully, since there is a fair amount of detail in this project. Also, the order of assembly must be followed accurately to avoid unnecessary work.

STEP 1
CUTTING PARTS

Saw out most of the larger parts per the cutting schedule, but ignore the machining of the louvers and their carriers for now. As for the cleat stock, pre-cutting it in one operation is quicker, but your accuracy will be improved if you trim it to length as you need it.

All flat head wood screws are driven into holes, pre-drilled with a combination bit to prevent splitting, especially near the ends of boards, and to provide a countersink for the flush seating of flat head screws.

STEP 2
ASSEMBLING THE ENCLOSURE

First, fasten the short cleats to the inner faces of the ends at the top. Center these cleats with a minimum of 1⅛ inches side clearance to both edges of the end. Then, screw the long and short cleats to the back—one long cleat to the top rail and one short cleat to the bottom rail.

The front assembly consisting of rails and dividers is next. Then, the back may be attached to the ends with all cleats in place. These cleats, together with the top cleat from the front, will be used to secure the top.

Note that the inner faces of the ends fit flush against the ends of the long cleat mounted to the back. The fit is the same when the front (rails, dividers, and cleats) is added to the back-and-end assembly. Check that

ASSEMBLING THE ENCLOSURE

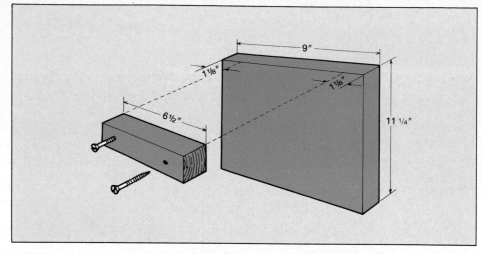

1. Begin to construct the enclosure by screwing the short cleats to the inner faces of the ends, flush with the top, and with the end clearances shown.

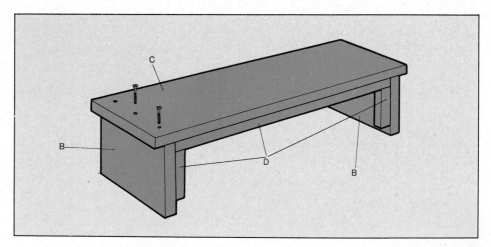

2. Place the back, with its cleats on the edges of the ends, so that the back cleats touch the inner faces of the ends. Drill holes with a combination bit and drive the screws.

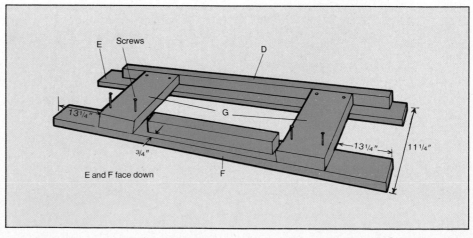

3. Join the top and bottom rails with the top dividers, 13¼ inches from the ends. Divider top butts against top cleat, and divider bottom is flush with bottom edge of bottom rail.

the overhang past the end is equal at back and front. An error here will have been caused by a cleat that was not properly centered; such a problem may be easily corrected.

The enclosure should now look like an open, four-sided box. Before installing the top, mark the positions of the cleats attached to the ends, front, and back below it; these will receive the screws that will hold the top in place. Draw centerlines on the top, representing centerlines of the cleats, for accurate drilling and screwdriving. When you align the top with the front and back and complete the assembly to this stage, the open box will be locked in place as a true rectangle. Check to see that the bottom brace fits properly between the back and front of the enclosure at the center and set it aside. If installed now, it will interfere with the fitting of the electrical parts, which must be added later.

STEP 3
ASSEMBLING THE POST

The post is made by combining two sides, a back, and a front, to form a long, rectangular redwood tube. Its entire top is sloped back at a 30° angle and later fitted with a top whose front edge tucks neatly under the edge of the enclosure top. The sides have long, 3/8-inch-deep notches at their upper ends to mount and support the enclosure. Additional support is provided by screws, driven through the back of the enclosure into the face of the post front.

Begin work on the post by sawing the miters at the upper ends of the sides and the corresponding bevels on the front and back respectively. Saw out the notch on both sides. Then, nail the sides to the front so that the side miters align with the front bevel and the front is set back 3/8 inch from the main edges of the sides. The front's face is even with the seat of the sawn notch, allowing the enclosure to fit therein.

Set the post on its back, and make a punch mark 3 inches down from the top on the centerline. Now, drill a 1 1/2-inch-diameter hole for passage of

ASSEMBLING THE ENCLOSURE (CONTINUED)

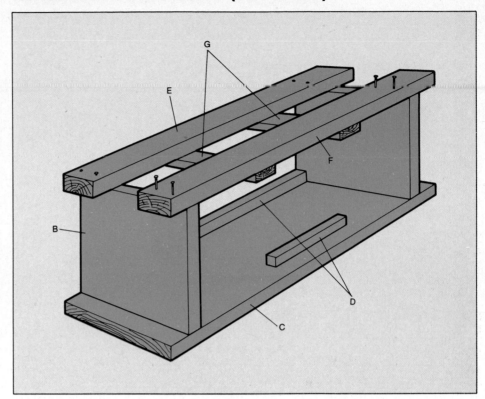

4. Line up the rail assembly with the ends so that the ends of the long cleat butt up against the inner faces of the ends. Check the assembly for square. Then drill the screw clearance holes with the combination bit and drive the screws.

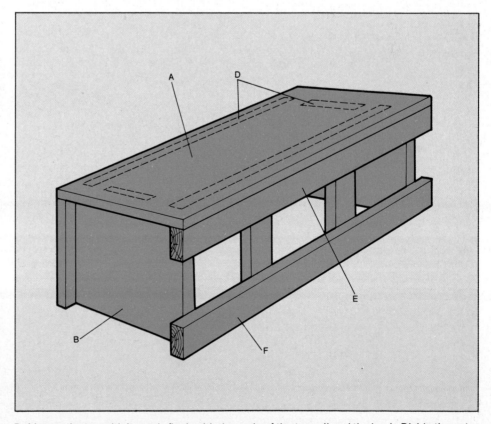

5. Line up the top with its ends flush with the ends of the top rail and the back. Divide the extra 3/4-inch overhang equally between the rail front and the back. Lay out the cleat locations. Then drill the clearance holes, and drive the screws to lock the top.

the UF cable and its sealed connector into the enclosure.

STEP 4
FITTING THE ENCLOSURE AND POST

Next, set the enclosure on its front face with the notched end of the post in proper position over the center part of the enclosure back. Make sure the enclosure back is fully seated on the ledge of the notches and prop; better yet, clamp it in this position. Continue the hole through the back of the enclosure. Fit but do not install the post top at this time. Although the enclosure can be joined to the post now, it will prove awkward when installing the electrical parts.

STEP 5
MAKING THE LOUVERED PANELS

The front is divided into thirds, each of which has a louvered panel. These louvers tend to deflect rain, but they still allow light to shine through the front face and the bottom opening.

Note that the louvers are exactly alike but their carriers, which orient and separate them, are not. Each louver section has a right-handed and a left-handed carrier. Therefore, for the entire front, three left-handed and three right-handed louver carriers are needed.

Make these carriers in groups of three (left- or right-handed) and cut them apart later, as it's easier and safer to handle a longer workpiece, whether working with a table saw or radial saw.

First, take two 24-inch lengths of the $1^1/_{16}$-inch-square stock and carefully lay out the $1/_4$-inch-thick slots at a 30° angle, observing the right- and left-hand orientation. If using a radial saw, lock in a pair of $1/_8$-inch-thick dado blades to make the $1/_4$-inch-thick cut. Then, set the arm at the 30° mark on the appropriate side, and adjust the post for the correct depth of cut. Test this on scrap for accuracy. If you're correctly set up, place the 24-inch length against the fence, and

ASSEMBLING THE POST

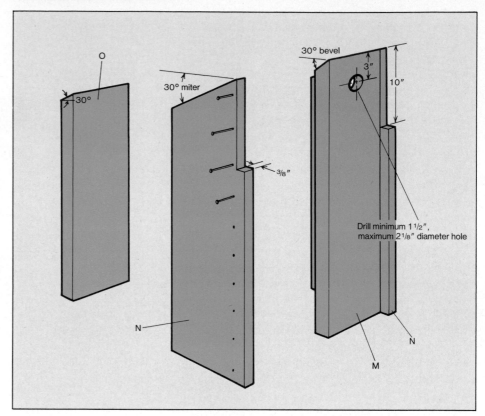

1. Machine the side miters, front and back bevels, and notches. Nail the sides to the front with the miters and bevels aligned and the front face flush with the depth of the side notches. Add the back, and drill the hole in the front to fit the electrical parts.

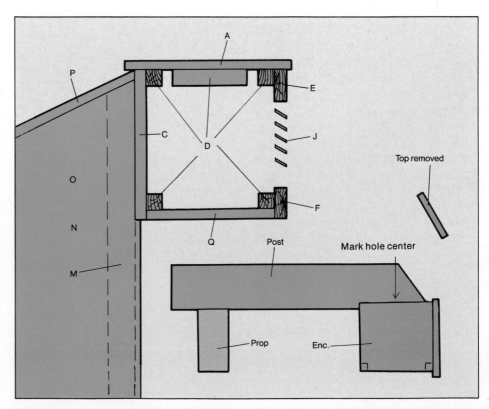

2. Place the enclosure face down. Set the top end of the post on it, with the notches fully home, and prop the lower end. Mark the hole center in enclosure back, and drill it.

align the blade path with the first cutting mark. For a splinter-free cut, back up the 24-inch workpiece with a piece of scrap of the same height. Then make the fifteen cuts carefully. Re-set the saw arm to cut the opposite-handed piece, and repeat the procedure.

If you're using a table saw, the marking steps are the same and the blades are handled in the same manner, including the depth of cut setting. The miter gauge will control the 30° angle for the left-handed cuts by using the 30° setting on one side, and for the right-handed cuts using the other side.

All fifteen louvers should be ripped to correct thickness and then trimmed to equal length. The 1/2-inch-square notches are gang-sawn with dado blades, either on a radial or a table saw.

To use a radial saw, load it with a 5/8–3/4-inch-thick dado set, set the arm at 0° for a straight crosscut, and adjust the post height for the correct depth of cut. Rack up the fifteen louver blanks and a scrap backup flat against the fence in the correct location for a 1/2-inch-wide bite. Finally, use a square to make sure that the pack forms a perfect rectangle. Clamp the entire pack, and cut the notches. Reverse the ends, reposition the scrap backup, clamp up the pack, and cut the notches on the other end.

If you have a table saw, squarely clamp the pack and backup scrap block. Set the 5/8–3/4-inch-thick dado set to cutting height and the miter gauge to 0°. Make sure that the clamp clears the miter gauge. Clamp a scrap block flat against the fence across from the blade, and set the fence so that the distance from the near face of the scrap block to the blade is correct for the first cut. Place the back of the louver pack against the miter gauge and the left end against the block, which serves as an auxiliary fence. Advance the miter gauge and pack to make the first cut. Make a similar set-up for the second notches and make the cut.

Assemble the three sets of louvers, carriers, and stiles, and hold

CUTTING THE LOUVER PARTS

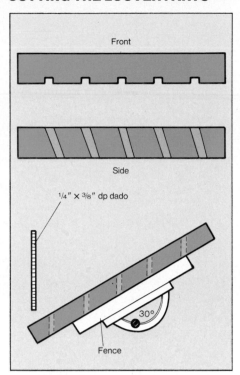

1. Cut the mitered slots in the louver carriers on the table saw, with the miter gauge set at 30°.

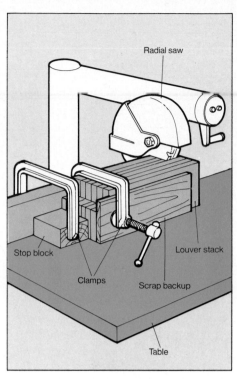

2. Gang-cut louver notches in a pack, squared up and clamped to the radial-saw fence.

ASSEMBLING THE LOUVERS

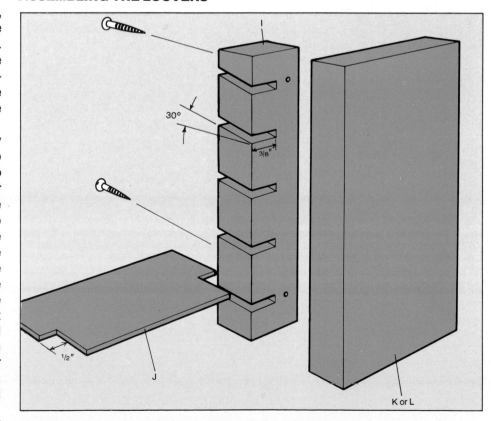

1. The enclosure front is divided into thirds—each partially covered by five louvers held in place by a pair of slotted carriers—and faced with a pair of stiles.

them aside until the electrical work is installed.

STEP 6
INSTALLING THE ELECTRICAL PARTS

Begin the electrical work by screwing a UF sealed connector into the rear threaded opening of a round weatherproof box. Determine the length of UF cable required to reach the next pull box or metal box within the house wall. Add 10 feet to this measurement, and cut off this total length of UF cable. Strip back the insulation about 6 inches from one end of the cable. Pass this through the 1½-inch-diameter hole in the back of the enclosure, insert the cable through the sealed fitting into the round box, and lock the fitting. Then, center the box over the hole, punch-mark the mounting holes, and drive in the mounting screws. Mount the two vaportight fixtures to the top of the enclosure near the ends, and install EMT compression fittings in all fixtures.

Make a cardboard template for the modified S curve needed for the ½-inch EMT tubing. Remove the compression-fitting nuts, and note that the tubing should bottom out in the fittings. Form the EMT to shape with a tubing bender, or hickey, and cut the tubing to length with tubing cutter or hacksaw; then, file the end smooth. To connect everything, you may have to dismount a box or fixture. When all is fitted up, tighten the compression nuts and drive home all mounting screws.

Check the weatherproof round box for a 10–32 (#10 screw, 32 threads to the inch) threaded hole for the green ground screw. If no threads exist, run a 10–32 bottom tap into the boss (small tower with hole). Route the black and white fixture wires through the EMT to the round box, and connect all black wires together with a wire nut; do the same with the white wires. Drive a green ground screw partly into the tapped hole, wind a loop of the bare ground wire from the UF cable around the screw, and drive it home. Since all electrical work must conform to your local

ASSEMBLING THE LOUVERS (CONTINUED)

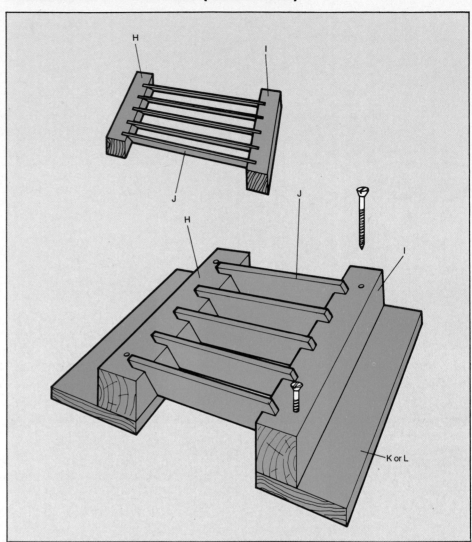

2. View of louvers assembled to louver carrier with epoxy shows Venetian-blind effect of slanted slots. Louver-carrier assembly is then screw-fastened to a pair of stiles (either center or outer), ready for installation on the housing.

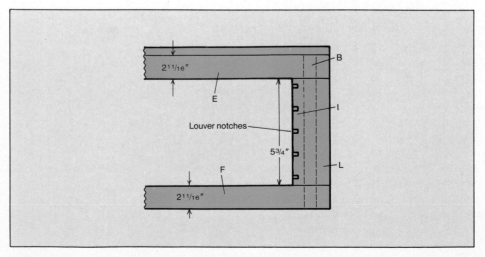

3. Phantom View from front shows the relative positions of louvers, carriers, top, top and bottom rails, end, stiles, and divider.

electrical code and be inspected by local authorities, leave the boxes open until your work has been approved. Note that the ground screw is mounted in the round box because from that point to the fixtures, the wires are enclosed in an all-metal raceway that serves the purpose of the ground wire in that area.

STEP 7
MAKING THE FINAL ASSEMBLY

Now, fit and mount the louver assemblies. Pass the UF through the hole in the front of the post, and mount the enclosure to the post. Run the UF down the post, into a ½" metallic sweep with end bushings and out of the post. Add the post top and the bottom brace. The unit is now ready for mounting in the ground as shown.

INSTALLING THE ELECTRICAL PARTS

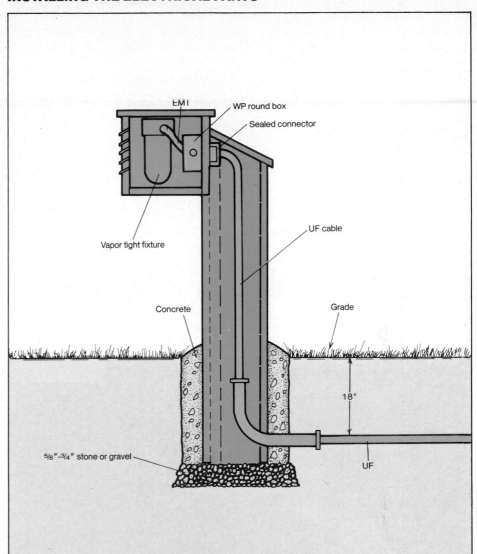

1. Post is set in foundation. UF cable enters post through bushed metal or plastic sweep; then it goes into a weatherproof box via a sealed UF connector.

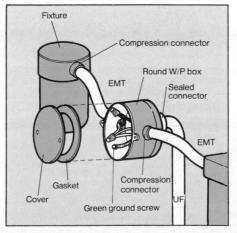

2. Formed EMT with compression connectors joins weatherproof box to both fixtures.

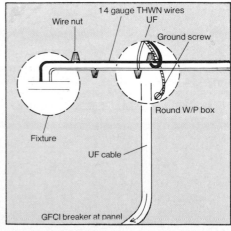

3. All connections made with wire nuts must be inside either the fixture or round weatherproof boxes.

DUCKBOARDS

Duckboards, or wooden walks, can be used to solve many different backyard problems. For example, they provide dry crossing for grassy areas that don't drain properly; they also make attractive dividers for large planting areas.

Whatever the purpose, this is a project that you will have to build just once in your lifetime, thanks to the properties of the construction material, pressure-treated wood (wood that has been saturated with copper-chromium-arsenate solution). This treated lumber resists the destructive effects of both water and insects. As a matter of record, tests on in-ground samples have shown that it retains its protective properties for more than thirty years.

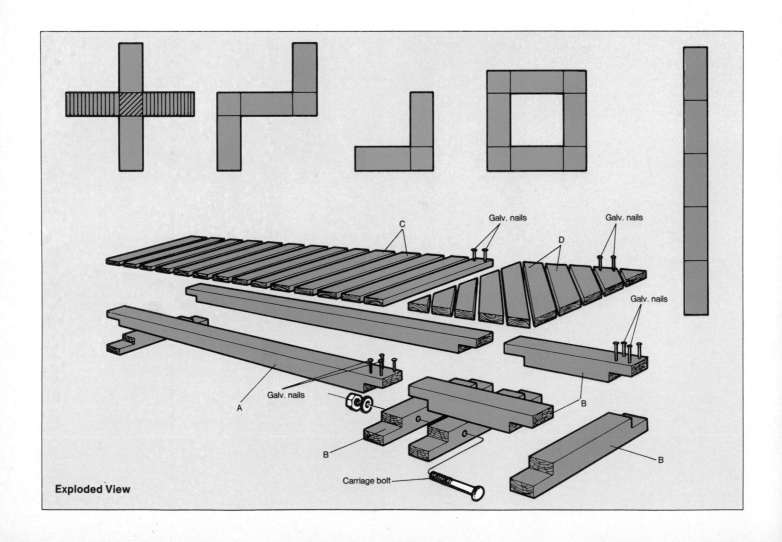

C

Galv. nails

D

Galv. nails

Galv. nails

A

Galv. nails

B

B

B

B

Carriage bolt

Exploded View

BILL OF MATERIALS

Qty	Size	Material
8	4 × 4 × 8'	Pressure-treated lumber
3	4 × 4 × 10'	Pressure-treated lumber
24	2 × 4 × 12'	Pressure-treated lumber
8	3/8 × 8"	Carriage bolts, nuts, washers
	10d	Oval head, galvanized nails

PARTS LIST

All parts pressure-treated lumber

Part Name		Qty	Description
A	Long sleeper	8	3 1/2" × 3 1/2" × 96"
B	Short sleeper	12	3 1/2" × 3 1/2" × 29 3/4"
C	Decking	88	1 1/2" × 3 1/2" × 32"
D	Center deck	10	1 1/2" × 3 1/2" to suit

GANG-CUTTING THE SLEEPERS

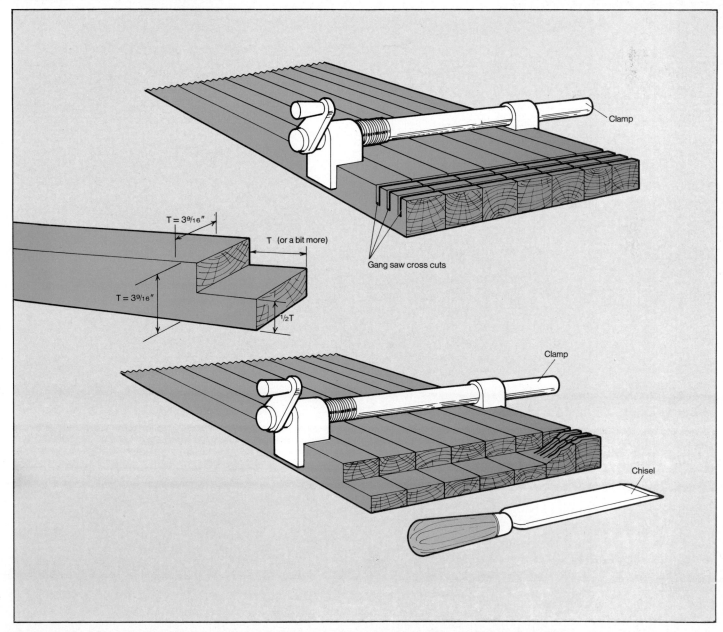

Gang-saw the crosscuts for the lap joints with the sleepers clamped together (top). Then chisel away the waste.

Our shopping list will make four 8-foot-long walks, plus one center section. It takes two 8-foot 4×4s plus one 5-foot 4×4 to frame each walk and seven 8-foot 2×4s to deck it. Each unit, whether an 8-foot walk or a center section, requires a 4×4 lap-jointed frame plus 2×4 decking.

STEP 1
GANG-CUTTING THE SLEEPERS

In this project, the 4×4s are gang-cut; in other words, several pieces are clamped together and sawn as a unit. Gang-cutting may be done on a radial saw, if available, or with a portable saw on a work surface.

First, make sure that the group of four or eight sleepers are all the same length. If not, clamp them up squarely and trim them to equal length. Then, mark both ends of the 4×4s with a line completely across the top surface, placed in from the end the actual width of your 4×4s (typically $3^{1}/_{2}$ or $3^{9}/_{16}$ inches). Set the blade for a cutting depth of half the actual width of your 4×4s, and cut across the group along the lines. Then, make three or four additional cuts between the first cut and the ends.

Then, mark the ends at the same depth of cut as the saw. Chisel away the waste carefully and match-mate the pieces for accuracy (A's to B's or B's to B's).

STEP 2
ASSEMBLING THE PIECES

Nail these sleepers into rectangular walks or square center sections. To cover the walks, cut twenty-two lengths of decking, nail the end pieces in place, with equal side overhang and with one end set back 1 inch. Stretch a string from end to end as an overhang gauge; use a piece of $^{3}/_{4}$-inch scrap plywood as a spacing gauge.

When planking a center section, nail the decking on a 45° angle. Start with the two longest center pieces and work outwards, again using a $^{3}/_{4}$-inch spacer. Allow extra overhang, and trim back with a saw along snapped chalk lines to provide a $^{1}/_{2}$-inch overhang.

ASSEMBLING THE SLEEPERS

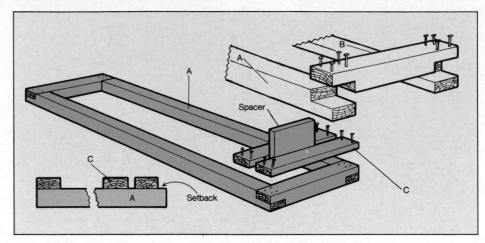

Nail the sleepers together at the half-lapped corners. Square up the sleepers, and nail on the deck boards, with equal overhang off each side. Insert a spacer gauge between boards as you proceed. Leave a gap at one end for center-section matching.

INSTALLING THE DECKING

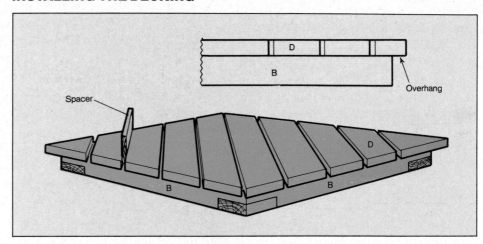

Center-section sleeper frame is constructed in the same manner as the straight section, but the boards are installed diagonally, with overhang on four sides. Install the boards, snap chalk lines, and saw on these lines.

JOINING THE SECTIONS

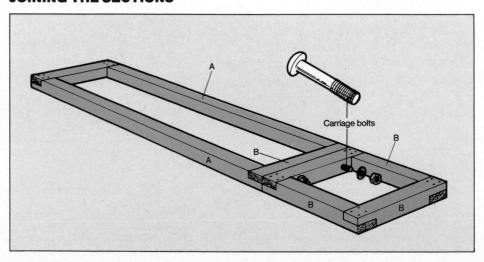

To join any two modular sections, align them as shown, drill through both short sleepers, and install bolts. Drill the holes slightly larger than the bolt size. Assemble prior to decking, as shown, or after, with the end deck boards removed.

SITTING PLANTERS

These planters may be used singly or in groups. The drawings, Materials List, and information are geared toward the construction of six ground-based planter boxes. A circle takes twelve boxes; if you wish this arrangement, simply double the formulas.

However, as few as three together will form a curved shape or a three-part straight line, if the center box is turned. Six boxes can make a semicircle or a dog-leg shape.

This feature, due to the 15° miters on the box ends, provides a unique versatility in garden design to fit in with a backyard of almost any shape with flat topography. Best of all, the project requires minimal expenses and building time.

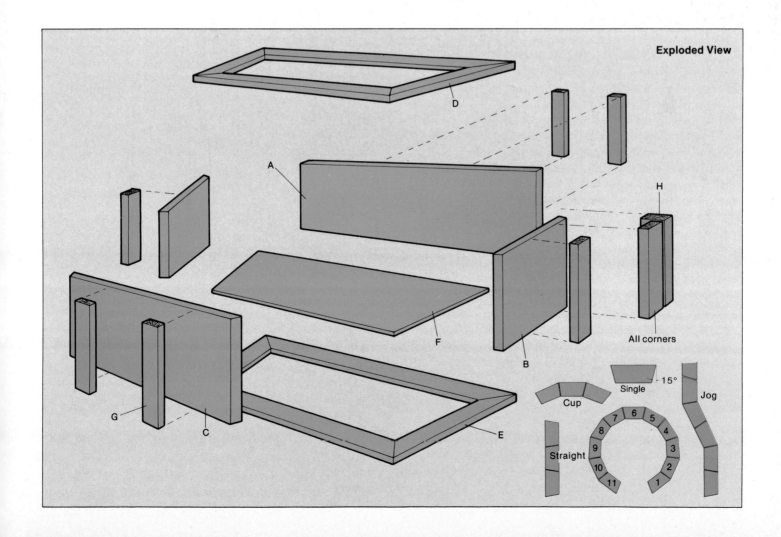

BILL OF MATERIALS

Qty	Size	Material
3	2 × 6 × 12′	Construction heart redwood (ConHR)
1	2 × 6 × 6′	Construction heart redwood
4	2 × 4 × 14′	Construction heart redwood
4	2 × 4 × 14′	Clear heart redwood (ClrHR)
1	1 × 12 × 8′	Clear heart redwood
1	1/2 × 4 × 4′	CDX plywood
48	1/2″ × 5	Corrugated fasteners
	10d	Oval head galvanized nails
	6d	Oval head galvanized nails

PARTS LIST

Part Name	Qty	Description	Part Name	Qty	Description
A Back	6	1 1/2″ × 5 1/2″ × 27″, ConHR	**E2** End cap	12	1 1/2″ × 3 1/2″ × 16 3/8″, ConHR
B End	12	1 1/2″ × 5 1/2″ × 9 1/2″, ConHR	**E3** Front cap	6	1 1/2″ × 3 1/2″ × 22 3/4″, ConHR
C Front	6	1 1/2″ × 5 1/2″ × 21″, ConHR	**F** Bottom	6	1/2″ × 23″ × 9 1/4″, CDX ply
D1 Back cap	6	1 1/2″ × 3 1/2″ × 31 3/4″, ClrHR	**G** Rib (flat)	36	3/4″ × 1 1/4″ × 5 5/8″, ClrHR
D2 End cap	12	1 1/2″ × 3 1/2″ × 16 3/8″, ClrHR	**H** Rib (corner)	48	3/4″ × 2″ × 5 5/8″, ClrHR
D3 Front cap	6	1 1/2″ × 3 1/2″ × 22 3/4″, ClrHR			
E1 Back cap	6	1 1/2″ × 3 1/2″ × 31 3/4″, ConHR			

Note: These materials will build six planters.

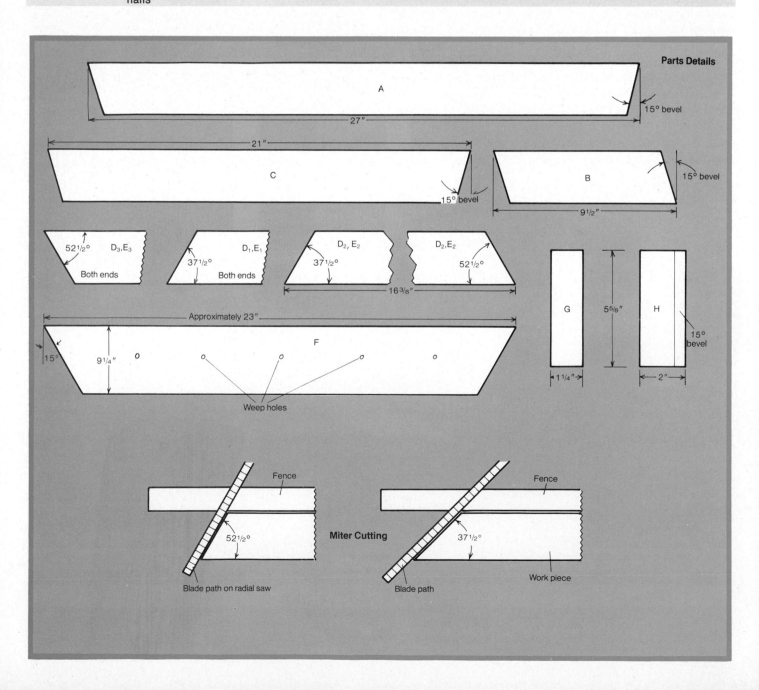

Parts Details

A 27″ 15° bevel

21″ C 15° bevel

B 15° bevel 9 1/2″

52 1/2° D₃, E₃ Both ends

37 1/2° D₁, E₁ Both ends

D₂, E₂ 37 1/2° 16 3/8″ D₂, E₂ 52 1/2°

G 1 1/4″ 5 5/8″ H 2″ 15° bevel

Approximately 23″

15° 9 1/4″ F Weep holes

Miter Cutting

Fence 52 1/2° Blade path on radial saw

Fence 37 1/2° Blade path Work piece

The Materials List and Parts List specify both construction heart and clear heart redwood to build these planters. The less expensive construction heart is used in the less visible places only to hold down cost. It may be replaced with clear heart, if desired.

Ends, fronts, backs, and corner ribs are beveled, while both upper and lower cap members and bottoms are mitered. All pieces may be flipped or reversed, end for end. There are no left- or right-handed pieces.

Note that the miters are equal on both ends of the cap backs as well as on both ends of the cap fronts. But the miters on opposite ends of the cap ends are different.

Bevels are equal on both ends of the backs and on both ends of the fronts. The bevels on the end pieces are not only equal but parallel as well.

If you rough-cut the lumber down to smaller lengths, you can do the beveling and mitering on a table saw, or you can use a portable saw or a saw with a guide. However, if a radial saw is available, it's the fastest and most accurate tool to use.

STEP 1
CUTTING THE MITERS

If you plan to cut the miters on a radial saw, first make a really accurate pattern for each particular angle; then hold it edge-flush against the fence, and move the arm until the saw blade contacts the pattern. When the arm is locked and the saw is moved in and out along the carriage, there should be constant contact between saw blade and pattern.

Now, cut the first miter on the end of what will be a cap piece. If the piece has the same miter on both ends (a back or front cap), flip it over, front for back and move it laterally to the proper place to cut the next miter.

The second cut completes the first cap piece and cuts one end of the second. Repeating this procedure will produce any given number of these pieces with great accuracy. You can improve on this system by setting up a stop on the table that will

ASSEMBLING THE PLANTER

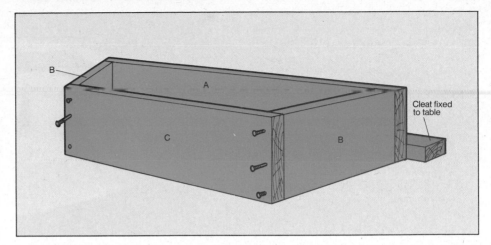

1. Nail or clamp a 2 × 4 cleat to your work surface. Then position the planter back against this cleat, followed by the ends and the front. Drive in nails to assemble.

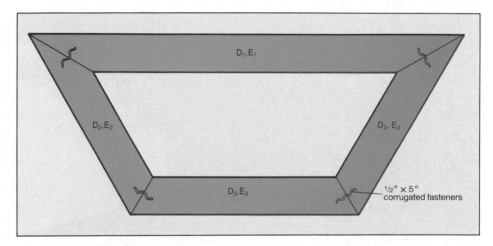

2. Position the cap parts in their proper order on the work surface for assembly, and lock the corner joints temporarily by driving in corrugated nails.

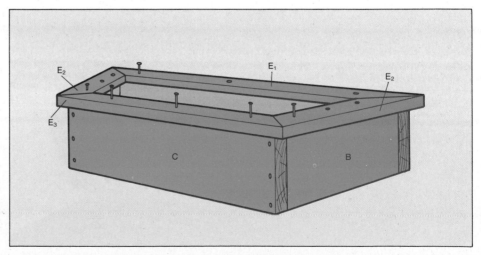

3. Place the bottom cap assembly on the box-frame assembly, allowing equal overhang on all sides. Drive nails through the cap into the edge stock of the box frame.

block the first mitered end and locate the piece for the second miter cut. Use the same mitering procedure for the plywood bottoms after ripping out eight foot-long strips of plywood to the proper width.

Those pieces that have different miters on each end are best cut as follows. First, crosscut the necessary number of pieces slightly longer than their final length. Then, with the saw set at one miter angle, cut that end on all pieces. Reset the saw angle and miter all the second ends.

STEP 2
CUTTING THE BEVELS

To make the bevels on the back and front, set the arm at zero and the saw bevel angle as required. Cut the first bevel, flip the board front for back, move it laterally to the proper location, and cut the second bevel. A stop block will speed this process.

For the end pieces (those with parallel bevels), no flipping is necessary; just move laterally to the stop block, and cut the second bevel.

STEP 3
CUTTING THE RIBS

The common ribs and the corner ribs with the bevels are ripped, beveled, and trimmed most easily on the table saw.

STEP 4
ASSEMBLING THE PLANTERS

Ends, backs, and fronts are screw-assembled. Cap assemblies are assembled with corrugated fasteners before nailing, and the bottom is supported by the bottom cap's inner ledge. Ribs are located and nailed in place as shown.

ASSEMBLING THE PLANTER (CONTINUED)

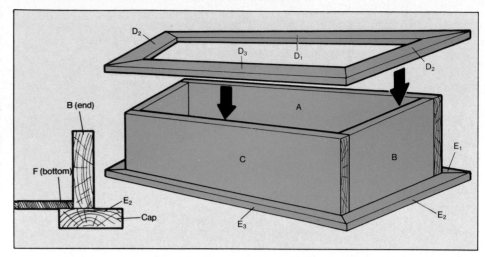

4. Set the box down on the surface on its bottom cap. Insert the plywood bottom. It rests on the bottom cap's inner edges and controls the box's shape.

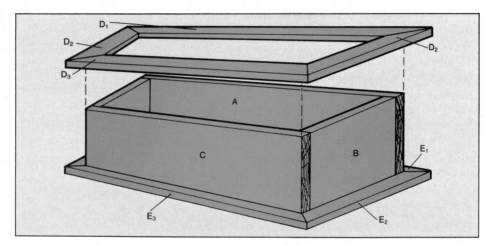

5. Drive nails or stainless steel screws through the top cap into the box-frame edges. Note that the bottom caps may be made of construction heart redwood, but the tops are clear.

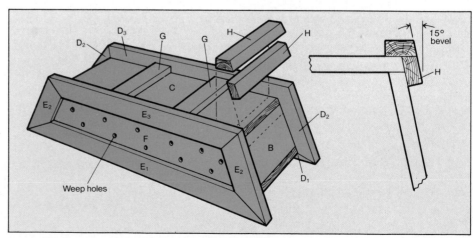

6. There are eight corner ribs and six straight ribs per box. Nail two ribs in the front face, four ribs on the rear face, and two beveled ribs at each corner.

SANDBOX

T his sandbox really gives you your money's worth. Not only is it attractive and a great play area for toddlers, but when the kids have outgrown it, you are left with a handsome, redwood, double-decked planter.

The all-redwood construction and stainless steel hardware are both beautiful and durable. The top L shape, which contains two hatch-covered storage areas, may be removed from the square base for easy transportation; the diagonal decking adds a stylish touch.

Construction is easy, due to both the light weight of redwood and the simplicity and symmetry of the design. This is a truly rewarding project.

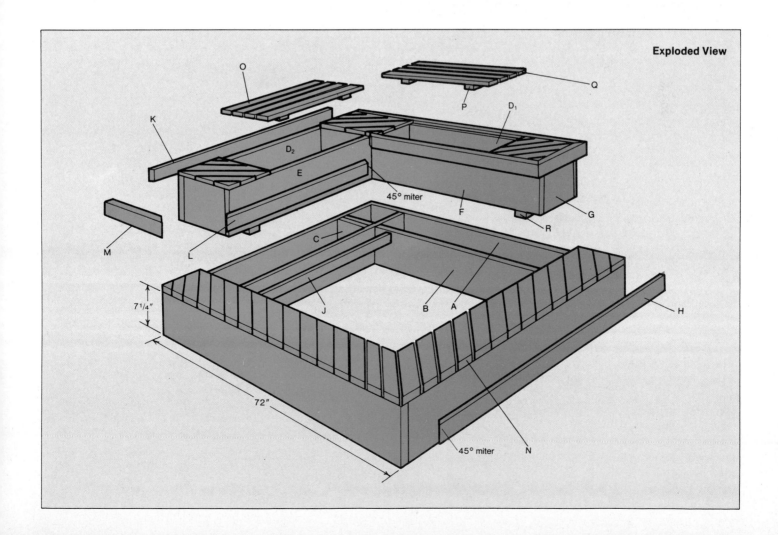

Exploded View

BILL OF MATERIALS

Qty	Size	Material
6	2 × 8 × 12'	Clear heart redwood
3	1 × 12 × 16'	Clear heart redwood
1	1 × 12 × 6'	Clear heart redwood
150	#10 × 3"	Flat head, Phillips head, stainless steel wood screws
270	#8 × 1½"	Flat head, Phillips head, stainless steel wood screws
32	#8 × 1¼"	Flat head, Phillips head, stainless steel wood screws

PARTS LIST

All parts clear heart redwood.

Part	Name	Qty	Description
A	Side, outer bottom	4	$1\frac{1}{2}'' \times 7\frac{1}{4}'' \times 70\frac{3}{8}''$
B	Side, inner bottom	4	$1\frac{1}{2}'' \times 7\frac{1}{4}'' \times 56\frac{3}{4}''$
C1	Bridge, bottom	4	$1\frac{1}{2}'' \times 7\frac{1}{4}'' \times 10\frac{3}{8}''$
C2	Blocking	1	$1\frac{1}{2}'' \times 3\frac{1}{2}'' \times 10\frac{3}{8}''$
D1	Side, outer top, long	1	$1\frac{1}{2}'' \times 7\frac{1}{4}'' \times 58\frac{1}{8}''$
D2	Side, outer top, short	1	$1\frac{1}{2}'' \times 7\frac{1}{4}'' \times 56\frac{3}{4}''$
E	Side, inner top, short	1	$1\frac{1}{2}'' \times 7\frac{1}{4}'' \times 44\frac{3}{4}''$
F	Side, inner top, long	1	$1\frac{1}{2}'' \times 7\frac{1}{4}'' \times 56\frac{3}{4}''$
G	Top ends, bridges	5	$1\frac{1}{2}'' \times 7\frac{1}{4}'' \times 10\frac{3}{8}''$
H	Trim, outer bottom	4	$\frac{3}{4}'' \times 2\frac{11}{16}'' \times 74\frac{1}{2}''$ *

Part	Name	Qty	Description
J	Trim, inner bottom	4	$\frac{3}{4}'' \times 2\frac{11}{16}'' \times 45\frac{1}{2}''$ *
K	Trim, outer top	2	$\frac{3}{4}'' \times 2\frac{11}{16}'' \times 60\frac{1}{2}''$ *
L	Trim, inner top	2	$\frac{3}{4}'' \times 2\frac{11}{16}'' \times 46''$ *
M	Trim, end top	2	$\frac{3}{4}'' \times 2\frac{11}{16}'' \times 16''$ *
N	Deck board	39	$\frac{3}{4}'' \times 3\frac{1}{2}'' \times 24\frac{1}{2}''$ *
O	Small hatch deck board	4	$\frac{3}{4}'' \times 2\frac{11}{16}'' \times 27\frac{1}{2}''$ *
P	Hatch nailer	4	$\frac{3}{4}'' \times 2\frac{11}{16}'' \times 10\frac{1}{8}''$ *
Q	Large hatch deck board	4	$\frac{3}{4}'' \times 2\frac{11}{16}'' \times 29\frac{1}{2}''$ *
R	Lock dog, top	4	$\frac{3}{4}'' \times 2\frac{11}{16}'' \times 6''$ *

*Cut from a 1 × 12 ($\frac{3}{4}$ × 11¼). Four pieces 2$\frac{11}{16}$" wide and 3 pieces 3½" wide can be cut from one 1 × 12.

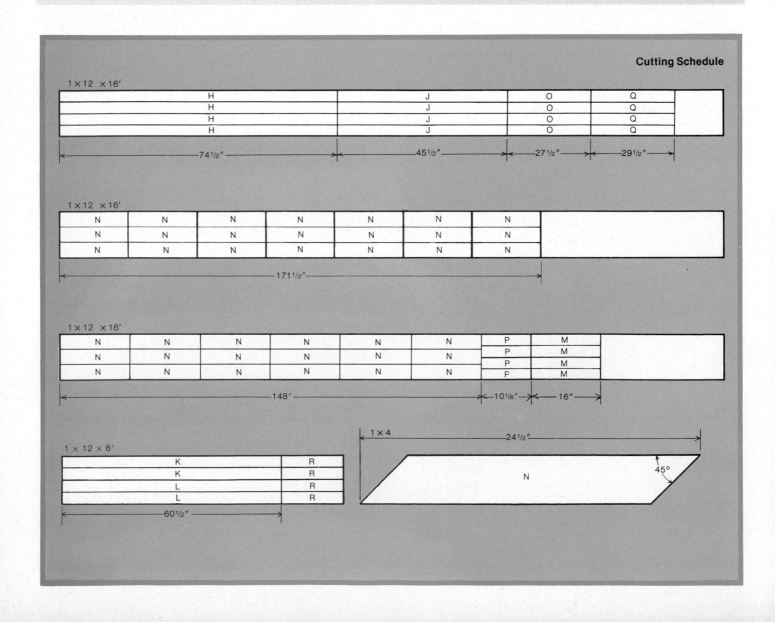

Cutting Schedule

STEP 1
ASSEMBLING THE BOTTOM SECTION

Saw out all structural parts from the 2×8s according to the cutting and parts schedule. Assemble the four inner bottom members with screws, driven into holes pre-drilled with a combination bit. Then, join the outer bottom members into an open square, 72 inches on a side.

Next, place the inner bottom assembly inside the outer bottom and draw centerlines representing the ends of the inner members on the faces of the outer members. Drill holes and drive the screws; it is more than acceptable—in fact, it is preferable—to countersink the holes and drive in the screws slightly below the surface as a safety measure. Add the bridging and blocking in the usual manner to complete the bottom structure.

STEP 2
DECKING THE BOTTOM SECTION

Saw out and miter both ends of thirty-nine or forty deck pieces (N) at 45°. Note that only two full sides of the bottom are covered with decking, specifically the area *not* covered by the smaller top section.

Select any convenient area on the bottom and mark off a line on the structure that makes a 45° angle with the sides. Start the first deck piece against this line and place any overhang so that it lies outside the outer member; this will make for easy sanding later. Continue to add decking, holding a ¼-inch spacer between adjacent pieces as a guide. Try to drill the holes and drive the screws in a straight line to create a neat appearance. At the ends and corners, the size of the deck pieces will diminish, but the installation is done in the same way.

STEP 3
ASSEMBLING THE TOP L SECTION

The top section, even though L-shaped, is constructed in much the same way as the bottom. Here, the bridges and ends are the same size,

ASSEMBLING THE BOTTOM

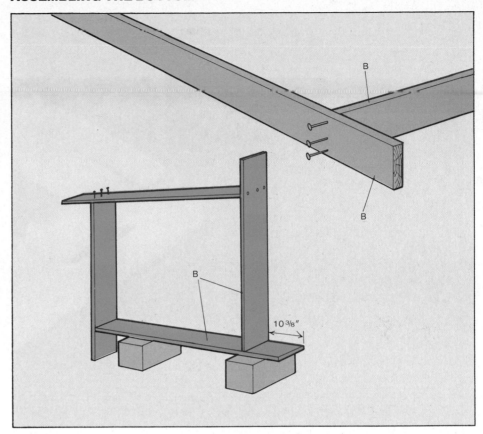

1. Assemble the inner bottom by screwing together two pairs of offset Ls. Be sure to keep the overhang dimension the same as that of the bridges, blocking, and upper section ends. Join the two Ls to form a square with four overhangs.

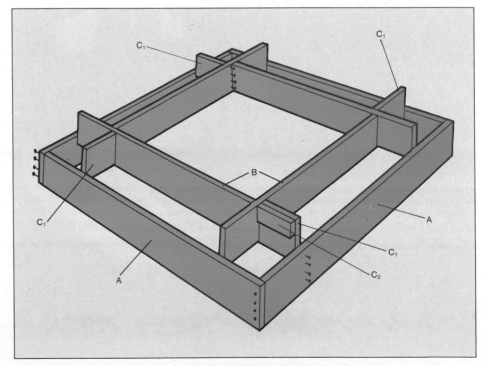

2. Assemble the outer bottom sides by pre-drilling the holes and driving the screws. This forms a square, 72 inches on a side, with each end overlapping the adjacent one. Place the inner bottom inside the square and join the two. Add blocking and bridges.

and the bridges help to outline the hatch-covered openings, in which toys can be stored when the structure is used as a sandbox. Later, these spaces may be fitted with plantings.

Before decking the top, make sure that the top section fits properly over the bottom. At this time, screw the lock dogs in place to the inner surfaces of the upper section. Then, except for the hatches, complete the corner and end decking on the upper section.

The hatchcovers are made from parallel boards with nailers attached from below and at right angles to them. The boards should be evenly spaced and held in place by screws that fasten them to the nailers.

STEP 4
ADDING THE TRIM

Before fitting any of the trim, belt-sand all decking flush with the inner and outer faces of both the top and bottom structures. Then, with a block plane held at a 45° angle, chamfer the edges of all decking edges, except for the decking on the lower section that faces the ends of the upper section. When the trim is in place, this chamfer will add a neat touch.

Make sure both the inner and outer faces of the lower section trim fit up flush with the top of the decking. Note that in areas that have no decking, this trim will cover about 3/4 inch of the bottom of the top section structure for an eye-appealing fit.

The upper section trim will require end pieces as well as long pieces, inasmuch as the ends are exposed at the top. As with the bottom, align the trim so it is flush with the top section decking. Note that the trim in areas that have no decking will serve as outer borders for the hatches.

In applying the trim, use butt joints on external corners and 45-degree miter joints on internal corners. Also, check the entire project over for any splinters or sharp spots, and sand or plane these smooth.

DECKING THE BOTTOM

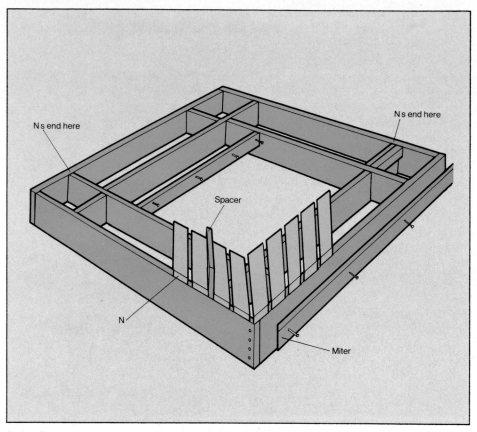

Check for squareness. Then start to attach the deck boards in a corner, orienting them 45° to the square. Try to get the inside miters flush with the inner faces of the inner sides; space the boards 1/4 inch apart. Saw and sand the outer miters flush. Install all bottom trim.

ASSEMBLING THE TOP L

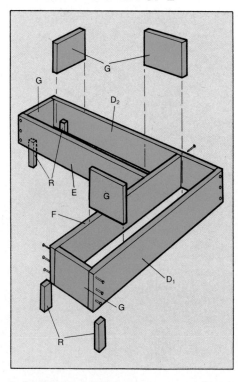

1. Assemble all major top section inner and outer members, forming an L. Then add the bridging and lock dogs.

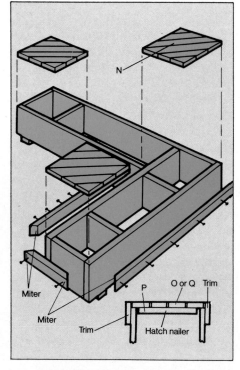

2. Install decking at the corner and ends. Add the trim on inside, outside, and ends. Fit and build hatches.

FIREWOOD STORAGE BIN

Fireplaces and wood stoves have been providing heat in many homes since the energy squeeze started in 1973. However, the price of commercial cordwood has also risen appreciably as demand for firewood has increased. Thus, many people are taking advantage of public lands as a source for their own firewood.

A generously sized firewood storage unit with integral sawbucks can be a big help for storing kindling and cordwood and for holding wood safely when sawing it to usable lengths.

The project is easy to build, it is sturdy, and it uses pressure-treated wood that assures years of rugged, trouble-free service.

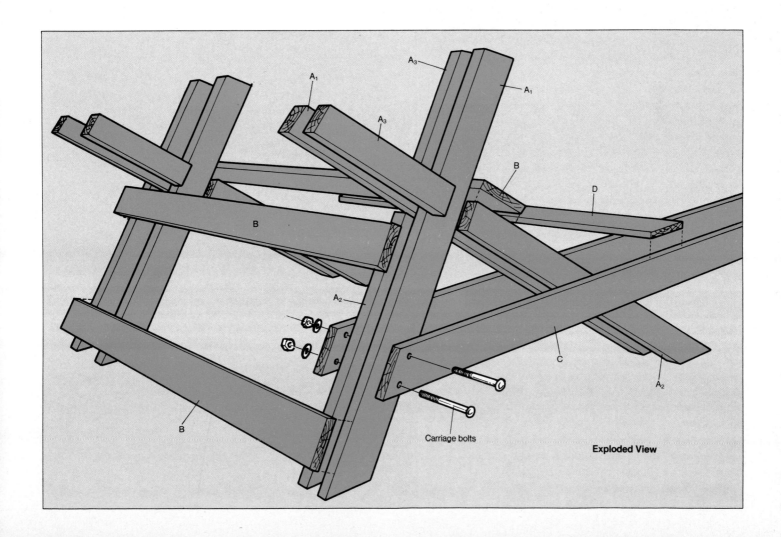

Carriage bolts

Exploded View

BILL OF MATERIALS

Qty	Size	Material
4	2 × 4 × 14′	Pressure-treated lumber
3	2 × 4 × 12′	Pressure-treated lumber
4	2 × 6 × 14′	Pressure-treated lumber
9	5/4 × 6 × 10′	Pressure-treated lumber
16	3/8 × 7″	Carriage bolts, nuts and washers, galvanized
	10d	Oval head, galvanized nails

PARTS LIST

All parts pressure-treated lumber

Part Name		Qty	Description
A1	Full leg	8	$1\frac{1}{2}″ \times 3\frac{1}{2}″ \times 54″$
A2	Medium leg	8	$1\frac{1}{2}″ \times 3\frac{1}{2}″ \times 38\frac{1}{2}″$
A3	Short leg	8	$1\frac{1}{2}″ \times 3\frac{1}{2}″ \times 12″$
B	Stretcher	6	$1\frac{1}{2}″ \times 3\frac{1}{2}″ \times 36″$
C	Base rails	4	$1\frac{1}{2}″ \times 5\frac{1}{2}″ \times 14′$
D	Slats	16	$1\frac{1}{16}″ \times 5\frac{1}{2}″ \times 40″$

Note: Slats inside X frames are cut to approximately 30″ instead of 40″.

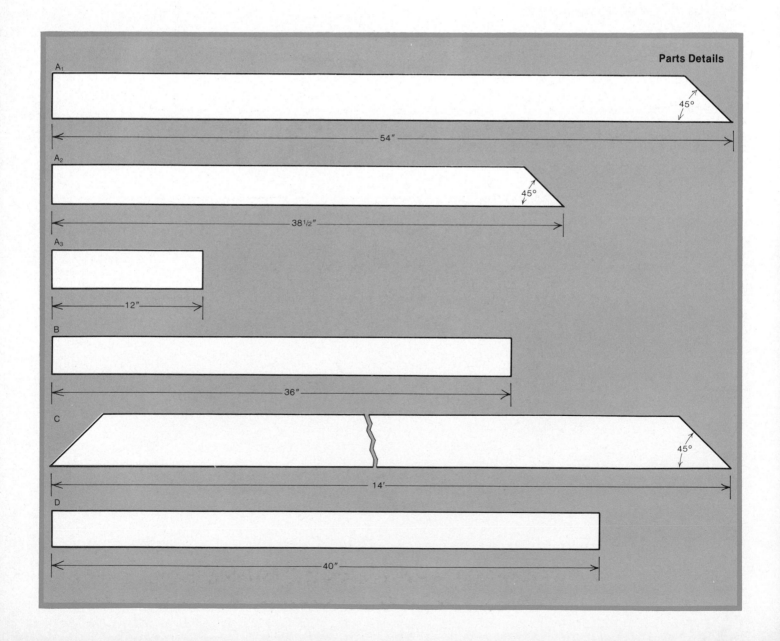

Parts Details

A₁ — 54″ — 45°

A₂ — 38½″ — 45°

A₃ — 12″

B — 36″

C — 14′ — 45°

D — 40″

A glance at the photograph will show you that the firewood storage and sawbuck project basically consists of two sturdy sawbucks joined by four rails, with a board floor running from end to end. Small branches or kindling may be kept in the end areas, while the central section holds firewood that has been sawn to convenient lengths.

Since the completed firewood storage unit is rather heavy, it's a good idea to build it where it will permanently stand. Firewood, like all dead wood, should be stored away from the house to avoid termite problems, especially in the more temperate and warmer areas.

STEP 1
CUTTING AND ASSEMBLING THE SAWBUCKS

Cut all thirty leg and stretcher parts to length at one time, using gang-cutting methods, if you wish. Next, saw the 45° miters on those leg parts that require it.

Then, start assembling the four X parts of the bucks with 10d oval head galvanized nails. Use plenty of nails in a zig-zag or staggered pattern.

The stretchers, which control the spacing between the X parts, are most easily nailed in place with the X part resting on and hanging over a worktable or similar support. Make sure that the X's and stretchers form true rectangles when viewed from the end; check the alignment with a rafter or a carpenter's square. Carry the completed sawbucks to their permanent home and set them on level ground, with the correct spacing between them.

STEP 2
CUTTING AND ASSEMBLING THE RAILS

Now, saw the 45° miters on all four rails, and carry them out to the sawbucks. Place these rails alongside the sawbuck legs to form sandwiches: rail—legs—rail.

Prop up the rails so that (1) their bevel ends are flush with the legs of the sawbuck; and (2) the rails are at equal height with respect to the sawbuck legs at all points of contact.

PLAN AND ELEVATION

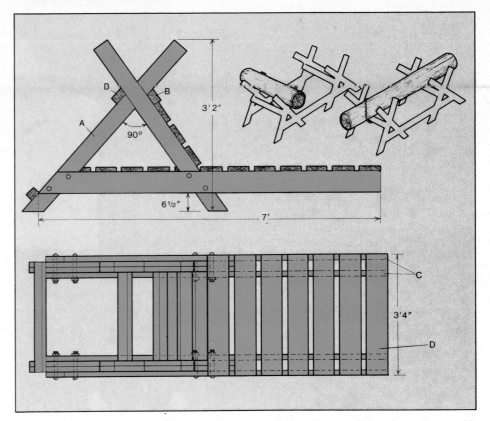

Sawbucks, joined by planked base rails, allow easy sawing of long and short logs. Firewood is stored in the center section, kindling on the sawbuck floor.

ASSEMBLING THE X PARTS

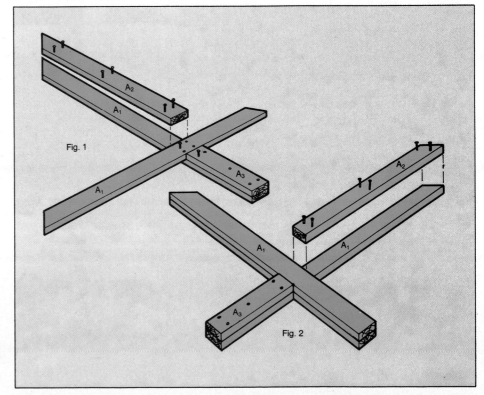

The × shapes are laminated in two layers so that any short members are paired with full-length members for strength. Galvanized nails hold pressure-treated lumber in place.

Check this carefully and clamp all contact areas, making sure that you can drill at least one hole at each position without hitting a clamp.

Drill 3/8-inch-diameter holes completely through the sandwich at each contact area, but stagger them so that they lie on different wood grain lines. You'll probably have to drill one hole, move the clamp, and then drill the second hole. Try to keep the drill bit vertical to the surface for the most accurate bolting. You'll have to persuade the bolts to slip through the sandwich with a soft-faced hammer or a scrap wood board hit with a steel hammer.

Place the washer and nut in position on each bolt and tighten it up with a hand or a socket wrench as you go along.

STEP 3
TRIMMING AND INSTALLING THE SLATS

Trim the slats that go in between the bucks to 40 inches. Then, deck the floor, allowing equal overhang on each side. Use a 3/4-inch spacer between adjacent slats when nailing, and check the accuracy with a tape every few boards.

Nominally, the distance between the inner leg faces should be 30 inches. However, in the real world, it's best to measure before cutting, in case of a slight difference. Use this measurement as the length to trim the short slats that fit underneath the bucks.

With these short slats in place, you can complete the inner-area slats. Hammering nails under the buck is best done with a bit of swinging room. So run the floor right up the legs to the inside stretcher; but as you do, check to see that you're forming a true rectangle. Also, it may be necessary to rip the last slat to fit in next to the inner stretcher.

As a final touch, check all exposed edges, especially where you have a long run of slats. You may wish to resaw or belt-sand these edges for a neater appearance. If you desire, the unit may be stained, but if left unfinished, it will weather to an attractive gray.

ASSEMBLING THE SAWBUCK

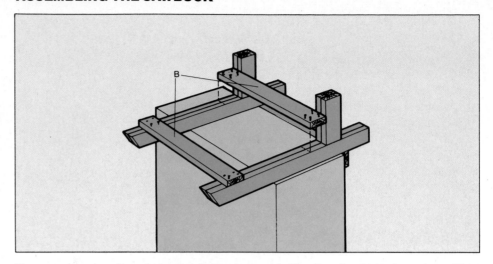

Place one leg of each × shape on a flat surface, and allow the other leg to hang down. Then place the stretchers in position, and nail them on the legs.

JOINING THE SAWBUCK AND BASE

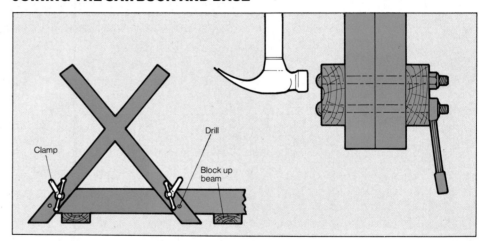

Position the sawbucks and base rails for assembly, and prop up the rails to height. Clamp the eight rail-leg sandwiches together. Drill and bolt them together.

INSTALLING THE SLATS

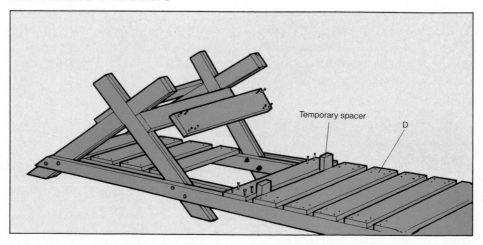

Nail down the slats, allowing equal overhang off each side, using a spacing gauge between each slat. Run the slats up the inside legs and beneath the ×.

DECK CHAIR

This deck chair is built of solid oak throughout, has wheels for mobility, and features a footrest that is removable for easy storage.

The chair has been designed as a mixture of steamship deck chair and a backyard lounger, and it is suitable for use with or without cushions. It is a smartly styled piece of outdoor furniture that is easy to build.

All tapered pieces are first cut out as blanks following a basic module, which permits an efficient cutting setup. The remaining parts are simple slats, which must be pre-drilled to accommodate the hardened assembly screws. The completed project is spar-varnished.

BILL OF MATERIALS

Qty	Size	Material
1	$5/4 \times 8 \times 14'$	Red oak
1	$4/4 \times 8 \times 7'$	Red oak
2	$4/4 \times 6 \times 11'$	Red oak
1	$4/4 \times 6 \times 9'$	Red oak
12	$5/16 \times 2^{1}/2''$	Carriage bolts, nuts, washers
4	$1/4 \times 2''$	Carriage bolts, nuts, washers
1	$3/4 \times 3'$	Maple dowel
1	$7/8 \times 3'$	Maple dowel
120	$\#8 \times 1^{1}/2''$	Flat head, Phillips head, assembly screws
30	$\#8 \times 1^{3}/4$	Flat head, Phillips head, assembly screws
1	$1/2 \times 36''$	Aluminum rod
4	$1/2''$	Clamp-type collars*
8	$1/2''$	Washers

PARTS LIST

Part	Name	Qty	Description
A	Seat sides	2	$1^{1}/16'' \times 5'' \times 40''$, oak
B	Backrest sides	2	$1^{1}/16'' \times 5'' \times 40''$, oak
C1	Armrest	2	$1^{1}/16'' \times 5'' \times 24''$, oak
C2	Chair leg	2	$1^{1}/16'' \times 3'' \times 20''$, oak
D	Slats	11	$13/16'' \times 2^{1}/2'' \times 24''$, oak
E	Slats	12	$13/16'' \times 2^{1}/2'' \times 22''$, oak
F	Backrest slat nailer	2	$1^{1}/16'' \times 2^{1}/2'' \times 22''$, oak
G	Slats	7	$13/16'' \times 2^{1}/2'' \times 32''$, oak
H1	Footrest side	2	$13/16'' \times 4^{5}/8'' \times 28''$, oak
H2	Footrest leg	2	$13/16'' \times 2^{1}/4'' \times 12''$, oak
I	Brace	2	$1^{1}/16'' \times 3'' \times 5^{1}/2''$, oak
J	Wheels	2	$1^{1}/16'' \times 5''$ diameter, oak

* Machine shop supply.

STEP 1
CUTTING THE PARTS

Cut out all the 44-inch-long basic tapered modules, six pieces from $5/4$ ($1^{1}/16$ inches) and two pieces from $4/4$ ($13/16$ inch) oak. Then perform the additional cutting operations on these modules. The seat sides and backrest sides require the small tip end to be trimmed back, while the footrest sides and legs need the large end trimmed. Some parts—such as the armrest and chair leg—need no trimming, but they require a mitered cut to separate them. Refer to the parts detail drawings as you proceed to avoid any waste.

The basic module approach not only simplifies the basic cutting, it also lets you control the accuracy of

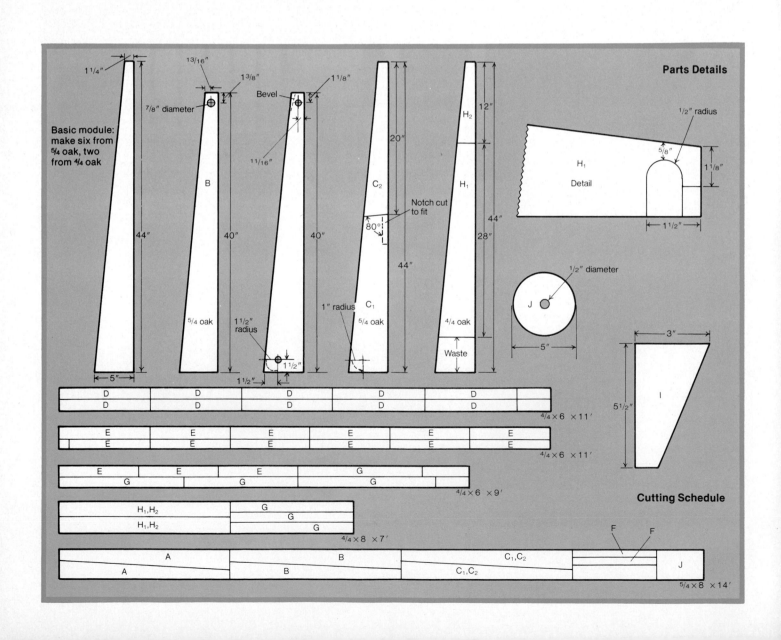

the cuts and check quickly to deal with any discrepancies early on. It's just as well to cut out the rest of the parts now, including the wheels, braces, slats, and nailers. How to make the wheels perfectly round and smooth is shown in the Portable Potting Bench project.

When making the hardwood slats, using a jointer helps to ensure speed and accuracy. Joint the first edge. Rip the workpiece slightly oversize, and joint the second edge. If you don't have a jointer, these operations must be done with a long (jointer) plane and/or a belt sander. Before assembly, sand all parts down to a #180-grit finish.

STEP 2
ASSEMBLING THE SIDES AND SLATS

Start the assembly by clamping each seat side to its matching backrest side and leg at the locations and orientations shown. With scrap or rough table surface backing up the bottom pieces, drill all the through holes for the assembly bolts, and install these bolts with their nuts and washers.

Notice that the seat sides are joined by some slats that are 22 inches long and others that are 24 inches long. Only two of the shorter slats are used at the front of the seat sides, and all edges are flush with them. The remaining slats are longer and overhang each side by 1 inch. As mentioned before, the slats are clamped or held in place, and the screwholes are pre-drilled using a combination bit. This is standard procedure when working with hardwood.

Each slat is fastened to each side with two screws and is spaced 3/8 inch away from the adjacent slat. As the assembly continues, be sure that the backrest sides remain parallel, constrained at the top with a piece of scrap wood and clamps. Keep this scrap in position while fitting and installing the slat nailers. These nailers should be level, and they should also be oriented and positioned so that they're parallel to the front edges of the backrest sides.

ASSEMBLING THE SEAT SIDES

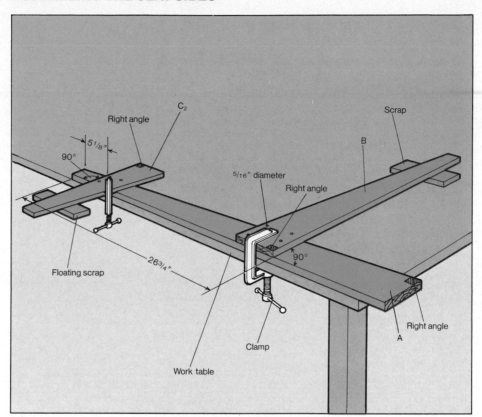

1. Mark off the positions of the chair leg and the backrest side on the seat side. Place the seat side on the work surface. Position the chair leg and the backrest side on their respective marks, and prop up the ends with scrap. Clamp, and drill.

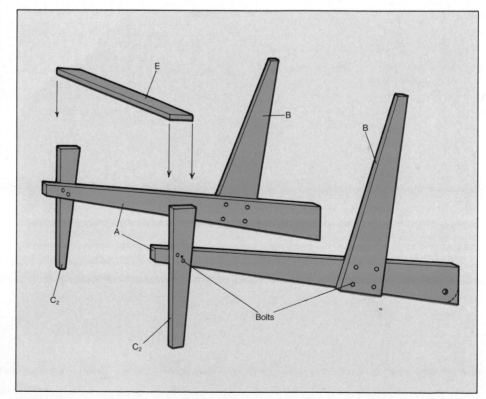

2. Assemble chair leg and backrest side to the seat side with carriage bolts. Join the two side assemblies by installing the seat slats with screws driven into pre-drilled holes. Keep the entire assembly squared up during this operation.

STEP 3
COMPLETING THE CHAIR

If you have not already done so, drill the holes for the dowels and axle, using a drill guide and scrap backup to prevent splintering as the bit exits. Install the dowels, and lock them in place with small nails driven through cross-drilled pilot holes.

Install the armrest braces. Then fit the arms. The arms are notched at the point where they are joined to the backrest side, so they can be installed parallel to the run of seat slats. This should be done before the seat-backrest slat installation, because there's sufficient room then. Cut the outside radius of the armrest corners to suit.

Install the seat-backrest slats with the outer ones against the inner faces of the backrest sides, with 3/4 inch between slats.

Now, assemble the wheels, axle, washers, and collars. Check the area at the rear of the seat sides for ground clearance, especially when the chair is cocked back and resting on its wheels. Cut the radius of the lower rear corner of the seat sides to accomplish this.

STEP 4
CONSTRUCTING THE FOOTREST

The footrest is constructed in essentially the same manner as the chair itself. However, before clamping, drilling, and bolting the legs to the footrest sides, drill the 1-inch-diameter holes in the narrow ends of the sides, and remove the waste to the bottom edge with a jig or band saw. Sand these notches smooth, and fit them to the chair's front dowel. Install the footrest slats. Sand the chair, and apply three coats of varnish.

DRILLING HOLES

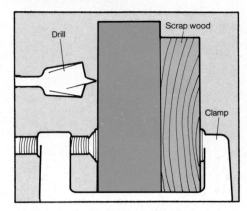

Back up the backrest side with a scrap block where the drill will exit and clamp. Drill hole for dowel.

INSTALLING DOWELS

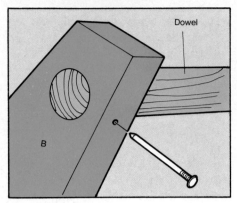

Work the dowel handle into the holes. Drill a cross hole through the side and dowel, and lock the dowel with a nail.

ASSEMBLING THE SLATS AND BACKREST

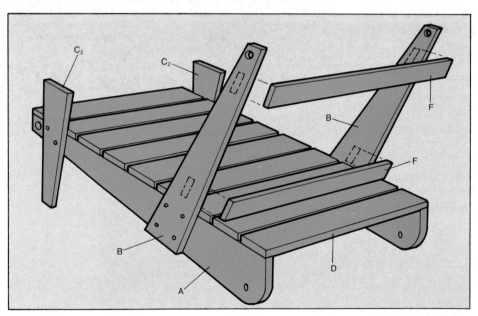

Square up the backrest sides by installing both the top and bottom backrest slat nailers. Gauge them so that when the backrest slats are installed, the slat surface will be flush with or lie slightly below the backrest side edges.

ATTACHING THE ARM RESTS

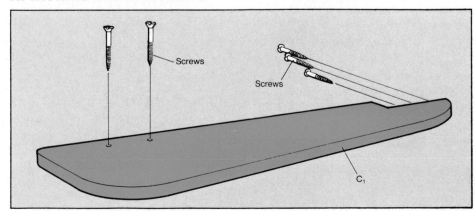

Position the armrest on top of chair leg. Scribe notch at backrest side, and cut notch to fit, including bevel angle at front. Drill, and assemble with screws.

Game Table (pages 30-33). You can play backgammon, checkers, chess, mah jongg, or any board game at this all-redwood game table.

The game board flips over easily to convert to the preferred game. And its lightweight construction makes the table easy to carry indoors.

Sandbox (pages 85-88). Here's a project the toddlers will surely love, but it won't outlive its usefulness after they've grown. When the children are still young, pails and shovels will store conveniently in the top L shape, which contains two hatched-covered storage areas. And when they are older, you'll have a handsome double-decked planter.

Large Standing Planter and Detail (pages 142-146). Want a simple and dramatic way to display flowers in your backyard? This large standing planter is nothing more than a four-posted rectangular tower, with four pairs of support arms at varying heights. It has a wonderful impact when filled with geraniums, petunias, or a combination of flowers.

Sitting Planters (page 81-84). The mitered end design of these redwood planters enables you to arrange them in either a straight line or a curve. They are ideal for adding accent to a deck or patio and for clearly defining borders.

Tree Surround (page 117-122). Encircle the base of a large tree trunk with this eye-pleasing surround, constructed of redwood and pressure-treated lumber, and discover the pleasures of relaxing in the shade with a friend, a cool drink, or an absorbing book.

Slat Chaise and Details (pages 133-138). Loll away a sunny afternoon on this classic chaise. You'll want to consider making more than one, since everyone will want to use this one. It has a pair of wheels that may be set down if you choose to move it, along with a wood dowel grab-bar at the foot end to facilitate shifting its position. The backrest adjusts from a prone to a sitting position.

Umbrella Table (pages 20-24). It's time for a barbecue dinner under the shade of this umbrella table. In fact, no backyard is complete without this handsome and easy-to-build item.

Barbecue Cart (pages 63-69). A rolling cart set up next to the barbecue provides a practical solution to organizing outdoor cooking. When open, it boasts 18 square feet of work surface, including a butcher block and a recess for a three-part acrylic server. It can be closed for smaller gatherings, as well as for storing when not in use.

Wishing Well (pages 123-128). Build this wishing well, a decorative descendant of the traditional working kind, and use it as a planter. The center can be shelved to house plants that do better in indirect light, while the sill can provide a home for sun-loving species.

Jungle Gym and Details (pages 147-155) This play center will keep the children happy for hours. It includes a seesaw, four ladders, two platforms, and an overhead trussed walkway. Beneath the walkway, you can install climbing ropes, nets, rings or swings.

Slat Chair and Details (pages 129-132). The simple lines of this slat chair are designed to complement the Slat Chaise project on pages 133–138. The two will add comfort to any lawn, patio, or deck.

Nest of Tables (pages 139-141). You can always find a use for these easy-to-build, lightweight snack or occasional tables, which will also complement the Slat Chair and Chaise projects.

Sling Chair and Detail (pages 25-29). A practical, knock-down design enables you to store this chair when not in use. The canvas sling can also be easily cleaned or replaced between seasons.

Portable Bar Unit (pages 38-42). Transfer your bar or wine cellar outdoors to this handy cart, which moves on casters and has ample storage space for bottles and glasses.

Perimeter Bench (pages 34-37). Try your carpentry skills on this contoured seat; it's relatively simple to construct, requiring only ten 2 × 4s and a length of 2 × 6.

Lighting Enclosure (pages 70-77). Light your walks, patio, deck, or garden with this attractive all-redwood lighting fixture. The front features removable louver assemblies, and the bottom is open, so maintenance is easy.

Duckboards (pages 78-80). These pressure-treated lumber walkways can be built and arranged in a variety of patterns to provide dry crossing in grassy or wet areas or to divide large planting areas attractively.

Garbage Storage (pages 48-51). Empty cans are filled through the top and, when full, removed through the front doors. You'll love this animal-proof storage!

Firewood Storage Bin (pages 89-92). Store kindling and cordwood in this generously sized unit. For convenience and safety, it contains two sawbucks for holding wood when cutting to size.

Portable Potting Unit (pages 52-57). Perfect for potting work and easy enough to move from garage to yard and garden, this unit will please every green-thumb gardener. Open and closed storage space plus a tiled top are all part of the plan for this redwood and plywood cart.

Folding Picnic Table (pages 113-116). When open, this table measures 30 × 60 inches for informal dining. When closed, it stores the parts needed for assembly, and it is small enough to fit in most car trunks.

Deck Chair (pages 93-96). Reminiscent of steamship deck chairs and constructed of oak, this contemporary version has wheels for mobility and a removable footrest for easy storage.

FOLDING PICNIC TABLE

Here are plans for building a basic, self-contained, folding picnic table. The box sides open up to provide a generous 30 × 60-inch surface for informal dining.

When closed, the table not only stores the parts necessary for its own quick assembly, but there's also plenty of room to keep on hand indispensable items such as plates, utensils, napkins, tablecloths, and cups.

The simple design is easy to follow and a snap to build. Standard, readily available hinges, latches, and miscellaneous hardware are used throughout. The folded table is small enough to fit in most car trunks.

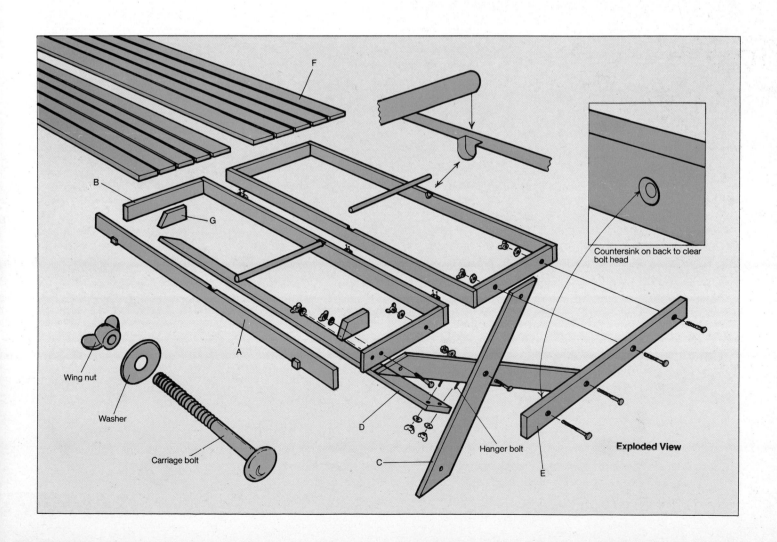

Countersink on back to clear bolt head

Wing nut

Washer

Carriage bolt

Hanger bolt

Exploded View

BILL OF MATERIALS

Qty	Size	Material
1	$5/4 \times 12 \times 16'$	Clear heart redwood
5	$1 \times 4 \times 12'$	Clear heart redwood
3	$2^{1/2}''$	Stanley #SP295 hinge
2	$3^{1/4} \times 1^{3/4}''$	Stanley #5366 chest latch
4	$1/4 \times 1^{1/2}''$	Hanger bolts
8	$1/4 \times 2^{1/2}''$	Carriage bolts
4	$1/4 \times 3^{1/2}''$	Carriage bolts
16	$1/4''$	Washers
16	$1/4''$	Wing nuts
72	$8 \times 1^{3/4}''$	Flat head, Phillips head, stainless steel wood screws
1	$3/8 \times 36''$	Aluminum drape rod

PARTS LIST

All parts clear heart redwood

Part	Name	Qty	Description
A	Long skirt	4	$1^{1/16}'' \times 2^{11/16}'' \times 60''$
B	Short skirt	4	$1^{1/16}'' \times 2^{11/16}'' \times 15^{5/8}''$
C	Legs	4	$1^{1/16}'' \times 2^{11/16}'' \times 43^{5/8}''$
D	Trestle	1	$1^{1/16}'' \times 4^{1/8}'' \times 57^{3/4}''$
E	Stiffener	2	$1^{1/16}'' \times 2^{11/16}'' \times 35^{1/2}''$
F	Boards	10	$3/4'' \times 3^{1/2}'' \times 62^{1/8}''$
G	Blocking	2	$1^{1/16}'' \times 2^{11/16}'' \times 4''$

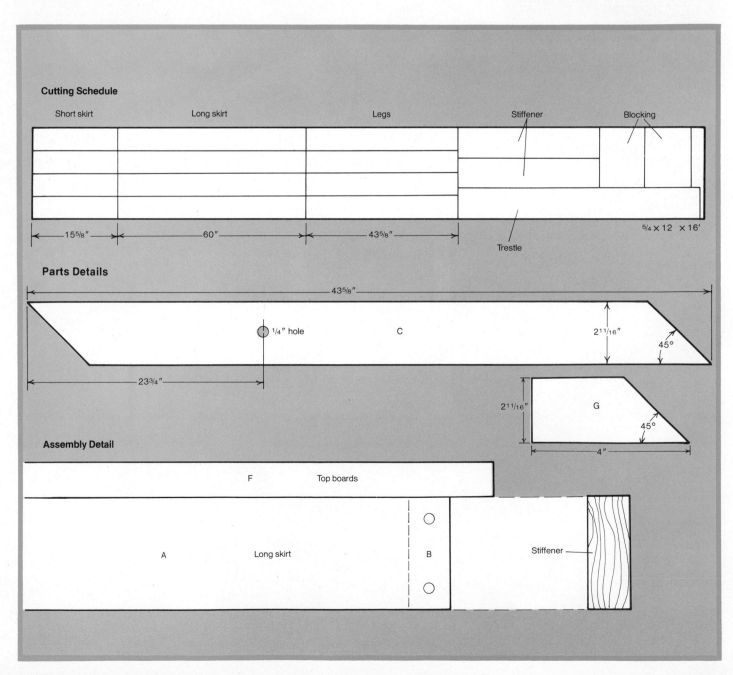

Cutting Schedule

Short skirt   Long skirt   Legs   Stiffener   Blocking

$15^{5/8}''$ $60''$ $43^{5/8}''$

Trestle

$5/4 \times 12 \times 16'$

Parts Details

$43^{5/8}''$

$1/4''$ hole   C $2^{11/16}''$ 45°

$23^{3/4}''$

$2^{11/16}''$ G   45° $4''$

Assembly Detail

F   Top boards

A   Long skirt   B   Stiffener

STEP 1
ASSEMBLING THE BOX FRAME AND BOARDS

Saw all redwood parts according to the cutting schedule and parts detail drawings. Start the box-frame assembly: screw the long skirt faces to the ends of the short skirts.

Chisel small notches in the middle of the top edges of all long skirts to hold an aluminum drape rod in each box frame, flush with the top edge. The rod provides central support for top boards.

Next, install the tabletop boards. Start the first board flush with the frame edge on one side, and provide ¼ inch spacing between each board. The last board will overhang the long skirt. Allow 1¹/₁₆ inches overhang past each short skirt.

STEP 2
INSTALLING THE HARDWARE

Now, set the two table halves with the two flush edges together and the boards facing down. Trace the hinge outlines on the long skirt edges at the middle and 4 inches from each end. Then, mark these outlines with a chisel, and remove the waste within them to the depth of the hinge leaves. Mount the hinges.

Set the folding table up on its flush, hinged edge with the opposite, overhanging edge facing up. Clamp or tape the two halves together, and mount the latches. Don't install optional handles now. Try using the completed table without them first.

STEP 3
ASSEMBLING AND ATTACHING THE LEGS

Saw 45° parallel miters on both ends of all four legs. Mark and drill the hinge bolt holes in the legs. Assemble the legs in pairs.

Open up the table and lay it face down on a smooth work surface. Then, place one set of legs just inside the short skirts, with an equal spread that is wide enough to make the miters flush with the underside of the top boards. You will find that the leg nearest the short skirt will fit flush with it, but that the other leg, 1¹/₁₆ inches away, must have a small

ASSEMBLING THE BOX FRAME

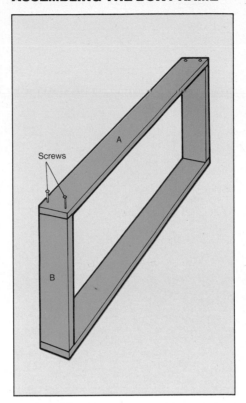

1. Place long skirt over short skirt ends. Drill and assemble with screws.

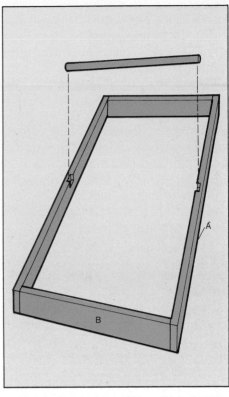

2. Notch upper edges of long skirt at center to hold aluminum support.

ATTACHING THE BOARDS

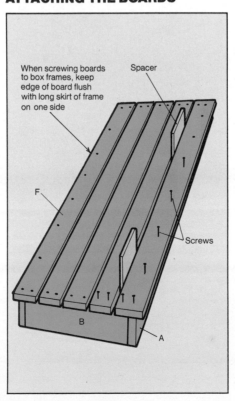

With proper overhang, position boards with spacer, drill and drive screws.

ASSEMBLING THE LEGS

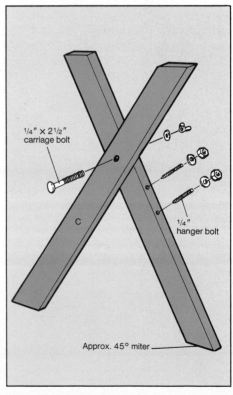

Drill legs for axle bolt, and install carriage bolt, washer, and wing nut.

blocking piece placed between it and the short skirt. Screw the blocking piece to the short skirt. This will also occur with the second set of legs, and blocking is installed on the same table half as well.

Place one set of legs in position and clamp one leg to one short skirt and the other leg to its blocking piece and short skirt. Drill a ¼-inch-diameter hole completely through at each position, and install a 3½-inch-long carriage bolt, washer, and wing nut where there is blocking. Remove the clamps. Repeat this procedure for the second set of legs.

STEP 4
DRILLING THE STIFFENER BOLT HOLES

Place the stiffeners on edge on the end board overhang at each end of the table. These should be almost flush with the board ends, flush at their ends with the faces of the long skirts, and flush at the top edge with the edges of the short skirts. Press the stiffener hard against the head of the bolt to make a mark. Then, remove the stiffener and countersink or counterbore it for bolt-head clearance. Return it to its original position. Repeat the procedure at the other end of the table. Make sure that the bottom edges of the stiffeners are in total contact with the underside of the top boards. Correct below the boards with wooden wedges.

Clamp each stiffener to the free leg and short skirt. Then, back-drill leg holes through the stiffener, and install a 3½-inch-long carriage bolt, washer, and wing nut. Now, drill a hole through the stiffener and short skirt near the blocking, but missing it, and drill another hole 3 inches away from and on each side of the hinge. Install 2½-inch carriage bolts, nuts, and washers in these holes.

STEP 5
INSTALLING THE TRESTLE

Clamp the trestle to the legs, and drill pilot holes through it into them. Install hanger bolts in the legs. Enlarge the pilot holes in the trestle to ¼-inch diameter, and install it with washers and wing nuts.

INSTALLING THE HARDWARE

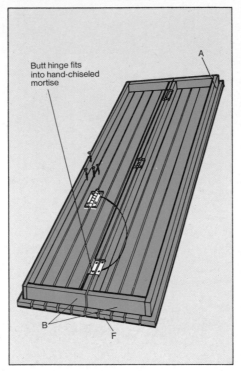

Butt hinge fits into hand-chiseled mortise

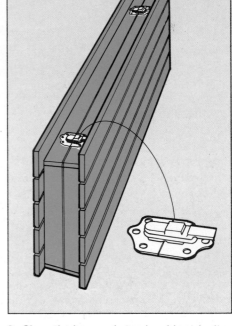

1. Place box halves face up. Mortise edges, and install hinges.

2. Close the box, and stand on hinged edge. Install latches on overhang-side skirts.

STIFFENER AND TRESTLE PLACEMENT

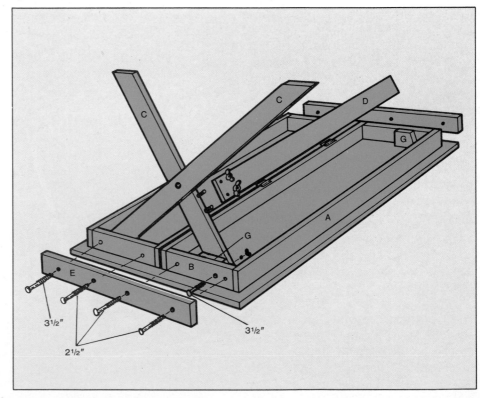

3½"

2½"

3½"

Install blocking. Place the legs in position, and drill through the short skirt, blocking, and one leg. Bolt the three pieces together. Line up stiffener, drill holes, and install bolts and nuts. Drill trestle and leg, and install hanger bolts.

TREE SURROUND

Do you have a large tree that grows inconveniently in the middle of your yard? Here is a project that encloses the base of the trunk with a smooth and eye-pleasing transition between the grass or ground cover and the tree trunk, branches and foliage. This particular design involves an octagonal-base plan, using pressure-treated lumber and redwood as the major materials.

There are four sections, each made up of two segments. Two of these sections are built-in seats, set at a comfortable height, while the other two are raised planters.

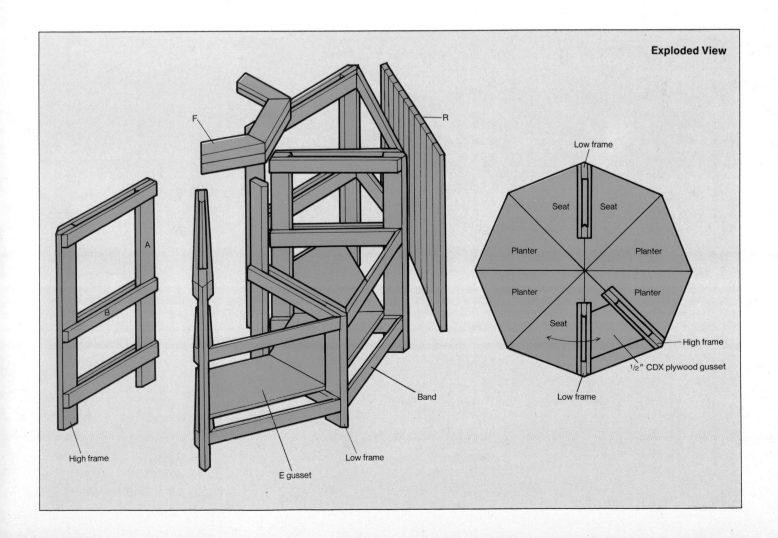

Exploded View

F

R

A

B

High frame

E gusset

Low frame

Band

Low frame

Low frame

Seat · Seat

Planter · Planter

Planter · Planter

Seat

High frame

½" CDX plywood gusset

BILL OF MATERIALS

Qty	Size	Material
21	2×4×8'	Pressure-treated lumber (P/T)
9	2×4×8'	Construction heart redwood (ConHR)
1	5/4×12×12'	Clear heart redwood (ClrHR)
8	1×12×16'	Clear heart redwood
2	1×12×14'	Clear heart redwood
2	1/2×4×8'	CDX plywood
700	#8×1½"	Flat head, Phillips head, stainless steel wood screws
100	#8×1½"	Flat head, Phillips head, hardened, assembly screws
	10d	Oval head, galvanized nails
100	Square feet	4–6 mil plastic
½	Cubic yard	Stone (3/8–5/8", type and color to suit)
100		Bricks
3	80-lb. bags	Dry concrete (aggregate) mix

PARTS LIST

Part	Name	Qty	Description
A	Long post	14	1½"×3½"×48", P/T
B	Stretcher	44	1½"×3½"×21½", P/T
C	Short post	2	1½"×3½"×24", P/T
D	Band	20	1½"×3½"×33", Con HR
E	Gusset	8	½"×13⅝"×29¼", CDX ply
F	Cap	16	1½"×3½"×18", Con HR
G	Horizontal nailer	4	1½"×3½"×21½", Con HR
H	Vertical nailer	4	1½"×3½"×16⅛", Con HR
I	Filler	4	1½"×3½"×23¼", Con HR
J	Seat boards	24	¾"×3⅛"×34½", Clr HR
K	Short wall boards	40	¾"×3⅛"×20", Clr HR
L	Seat side boards	24	¾"×3⅛"×23¼", Clr HR
M	Seat face boards	4	¾"×4"×23¼", Clr HR

Part	Name	Qty	Description
N	Shelf ledger	8	1½"×3½"×21½", Clr HR
O	Flower shelf	2	½"×19"×33¾", CDX ply
P	Cap sill	4	¾"×4"×22½", Clr HR
Q	Cap face	8	¾"×2⅜"×18¾", Clr HR
R	Long wall boards	40	¾"×3⅛"×44½", Clr HR
S	Outer wall top faces	4	¾"×5½"×38¾", Clr HR
T	Seatside board top face	4	¾"×7"×19", Clr HR
U	Divider top face	2	¾"×5½"×17", Clr HR
V	Seat back nailer	4	1¹¹/₁₆"×1¹¹/₁₆"×17", Clr HR
W	Seat back boards	24	¾"×3⅛"×26½", Clr HR
X	Cap trim	8	1¹¹/₁₆"×11¼"×19¾", Clr HR
Y	Molding	—	¾"×1½", Clr HR

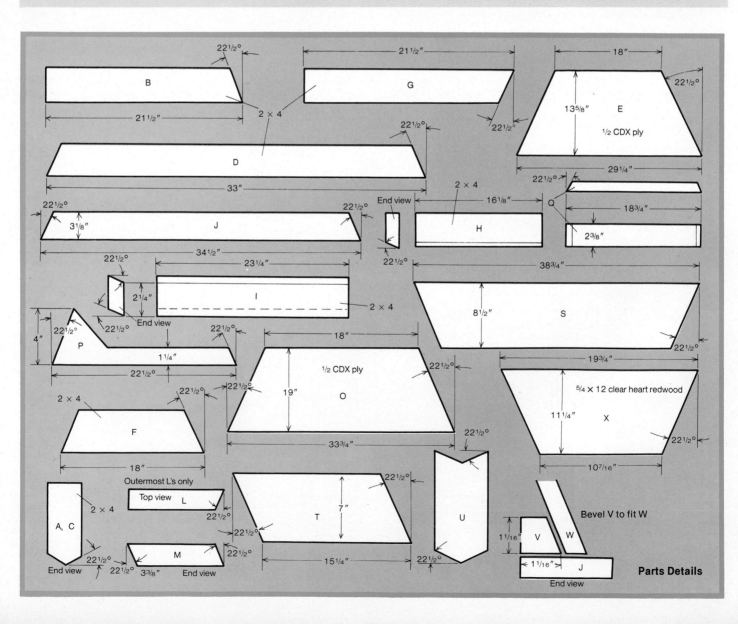

Parts Details

This is one of those good-looking projects that may appear quite difficult to build at first glance. It really is not, because: (1) there is a lot of symmetry in the design, hence, a lot of repetitive work; (2) the finish material, redwood, is soft and easily worked; (3) once past the foundation and base structure, everything is stabilized and easy to visualize and construct; (4) the same operations—ripping, trimming, beveling and mitering—are used throughout the machining and building of the entire base structure; (5) the bevel and miter angles are almost always 22½°, as dictated by the octagonal design.

Review the plans carefully to get a better understanding of the design.

STEP 1
BUILDING THE BASE
STRUCTURE

The base consists of both high and low frames, gussets, caps, and bands, with the bottoms of all sixteen frame posts embedded in small concrete footings. The octagonal shape is mainly provided by the gussets, which, on assembly to the frames, form an eight-sided ring.

Start by sawing out the posts, bands, caps, stretchers, and gussets. All posts have a double bevel at the front edge, all stretchers have a single bevel at one end, and all bands have a single bevel at each end. Caps and gussets have miters at each end.

Build up the high and low frames by nailing the stretchers to the posts. Note that there are six high frames and two low frames and that the double bevel of the outer posts and the single bevels of the stretchers form continuous beveled surfaces.

Move the frames, gussets, bands, and caps to the tree area and continue the assembly there. Join the frames to the gussets by driving screws through the gussets into the top edges of the lower stretchers on the frames. Make sure that the joint between adjacent gussets falls on the imaginary frame centerline between the inner and outer post centers (cusps).

ASSEMBLING HIGH AND LOW FRAMES

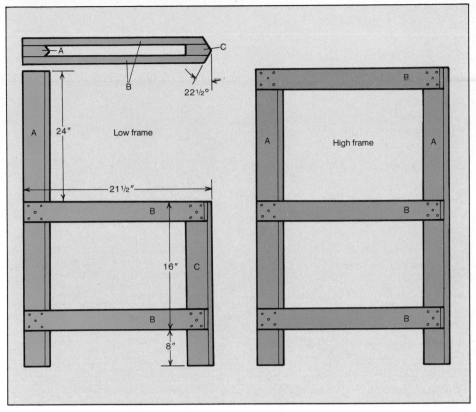

1. Six high frames and two low frames form the inner structure of the tree surround. Low frames are in the seat area. Frames, made of long posts, short posts, stretchers, and gussets, provide shape and anchor the structure to the ground.

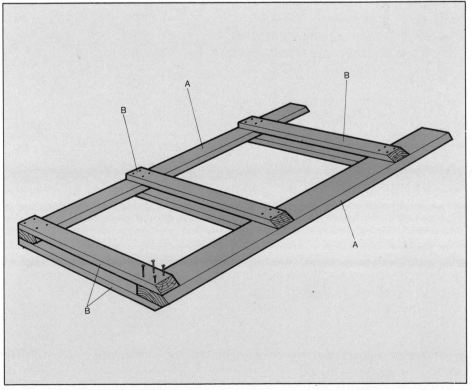

2. Viewed isometrically, the bevels on the front posts and those on the stretchers form continuous beveled planes, which are the eight outer corners of the octagonal surround. Bands and other members are attached to the bevels.

Lay out the post holes and dig them to a depth of about 10 inches. Then pour 4 inches of $^5/_8$–$^3/_4$-inch stone into the holes to drain water away. Separate the frame-gusset assembly into two halves by removing screws from joints that are 180° (semicircle) apart.

You'll need some help to lift the halves into position and place the posts in the holes. Rejoin the free ends of the gussets to their respective frame stretchers with the screws. You are now at a critical point in the project, so move slowly, patiently, and deliberately, in order to set the base structure correctly.

First, place both inner and outer posts of all frames level and plumb by adjusting the height of the stones in the holes. Frequent use of a level is necessary here. To plumb the sides of the frames, simply rock them until they're vertical. Add the bands to the front edges of the outer posts and the caps (two layers) to the tops of the inner posts. The cap joints should be over the centerlines of the inner posts, and the band joints over the vertical centerlines (cusps) of the outerposts. Any discrepancy in plumb, level, or alignment will be obvious now and must be corrected. Mix the concrete and backfill the post holes with it, constantly rechecking the plumb and level attitude of the frames with a level. Allow the concrete to set for a day or two.

STEP 2
SEATS, NAILERS, FILLERS

Saw out all seat boards, and miter one end of each. The seat boards meet miter-to-miter over the centerline of the low frame. To accomplish this, some trimming will be necessary at the other ends, which are screwed to the middle stretcher of the high frame. The outermost seat boards rest on and overhang the middle bands by 1½ inches. Once fitted, drill two screw clearance holes at each end of each board, using a combination bit, and drive the screws home.

With the seat surfaces covered, add the horizontal and vertical nailers to the high frames at the ends of

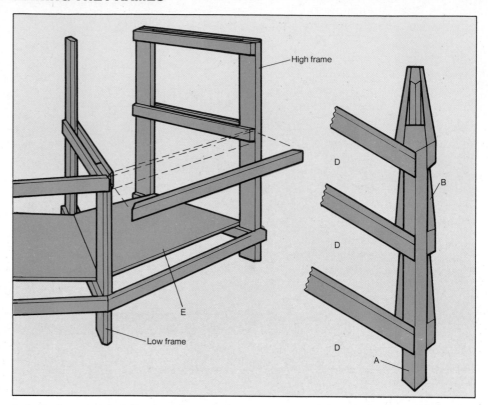

1. In the tree surround, the ring of gussets forms an octagon joined at the lower stretchers of the eight frames. At the outer perimeter, the shape is held by the addition of horizontal bands, which also serve as wall-board nailers.

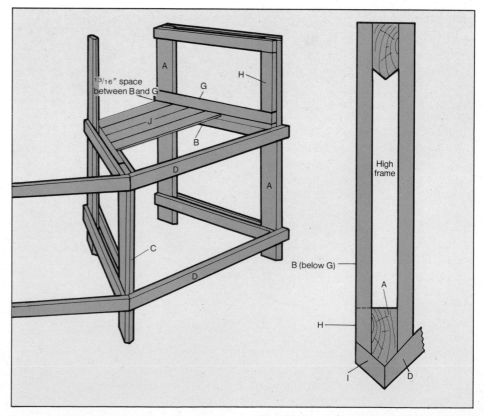

2. The seat boards rest on the middle stretcher of the high frames and the top stretchers of the low frames. Just above these boards, horizontal and vertical nailers, fastened to the posts, serve as backing for the side seat boards.

the seating areas. The horizontal nailers are, of course, parallel to the stretchers and rest down flush on the seat boards. The vertical nailers are fastened to the outer post between the horizontal nailer and the top stretcher.

To close the gap at the outer ends of the top stretchers and horizontal nailers, install the fillers. The filler sits on the seat boards with its inner face covering the beveled ends of the horizontal nailer, the top stretcher, and the exposed bevel on the outer post. Its outside bevel meets the end bevel of the adjacent top band. These parts serve as nailing bases for the seat-side boards and the seat-face boards.

STEP 3
THE VERTICAL SIDING

Now, saw out the pieces that make up most of the vertical siding. These include the short wall boards, the seat-side boards, the seat-face boards, and the long wall boards.

The seat-side boards are fastened to the horizontal nailer, top stretcher, and filler. They butt down flush on the seat boards, and the outermost seat-side board is beveled to be flush with the filler.

The short wall boards are screwed to the bands at the front of the seating area, and their top ends are flush with the seat overhang. Where the two center short wall boards meet at the cusp of the low frame outer post, they should be beveled for a neat-looking joint.

The seat-face boards are fitted next. They are beveled on the seat-side edges, which cover the edges of the last seat-side board. They are also beveled on the opposite edge, which meets the first long wall board over the cusp of the outer post of the high frame bordering the seat area.

Now install the long wall boards. There are four sections, just as there were for the short wall boards. The end boards in each section are beveled—one board to meet the bevel on the seat-face board, and the other to meet the bevel on the first board of the adjacent long wall section.

INSTALLING SEATS, NAILERS, AND FILLERS

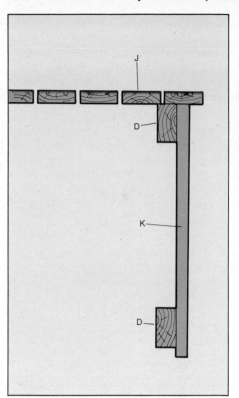

Cross-sectional view of seat shows seat boards, lower bands, and short wall boards at seat front, with seat board overlap.

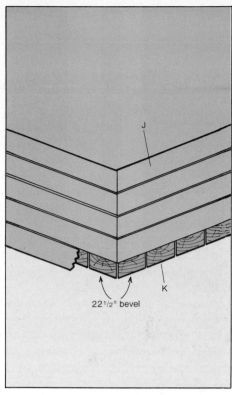

Plan view of seating area shows seat board miters meeting over low frame. Note bevels on short wall board at center.

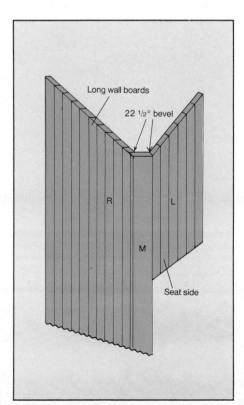

Six seat side boards line the side of the seating area. At the cusp is a beveled seat face board and ten long wall boards.

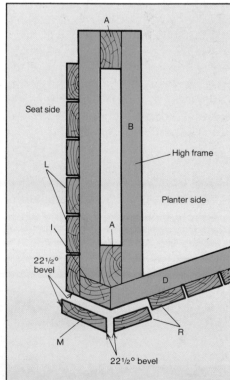

Plan view shows high frame, seat side boards, filler, beveled seat face board, and long wall board (first one beveled).

All vertical pieces are cut and sanded flush with the top band or top stretcher edge.

STEP 4
SEAT BACK NAILER, CAP FACES, SEAT BACK BOARDS, CAP SILL, AND CAP TRIM

Fit and install the four cap sills, noting that the thinner, mitered ends join over the centerline of the inner post of the center high frame of each double planter section. The hooked end of each cap sill covers the small exposed triangle at the rear corners of the seating area.

Then fit and bevel both ends of all eight cap faces, and screw them in place, flush with the top edges of the caps.

Next, use scrap pieces to make a dummy backrest, to determine the most comfortable seating angle; mark the seatboards accordingly for the placement of the seat-back nailers. Saw or plane the rake angle on these nailers, and install them.

The seat-back boards will be fastened at the bottom to these nailers and flush at the top to the cap faces. However, due to their rake angle and the angle of the seat-side boards, the seat-back boards will be narrower at the top than at the bottom.

So, as you're fitting these boards, bevel the edges of the two center boards where they join, and taper the outermost boards toward the top. Bevel them to match the side boards.

STEP 5
FINISHING UP

Nail in the eight horizontal planter shelf ledgers to the inner faces of the high frames at a height to suit your plants. Next, screw the plywood flower shelves to these ledgers. Miter and install the eight cap-trim pieces, which overhang the cap faces.

Now, fit and install all remaining surface pieces for each planter. These include outer wall top faces, seat-side board top face, and divider top face. The overhang at the long wall faces and seat-face boards will cover the top of the molding to be fitted in these areas.

INSTALLING BACK AND TRIM

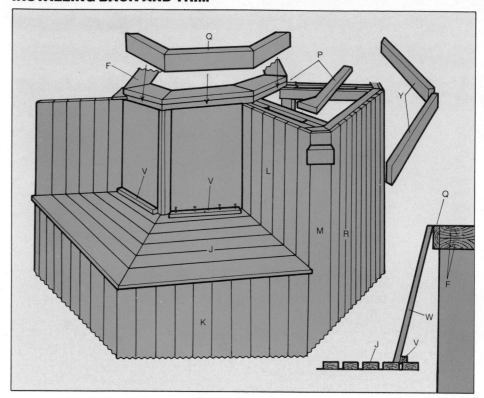

1. An isometric view shows seat boards, short wall boards, seat side boards, long wall boards, seat face boards, seat back nailers, cap, cap faces, cap sill, some molding, and the planter area. Cross-section shows seat boards, nailer, seat-back boards, cap faces.

2. Final isometric view shows cap trim and faces bordering the planter area. Within the four planters, nail the shelf ledgers to the frames inside and rest the planter shelf on them. Ledger height depends on plant height. Plan view shows planter design.

WISHING WELL

This wishing well is a decorative descendant of the traditional working water well. These old wells, plentiful prior to the advent of public water utilities, were easy to spot. Typically, they had a hip roof for protection, a windlass and bucket to haul up the water, and a lot more charm than a mechanical pump.

Our wishing well is a trip back to the past, and, although it does not provide water, it can be used as a planter. The center can be shelved to contain plants that can't receive direct sunlight, while the sill can be a home for sun-seekers and ivy.

Exploded View

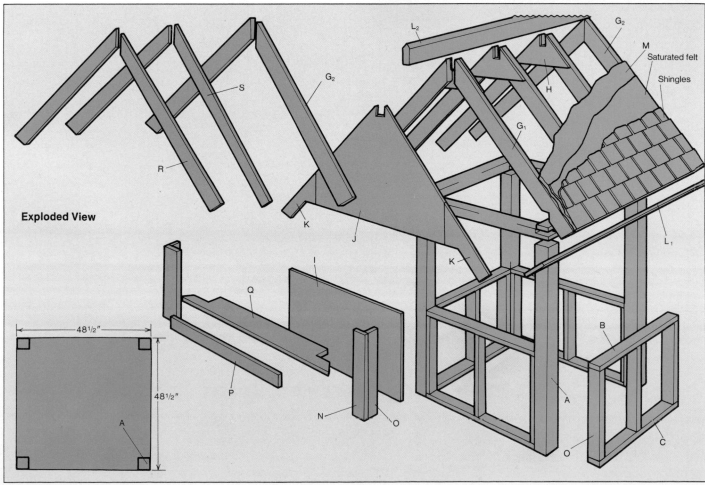

BILL OF MATERIALS

Qty	Size	Material	Qty	Size	Material	Qty	Size	Material
3	⁵/₈ × 4 × 8′	T1–11 panel	5	2 × 4 × 8′	Douglas fir		³/₄″	Roofing nails
2	¹/₂ × 4 × 8′	CDX plywood	3	2 × 4 × 7′	Douglas fir			Staples
4	4 × 4 × 8′	Pressure-treated lumber (P/T)	2	⁵/₄ × 6 × 10′	Pressure-treated lumber		8d	Oval head, galvanized nails
2	2 × 4 × 14′	Pressure-treated lumber	2	1 × 6 × 8′	White pine			
3	2 × 4 × 12′	Pressure-treated lumber	4	1 × 3 × 6′	White pine		6d	Oval head, galvanized nails, stain
1	2 × 4 × 14′	Douglas fir	2	1 × 3 × 8′	White pine			Exterior primer
2	2 × 4 × 10′	Douglas fir	3	3 × 7′	Pieces 15# saturated felt			Exterior trim paint
			2	bundles	Asphalt shingles			

PARTS LIST

Part	Name	Qty	Description	Part	Name	Qty	Description	Part	Name	Qty	Description
A	Post	4	3¹/₂″ × 3¹/₂″ × 7′, P/T	H	Rafter gusset	3	¹/₂″ × 23¹/₂″ × 11³/₄″, CDX ply	M	Roof sheathing	2	¹/₂″ × 48″ × 74″, fir
B	Rough sill	4	1¹/₂″ × 3¹/₂″ × 41¹/₂″, P/T	I	Base sides	4	⁵/₈″ × 48¹/₂″ × 36″, T1–11 panel	N	Corner trim, wide	4	³/₄″ × 2¹/₂″ × 36″, pine
C	Stretcher	4	1¹/₂″ × 3¹/₂″ × 41¹/₂″, P/T	J	Gable ends	2	⁵/₈″ × 48¹/₂″ × 30″, T1–11 panel	O	Corner trim, narrow	4	³/₄″ × 1³/₄″ × 36″, pine
D	Stud	12	1¹/₂″ × 3¹/₂″ × 32″, P/T	K	Gable end extensions (2LH, 2RH)	4	⁵/₈″ Fitted, T1–11 panel	P	Apron trim	4	³/₄″ × 2¹/₂″ × 48″, pine
E	Long top plate	4	1¹/₂″ × 3¹/₂″ × 48¹/₂″, fir	L1	Rafter tail faces	2	1¹/₂″ × 3¹/₂″ × 67¹/₂″, fir	Q	Sill	4	⁵/₄″ × 5¹/₂″ × 54″, pine
F	Short top plate	1	1¹/₂″ × 3¹/₂″ × 41¹/₂″, fir	L2	Ridge board	1	1¹/₂″ × 3¹/₂″ × 67¹/₂″, fir	R	Rafter fascia	4	³/₄″ × 3³/₄″ × 48″, pine
G1	Rafter	6	1¹/₂″ × 3¹/₂″ × 45¹/₂″, fir					S	Gable and roof trim	4	³/₄″ × 1¹/₂″ × 45¹/₂″, pine
G2	Outboard rafter	4	1¹/₂″ × 3¹/₂″ × 48″, fir								

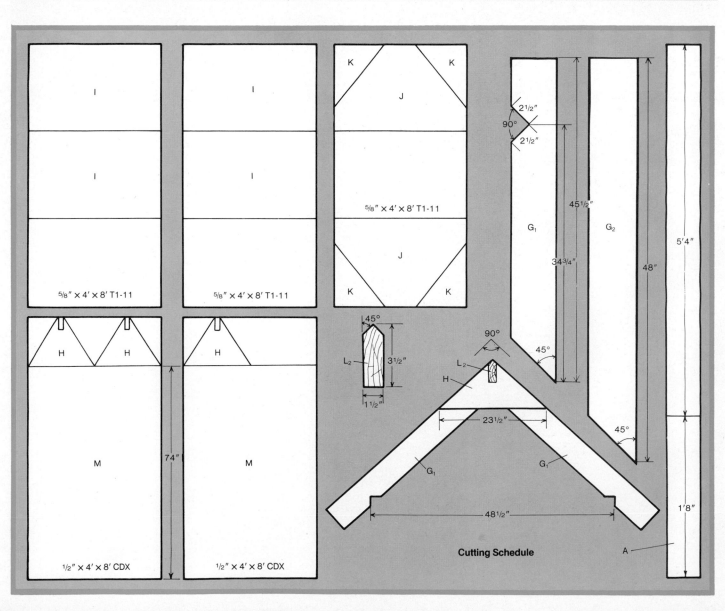

Cutting Schedule

STEP 1
LAYING OUT THE GROUNDWORK

Decide on the location, considering the topography of your yard and, if you'll be using the wishing well as a planter, the path of the sun. Then set up a network of stakes, and stretch mason's cord between them. The post holes should be centered under the cord intersections. These intersections should be 45 inches on center, and of course they should be square. If the sides are 45 inches, the diagonals must both be 63½ inches to ensure this.

Dig down 24 inches below grade with a post-hole digger (you can rent this tool). Throw about 4 inches of ⅝–¾-inch stone into the holes to drain away water and place the posts in the holes.

STEP 2
SETTING THE POSTS

Using either temporary braces or a second person to hold the posts steady, backfill the post holes with concrete or dirt. As you're backfilling, keep checking that the posts are plumb by applying a level to two adjacent faces of each post. Also, make sure that the span from the inner face of one post to the next remains a constant 41½ inches from top to grade. The 7-foot posts should be embedded in the ground 1 foot, 8 inches, below grade and be 5 feet, 4 inches, above grade.

STEP 3
MAKING THE INTER-POST LADDERS

The posts will support ladder-like 2 × 4 assemblies nailed to their inner faces at the lower portion, as well as lapped, doubled 2 × 4 plates nailed to their top ends.

The ladder structures are flush with the outer post faces and serve as a structural base (nailers) for the T1–11 side panels. They also function as a rough sill for each finished sill. The plates at the top, along with the posts, support the rafters, ridge, roof sheathing, and shingles.

LAYING OUT THE POST HOLES

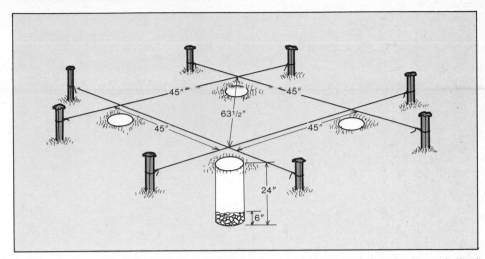

Set up stakes, and stretch mason's cord between them so that the cords intersect over desired post-hole centers. Mark centers with stakes, and remove the cords. Then pull the stakes, one at a time, dig the holes, and drop in the stone.

SETTING THE POSTS

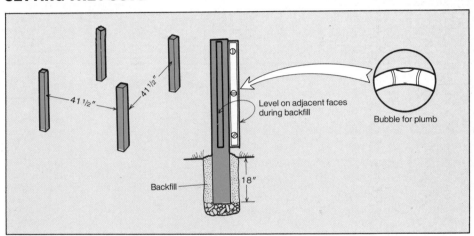

Place the first post in its hole, plumb it on adjacent faces with a level, and tack in temporary bracing. Backfill the hole with concrete, tapering the top of this collar to shed water. Align the other posts with the first, plumb them, and backfill them.

ASSEMBLING THE INTER-POST LADDERS

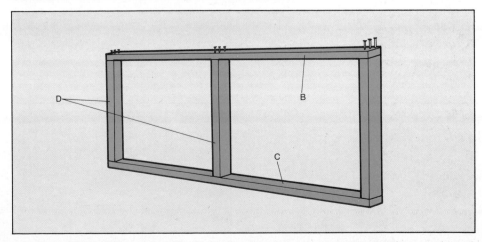

Assemble the ladderlike base side frame structure from short studs, stretchers, and rough sills. By nailing vertically, as shown, the lateral forces that would tend to spread the structure are directly opposed by the nails.

Start the ladderlike assemblies by cutting the studs, stretchers, and rough sills to length. You might wish to gang-saw these to save some time. Then nail the parts together to form the four ladders.

Place these ladders in position, one at a time, and face-nail the end studs to the inner faces of the posts, at about 37 inches above grade. This will allow any rainwater that might get inside to run out quickly.

Check with a level that the ladders are really horizontal. Then toe-nail the rough sills and stretchers to the posts. As you proceed from one side installation to the next, check for the horizontal alignment with the level.

STEP 4
INSTALLING THE SIDING

Saw out the four side pieces from T1–11 panel. Before nailing on the panels, make a final check to ascertain that the posts are plumb and the ladder structures are square. Do this now because once you nail on the panels, there won't be any flexibility for further adjustment. Note that the full panel width, including the edge laps, is 48½ inches. Thus they will span from post corner to post corner exactly. They should be positioned vertically so that the top edge is flush with the rough sill.

STEP 5
INSTALLING THE TOP PLATES

Cut to size the four short and four long top plates. Mark the positions of the short plates on the long plates and make four sub-assemblies by nailing one short plate to each long.

Place one double-plate sub-assembly on the top ends of two adjacent posts, short plate facing up. Nail through the two exposed long plate faces into the tops of both posts. Repeat this step on the two opposite posts so that both double-plate sub-assemblies are parallel.

The remaining two double-plate sub-assemblies will neatly lap with the first two when placed in position with their short plates facing down. Nail them in place that way.

INSTALLING THE LADDERS

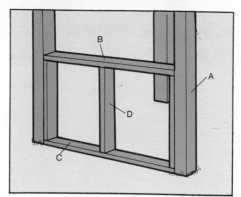

Fit the frames between the post faces, level them, and nail them solidly to the posts, flush with the outer faces.

INSTALLING THE TOP PLATES

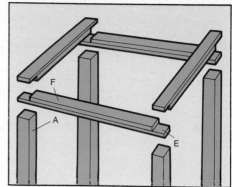

Check that the post tops are level; correct if necessary. Nail the lapped top plates in place to the post tops.

CUTTING AND ASSEMBLING THE RAFTERS

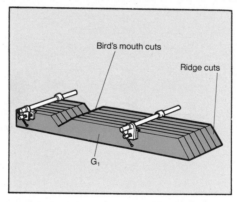

1. Saw the rafter ridge cuts individually. Then clamp the rafters together, and gang-saw the bird's mouths.

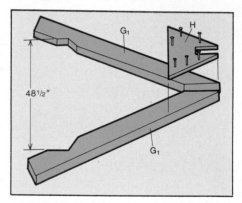

2. Nail the gussets to the rafters, maintaining the notch at the top and the spread between the bird's mouths below.

INSTALLING THE RAFTERS

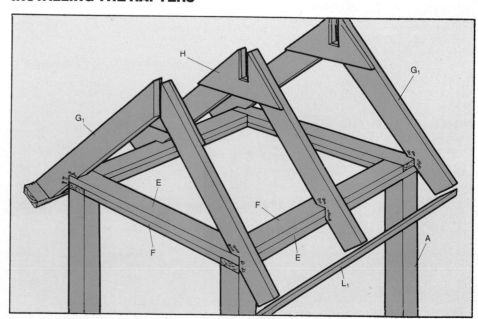

Place the rafter assemblies on the top plates with the outer rafters flush with the ends and their gussets facing inward. Toe-nail the rafters to the top plates.

STEP 6
MAKING THE RAFTERS

Cut out all rafters and their plywood gussets. This includes six G1s and four G2s. Clamp all the G1 rafters together, and gang-saw the lower notches (bird's mouths). Now, nail the G1s and their gussets into assemblies. Maintain the angles during the assembly, and make sure that the ridgeboard notches at the top of the gussets have enough clearance. Make this one final check: try the rafters on the plates to see if the bird's mouths fit them properly. Once you've verified this, clinch the rafter-assembly nails by bending them over and hitting flat against the 2×4s.

STEP 7
BUILDING THE ROOF

Mark off the centers of the plates where the middle rafter assembly will be fastened, position it, and toe-nail it in place so that the faces are plumb. Now, position the other two rafter assemblies with their gussets facing inward, and secure them to the ends of the top plates, with their faces plumb as well.

Check the alignment of the rafter tails (the parts that overhang the plates). If their ends are in a dead straight line, nail the rafter tail faces to them, allowing equal overhang on both ends. If the ends aren't aligned, snap a chalk line across them, trim as necessary to get a straight line, and then add the faces.

Now, center the gable end T1–11s over the outer rafters, allowing their bottom edges to hang down 1½ inches below the lowest of the top plates. Scribe lines on the reverse sides of the gable ends, tracing the upper rafter edges. Remove these ends, trim to the lines, and nail up the resulting triangular gable ends.

The small pork-chop-shaped extensions on both sides of each gable end are made from the triangle shaped scrap just trimmed off. But use those pieces that match the edge laps of the gable ends. Tack them in place. Then mark, remove them, trim, and replace them permanently.

CUTTING THE GABLE ENDS

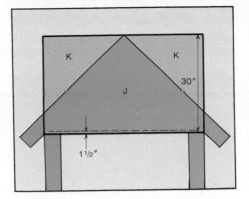

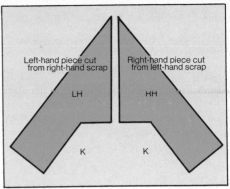

1. Tack up the gable end piece of T1–11, scribe the rafter outline on the back, remove it, and saw out the gable-end shape.

2. Use the triangular cutoffs to make the gable-end extensions. Match edge laps, scribe, cut, and nail in place.

ASSEMBLING ROOF PARTS

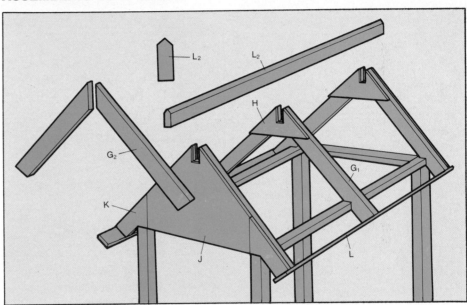

Nail in the ridge, allowing equal overhang past each end. Nail rafter tail faces to rafters, allowing equal overhang as well. Join outboard rafters at the top, and nail to ridgeboard end. Nail rafter tails to the end of the rafter tail faces.

INSTALLING SHEATHING

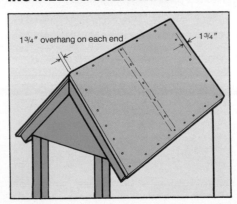

Nail the pre-cut roof sheathing to the roof structure, allowing equal overhang beyond each end.

INSTALLING FELT

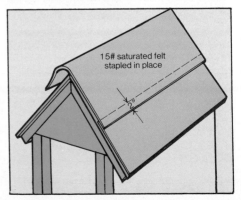

Staple saturated felt or building paper to the sheathing, starting at the lowest part; overlap the first piece with the next.

Saw the two 45° bevels on the top edge of the ridgeboard, and nail it in place in the rafter assembly top notches, allowing equal overhang on each end.

Note that the outside G2 rafters are 2½ inches longer than the G1s and have no bird's mouths. This is because their top miters meet directly over the ridgeboard end and do not rest on the top plates. So nail them in place at the ridgeboard ends and at the ends of the overhanging rafter tail faces.

Next, nail the roof sheathing to the rafters, ridgeboard, and faces, keeping the rafters square with the sheathing edges. Paint the rafter faces, and when they're dry, add the saturated felt and shingles (see the doghouse project for procedures).

STEP 8
FINISHING UP

Stain all T1–11 surfaces, and let them dry. While the stain is drying, saw out all trim pieces. This group includes narrow and wide vertical corners, sills, apron, gable-end roof trim, and rafter fascia. Prime and finish paint them, and allow them to dry.

The gable-end roof trim pieces are 45°-mitered at the top and butt cut at the bottom. They fit against the top edge of the gable ends, between the ridgeboard and the rafter tail faces. The rafter fascia are also 45°-mitered at the top and butt cut at the bottom. They completely cover the outside rafters and the ends of the tail faces. The corners are pre-nailed in L-shaped assemblies and installed, while the aprons are horizontal and fitted between the corners and flush at the top with the rough sills. The sills are fitted between the post inner faces, around the adjacent outer face, and then 45°-mitered to join the adjacent sill.

INSTALLING SHINGLES

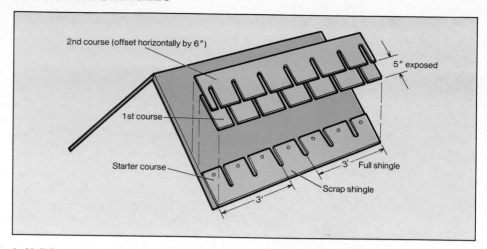

1. Nail the starter shingle course at the bottom, inverted to fill the area beneath the first-course slots. Offset the end shingle of the first course by 6 inches, and allow the butt ends to overhang the starter-course eave by ½ inch.

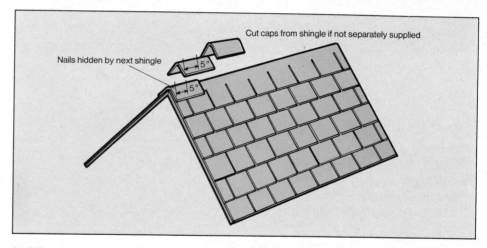

2. Offset the second course by another 6 inches. Leave 5 inches of the first course exposed to the weather. Continue this offset and exposure through all courses. Cut ridge caps from regular shingles (three per shingle), and nail them to ridge with 5-inch exposure and overlapping.

FINISHING UP

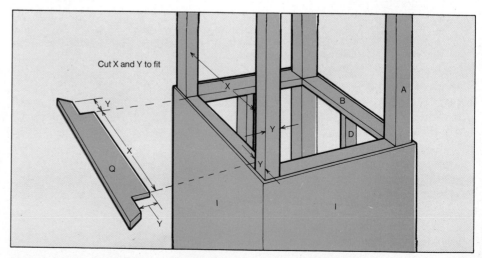

Fit inner edges of sills between the post faces. Then deepen the notches until the outer faces of the posts are covered. Finally, mark the miters on the ends, matching adjacent sills. Saw them, and nail the sills in. Add corner and apron moldings.

SLAT CHAIR

This all-redwood slat chair will fit comfortably on almost any backyard lawn, patio, or deck. Its combination of simple lines and modern styling are both esthetically pleasing and functional.

The slat chair itself is mounted on a sturdy, well-balanced base; the same base supports a companion piece to the slat chair, the slat chaise. Both pieces may be used as they are or with cushions.

You'll find that building the base with its sculptured sides is simpler than it appears; most of the initial work is done with straight lines, while the curves are added as a final decorative touch.

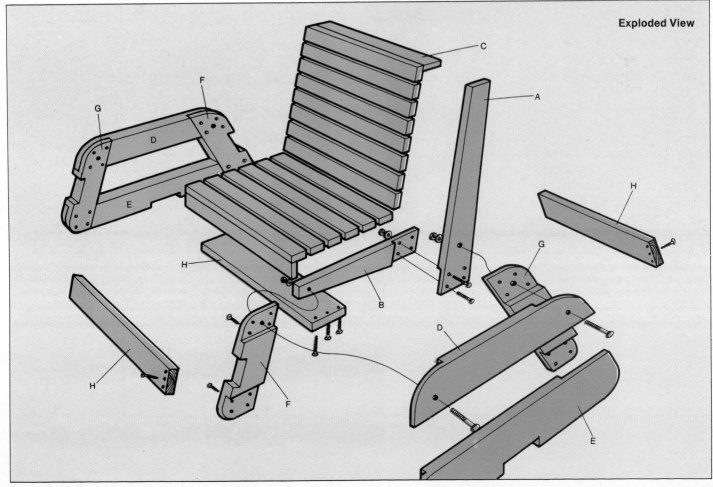

Exploded View

BILL OF MATERIALS

Qty	Size	Material	Qty	Size	Material	Qty	Size	Material
1	2×6×12'	Clear heart redwood	8	3/8 × 5 1/2"	Carriage bolts, nuts, washers	18	#10 × 3"	Flat head, Phillips head, stainless steel wood screws
1	2×6×8'	Clear heart redwood	76	#8 × 1 1/2"	Flat head, Phillips head, stainless steel wood screws	8	1/4 × 1 1/4"	Carriage bolts, nuts, washers
1	5/4 × 12 × 9'	Clear heart redwood		8d	Galvanized nails	4	1/4 × 3"	Carriage bolts, nuts, washers
1	1×12×8'	Clear heart redwood		10d	Galvanized nails			
2	2×4×14'	Construction heart redwood	110	#8 × 1 1/2"	Flat head, Phillips head, stainless steel screws			
3	2×4×10'	Clear heart redwood						
2	2×4×12'	Clear heart redwood						
2	1×12×14'	Clear heart redwood						

PARTS LIST

All parts clear heart redwood

Part Name		Qty	Description	Part Name		Qty	Description	Part Name		Qty	Description
A1	Right-side backrest	1	1 1/16" × 5 5/8" × 27 1/4"	B2	Left-side seat	1	1 1/16" × 5 5/8" × 22 3/4"	F	Base side end	2	1 1/2" × 5 1/2" × 19 3/4"
A2	Left-side backrest	1	1 1/16" × 5 5/8" × 27 1/4"	C	Seat slat	16	3/4" × 2 11/16" × 19"	G	Base side end	2	1 1/2" × 5 1/2" × 19 3/4"
B1	Right-side seat	1	1 1/16" × 5 5/8" × 22 3/4"	D	Base side top	2	1 1/2" × 5 1/2" × 30 3/4"	H	Base stretcher	3	1 1/16" × 5 1/2" × 22 1/2"
				E	Base side bottom	2	1 1/2" × 5 1/2" × 42"				

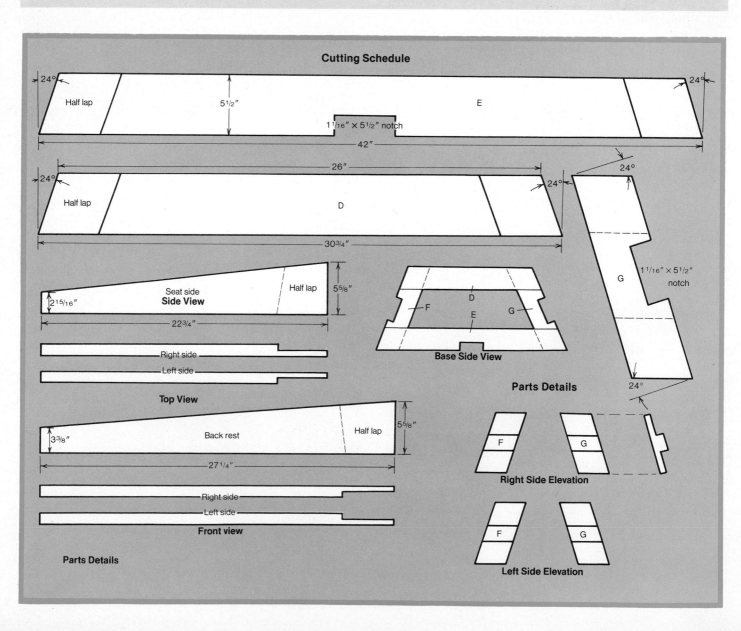

Cutting Schedule

Saw out the parts as shown in the Cutting Schedule and Parts Details drawings. Base and seat parts require that half lap joints be marked and machined with a dado set on a radial or table saw before assembly. There are left- and right-handed seat sides and backrest side assemblies.

STEP 1
MARKING THE PIECES FOR MACHINING

To mark the pieces, lay a seat side flat with its small end to the *left* and its right angle to the right. Then, set the backrest side over the first piece so that its small end is farthest from you and the right angles of both pieces are at the right. Support the far end of the top piece so that it is flat over the first, and make sure that their outer edges form a right angle at the right hand corner.

Using the inside edge of the top piece as a guide, mark a line on the first piece. Now, flip both pieces over. Support the small end of the top piece (which is now the seat side), and position the right angles at the corner as before. Check that their outer edges form a right angle, and mark the backrest side using the seat side as a guide. These two pieces become the left-hand assembly. To mark the right-hand assembly, set up the seat side and backrest as a mirror image of the first pair.

STEP 2
MACHINING THE JOINTS

On a radial saw, hold the workpiece against the fence, the miter angle set with the arm, and the post adjusted for a cut that will remove half the thickness of the wood.

With a table saw, the workpiece must be held against the miter gauge, which is set for the angle, and the blades raised to a cutting depth that will remove half the thickness. With either machine, perform a test cut on scrap.

STEP 3
ASSEMBLING THE SIDES AND BACKRESTS

To assemble, clamp the side pieces together, drill holes through

ASSEMBLING THE BACKREST AND SEAT

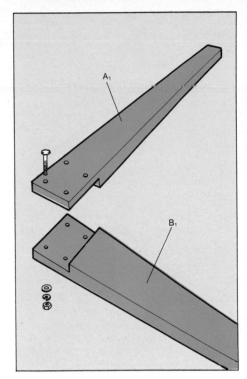

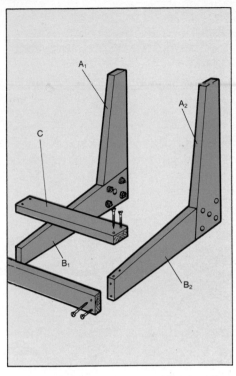

1. Clamp the machined backrest and seat side pieces together, drill bolt holes, and install carriage hardware to assemble.

2. Start joining the side assemblies together by drilling holes and driving screws through slats into sides.

ASSEMBLING THE SIDES

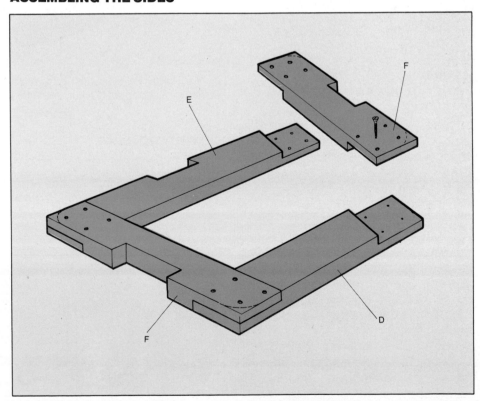

The notches for the stretcher and the half laps have already been machined. Position the pieces, clamp the corners, drill holes, and drive screws. Don't put screws in outer corners.

them, using a drill guide, and bolt them together.

STEP 4
CUTTING AND INSTALLING THE SLATS

Cut and sand the slats. Draw light pencil lines with a try square across them $9/16$ inch from both ends. Drill all screw holes along these lines. Install the seat slats, flush with the seat sides, starting at the small end at the front. Use a $1/4$ inch spacing gauge between slats.

STEP 5
CUTTING AND MACHINING THE BASE PIECES

Saw out the base members, trim them to length, and saw miters on both ends of each. Place end pieces over the top and bottom pieces, and mark the tops and bottoms for half laps. Then, flop all four pieces, and mark the ends for half laps. Mark these tops, bottoms, and ends as you marked the seat half laps.

Again, use a dado set on a radial or table saw to make the half laps. Test the settings on scrap first. Mark off the three notches in each base side to receive the stretchers. These notches may be made with the miter gauge and dado blade set on a table saw or with a jig or band saw.

STEP 6
ASSEMBLING AND ROUNDING THE BASE

Now, screw the base sides together, but avoid driving screws in the corners that will be rounded. With a compass, draw a $1\frac{1}{2}$-inch radius at each corner, cut with a jigsaw, and belt-sand smooth.

Install the three stretchers in the base-side notches, keeping the ends flush with the sides. Clamp one base to a work surface, and sand the top surface. Rout both edges with a rounding-over bit, observing the feed directions shown. Repeat on the opposite side.

Set the base upright and place the slat chair in it. Block the chair up, adjusting the position until you find a comfortable angle. Clamp the seat and base together, drill holes, and bolt the chair together.

ROUNDING THE CORNERS

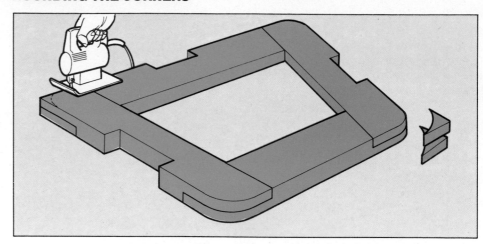

Mark the corner curves with compasses, cut them with a jig saw, and sand all edges smooth.

ASSEMBLING THE BASE

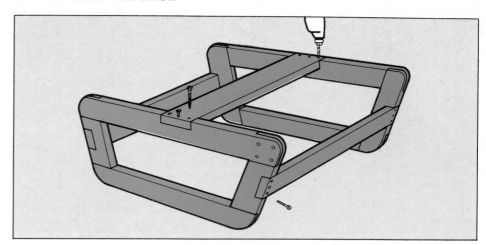

Join the two base sides by first installing the bottom stretcher and then the front and back stretchers, using screws in pre-drilled holes. Sand edges flush.

ROUTING THE EDGES

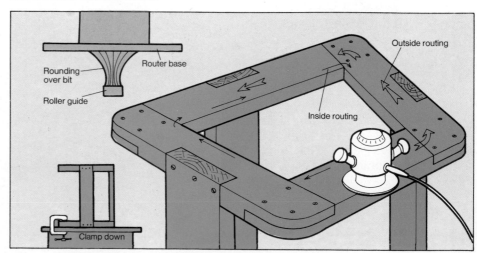

Clamp the base assembly to a work surface, and machine the perimeters of both sides with router and rounding-over bit. Be sure to clear all assembly screws.

SLAT CHAISE

O ur redwood slat chaise is the companion piece of the redwood slat chair, as can be readily seen by comparing wood, slat size and arrangement as well as the bases.

A simple but sturdy box frame, built of redwood lumber, forms the base for the chaise.

The major advantages of this large base are strength and stability. But it also has a pair of wheels that may be flipped down if the chaise must be moved. A wood dowel grab bar at the foot end serves as a lift handle to facilitate this.

The backrest section may be used in a horizontal position or elevated, by changing the position of a hinged prop whose wood dowel fits into the backrest notch.

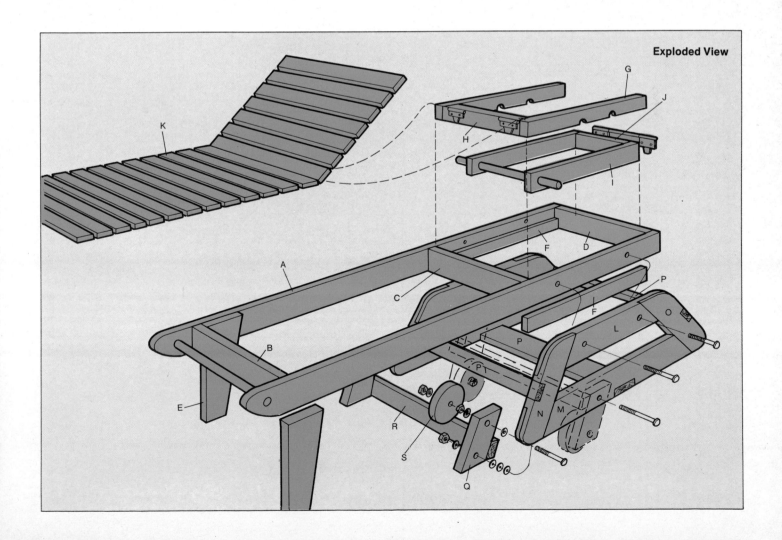

Exploded View

BILL OF MATERIALS

Qty	Size	Material
1	2 × 6 × 12′	Clear heart redwood
1	2 × 6 × 8′	Clear heart redwood
1	5/4 × 12 × 14′	Clear heart redwood
1	5/4 × 12 × 6′	Clear heart redwood
1	1 × 12 × 12′	Clear heart redwood
2	36″	1″ diameter maple dowel
2	Packages	Stanley #V908-4 hinges
18	#10 × 3″	Flat head, Phillips head, stainless steel wood screws
200	#8 × 11/2″	Flat head, Phillips head, stainless steel wood screws
4	5/16 × 21/2″	Carriage bolts, nuts, washers
4	5/16 × 31/2″	Carriage bolts, nuts, washers

PARTS LIST

All parts clear heart redwood

Part Name		Qty	Description
A	Side	2	11/16″ × 51/2″ × 75″
B	Cross member	1	11/16″ × 51/2″ × 19″
C	Cross member	1	11/16″ × 51/2″ × 19″
D	Cross member	1	11/16″ × 51/2″ × 19″
E	Legs	2	11/16″ × 51/2″ × 18″
F	Cleats	2	11/16″ × 51/2″ × 26″
G	Backrest side	2	11/16″ × 51/2″ × 251/2″
H	Backrest cross member	2	11/16″ × 51/2″ × 163/4″
I	Prop side	2	11/16″ × 2″ × 16″
J	Prop cross	1	11/16″ × 2″ × 141/2″

Part Name		Qty	Description
	member		
K	Slats	23	3/4″ × 211/16″ × 221/8″
L	Base top *	2	11/2″ × 51/2″ × 303/4″
M	Base bottom †	2	11/2″ × 51/2″ × 42″
N	Base end‡	2	11/2″ × 51/2″ × 193/4″
O	Base end§	2	11/2″ × 51/2″ × 193/4″
P	Stretcher	3	11/16″ × 51/2″ × 241/2″
Q	Wheel legs	2	11/16″ × 2″ × 71/2″
R	Leg brace	1	11/16″ × 2″ × 211/8″
S	Wheels	2	11/16″ × 5″ diameter

* Same as D in Slat Chair project.
† Same as E in Slat Chair project.
‡ Same as F in Slat Chair project.
§ Same as G in Slat Chair project.

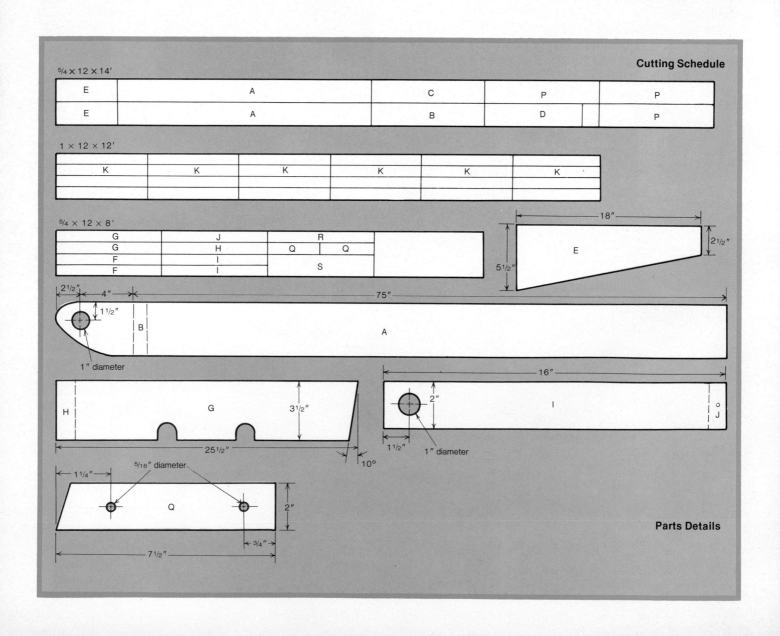

Cutting Schedule

Parts Details

BUILDING THE BASE

The base is identical to that of the companion piece, the Slat Chair project, except for the width of the sides, due to longer stretchers.

When you start building the base, refer to the Slat Chair project, and proceed in exactly the same way, except for the stretcher length. The sizing, machining, and assembly of all base side parts is unchanged.

CONSTRUCTION SEQUENCE

We suggest that you build the frame first. Then, add the dowel handle, front legs, and rear inside cleat for the backrest. If you wish, build the base at this point, as well as its wheel and leg assemblies. You can also now mount the wheel and leg assemblies to the base.

But, rather than assemble the base to the frame at this stage, prop up the rear end of the frame. In this way, working at the rear with the hinged assemblies will be much easier, with no awkward places to poke into or dead weight to lift.

The hinged assemblies should be built, fitted, and mounted, including the locations of the backrest notches for both up and down positions. After this work is finished, combine the chaise with its base and begin to install the slats. Since the backrest can be raised and lowered, you will have to determine the exact location for the break between the fixed and movable slats.

STEP 1
CUTTING OUT THE PARTS

Begin by sawing out the parts according to the cutting schedule and parts details, but delay machining the base side parts and any hole drilling and notching until you actually need to perform these operations.

STEP 2
ASSEMBLING FRAME AND LEGS

In setting up for the chaise frame, note that all cross members are the same and that the distance between the middle cross member and the one on the base end is the length of the cleat (F). Also, the front face of the cross member at the foot end is 6 inches back from the end of the side,

ASSEMBLING THE FRAME

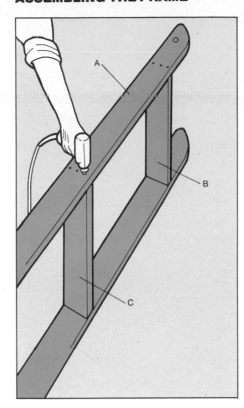

1. Position the cross members between the base sides, drill, and drive screws.

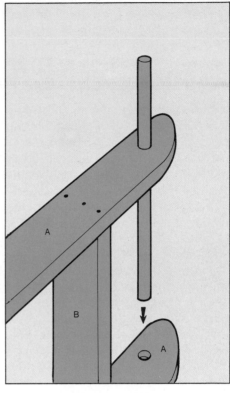

2. Drill dowel-handle holes. Insert dowel, cross-drill, and lock with nails.

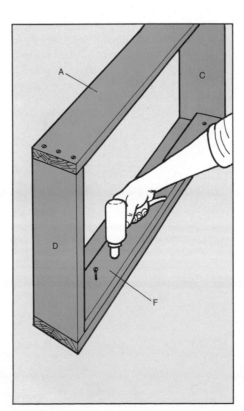

3. Screw both cleats in place between the center and rear cross members.

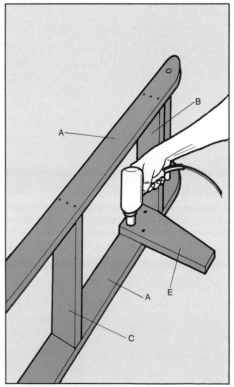

4. Install front legs at inner junctions of side and front cross members.

and 4 inches behind the dowel handle hole center.

Now, mark out a left and right side, including the locations of all three cross members, the dowel-hole centers, and the curved shape at the foot end of the side.

With the aid of a drill guide, bore the dowel holes, using scrap backup behind the holes to avoid splintering when the bit leaves the holes. Then, clamp up both sides and all cross members at the marks, and set the group up on props or blocks. Your setup should allow access to the clamp screws and be at a suitable height for drilling holes and driving screws.

First, drill through the sides into the cross members along the marked lines with a combination (pilot, clearance, and countersink) bit. Then, drive in the flat head screws until they are just slightly below the wood surface. Drill the holes, and screw the cleats to the inner faces of the sides flush with their bottom edges, between the center and rear cross members.

Next, clamp the front legs in place, flat against the inner faces of the sides, flush with the tops of the sides, and with the leg's front edge flat against the rear face of the front cross member. Then, drill through the legs, and screw them to the side. Also, drill through the front cross member, and screw into the front edge of the legs.

Work the dowel handle into its holes on both sides and saw or sand the ends flush. If the fit is tight, leave it that way. If the fit is loose, drill through the edge of the side through the dowel using a 1/8-inch-diameter bit from the nearest access point, and drive in a 10d oval head nail to lock the dowel.

STEP 3
ASSEMBLING THE BACKREST

Begin work on the backrest by marking out the screw-hole lines in both backrest sides. Then, clamp up both sides with the backrest cross member and a piece of scrap equal in length to the cross member, thus forming a rectangle. Drill through the

ASSEMBLING THE BACKREST

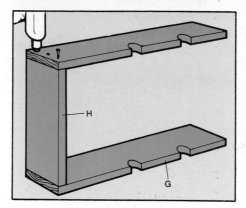

Assemble the backrest sides to their cross member with screws. This is easily done with support at the opposite end.

MAKING THE WHEELS

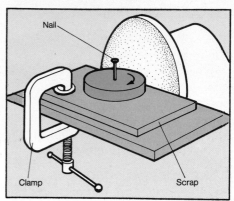

Saw out wheel, and drill pilot hole through center. Nail wheel through hole to scrap block, and smooth against disk sander.

ASSEMBLING THE WHEEL FRAME

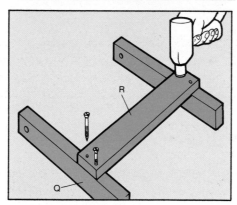

Position the brace over the legs, check for square, and screw the leg brace to the edges of the wheel legs.

ASSEMBLING THE WHEELS

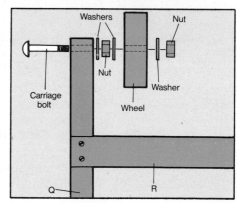

Drill axle holes in legs and wheels. Then assemble them with carriage hardware in the order shown (see text).

MOUNTING THE WHEEL ASSEMBLY

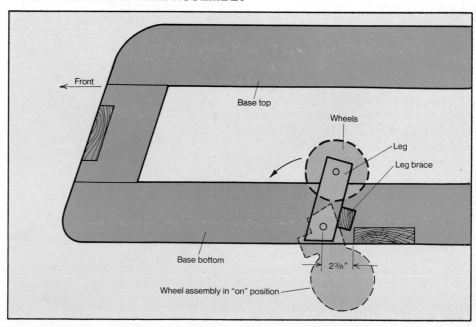

Although shown upright, it's easier to invert the base to drill the assembly axle holes in it and install the assembly. Make sure that both up and down positions are stable.

sides into the cross member, and drive the screws. Then, remove the clamps and set this assembly aside.

STEP 4
MAKING THE WHEELS AND WHEEL-AND-LEG ASSEMBLY

Draw circles for the wheels, and cut them out with a board or jigsaw. To sand their edges smooth, drill a 1/8-inch-diameter hole all the way through at the center mark. Then tap a 10d nail through this hole into a scrap board just below. The nail will serve as an axle for the wheel to be turned by hand. The scrap board may then be clamped to any surface adjacent to a sanding disk (such as one on a table saw) or to the table of a vertical sander.

The wheels are attached to an assembly consisting of two short legs and a leg brace. This assembly, in turn, is attached to the bottom member of the base side. To do this, first drill the axle holes in each end of both legs, using a drill guide.

Then, mark the location of the cross brace on the edges of both legs, and clamp it in place. Drill holes with a combination bit, drive the screws, and assemble the wheels and legs. Drill holes in the bottom members of the base sides, and mount the wheel-and-leg assembly in place with bolts. Make sure everything clears and that the wheel-and-leg assembly will lock in both up and down positions.

These wheels are designed only for occasional movement. If you foresee frequent movement, substitute a 21 1/8-inch-long threaded rod for the short wheel axles, and counterbore the outside faces of the legs to bring the outer nuts flush with those faces.

STEP 5
ASSEMBLING THE BACKREST PROP

Make the backrest prop assembly now. First, mark the dowel-hole centers, and drill 1-inch-diameter holes. Clamp up the two prop sides, the cross member, and a piece of scrap equal in length to the cross member, forming a rectangle.

ASSEMBLING THE BACKREST PROP

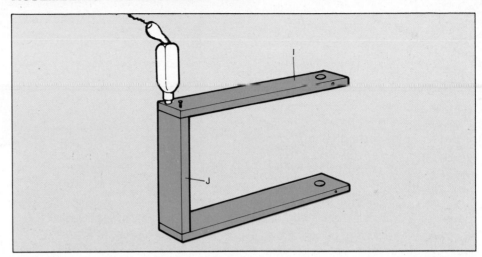

1. Drill the dowel holes in the prop sides. Then, position the prop cross member between the prop sides, and assemble the pieces by drilling screw holes and driving the screws; hold the opposite ends apart.

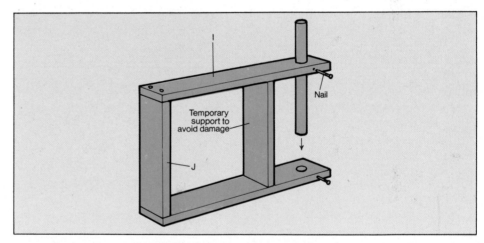

2. Keep the prop between the sides, and place the assembly on a work surface so that the dowel holes overhang it. Work the dowel into both holes, allowing equal overhang off each side. Drill cross holes, and drive nails to lock the dowel.

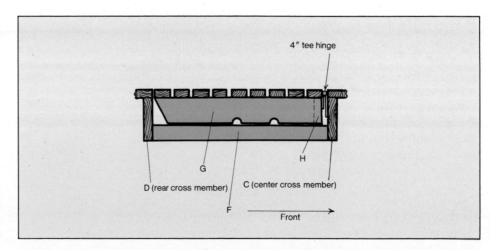

3. Mount one leaf of each T hinge to the front face of the backrest cross member. The assembly can be installed with or without its slats. Position the backrest to locate the hinges on the rear face of the center cross member, and install the second leaves.

Drill through the side faces into the cross member with a combination bit, and drive the screws home. Then, with the assembly still clamped up, work the dowel into position. The dowel is 18$7/8$ inches long, and the total width of the prop sides is 16$5/8$ inches, so the overhang on each side is 1$1/8$ inches. Drill $1/8$-inch-diameter holes through the prop side edges into the dowel, and drive 10d oval head nails into these holes to lock the dowel.

Attach the butt (rectangular) leaves of a pair of 4-inch T hinges to the cross members of both the backrest and backrest prop. Space these hinges about 1$1/2$ inches from the ends. Support the back end of the chaise frame. Then, mark the inner face of the last frame cross member (D) 1$1/2$ inches down from the top edge. Mount the backrest prop to this cross member so that its top edge touches the mark just made.

Mount the backrest on the rear face of the center cross member (C), with its top edge flush with the top edge of the frame. The backrest prop's dowel will rest on the cleats (F), but the backrest sides will not be able to touch the cleats because they will hit the dowel. Therefore, mark the backrest side notches for the down position and for the up position of your choice. Then, cut out these notches with a coping saw or a jigsaw.

STEP 6
INSTALLING THE SLATS

Slats are placed in position over the frame or backrest and then drilled and screwed in place. As usual, use a spacing gauge to keep the slats parallel. Give special attention to the innermost slat of the fixed section and to the bottom slat of the backrest. You may have to adjust the spacing and make a beveled edge on each slat in order to accommodate both the up and down positions of the backrest.

Remove the support, clamp the chaise in position on the base, drill and counterbore for the bolts, and lock it up.

ASSEMBLING THE BACKREST PROP (CONTINUED)

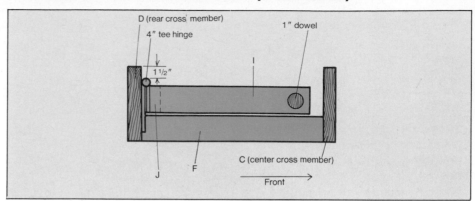

4. Flip the backrest forward to get it out of the way. Mount the second pair of hinges on the rear face of the prop cross member. Then position it so that you can locate the hinges on the inner face of the rear cross member. Install these second leaves.

ASSEMBLING THE BASE AND FRAME

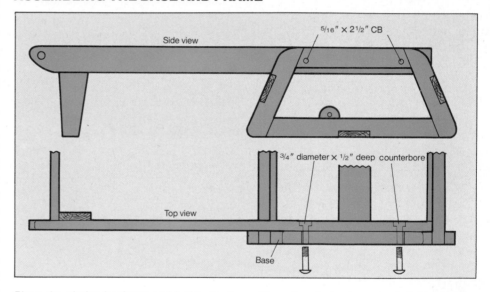

Place the chaise backrest end inside the base. Move the chaise to a comfortable position within the base, and clamp it. Drill two holes in each side through base and chaise. Bolt them together.

INSTALLING THE SLATS

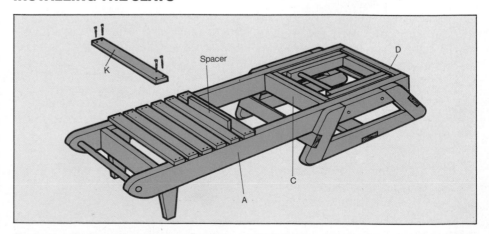

Start to install the slats. They should be fastened with two screws through pre-drilled holes in both sides of each slat. Use a spacer guide between each slat, and adjust them so that they're flush with the sides. Leave extra space at backrest-hinge joint.

NEST OF TABLES

If your backyard needs more tables to handle an occasional overflow crowd, or if a picnic in the park is the order of the day, small snack tables can guarantee comfortable dining.

The tables shown are attractive, lightweight, not easily affected by the weather, and easily carried around by hand or in the family car in a nest of three. In fact, altogether they fit into a space only 19½ inches square by 16 inches high.

Built to coffee-table height for maximum convenience, this project will put an end to having to juggle food and beverages. The tables are modest in cost and require a day's work at most.

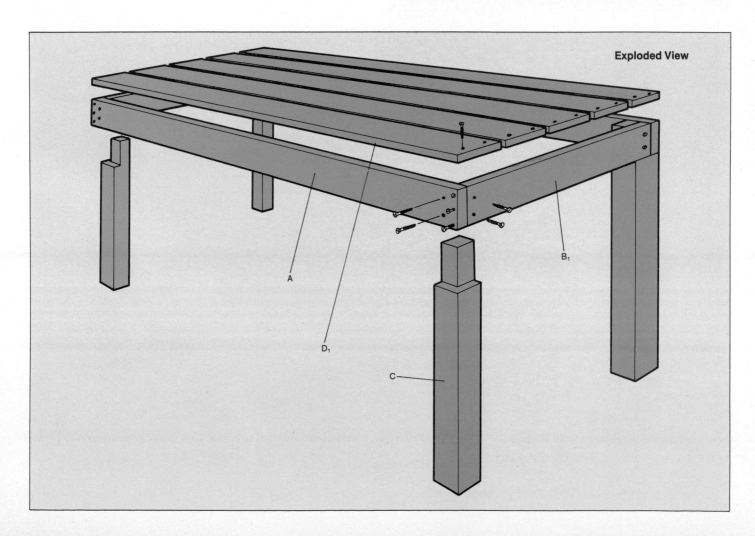

Exploded View

BILL OF MATERIALS

Qty	Size	Material
1	2×4×8'	Clear heart redwood
1	1×12×12'	Clear heart redwood
1	1×12×6'	Clear heart redwood
125	#8×1½"	Flat head, Phillips head, stainless steel wood screws

PARTS LIST

All parts clear heart redwood

Part	Name	Qty	Description
A	Side	6	³/₄" × 3¹/₂" × 19¹/₂"
B1	End	4	³/₄" × 3¹/₂" × 13"
B2	End	2	³/₄" × 3¹/₂" × 18"
C	Leg	12	1¹/₂" × 1¹/₂" × 16"
D1	Top board	10	³/₄" × 3" × 21"
D2	Top board	6	³/₄" × 3⁵/₁₆" × 21"

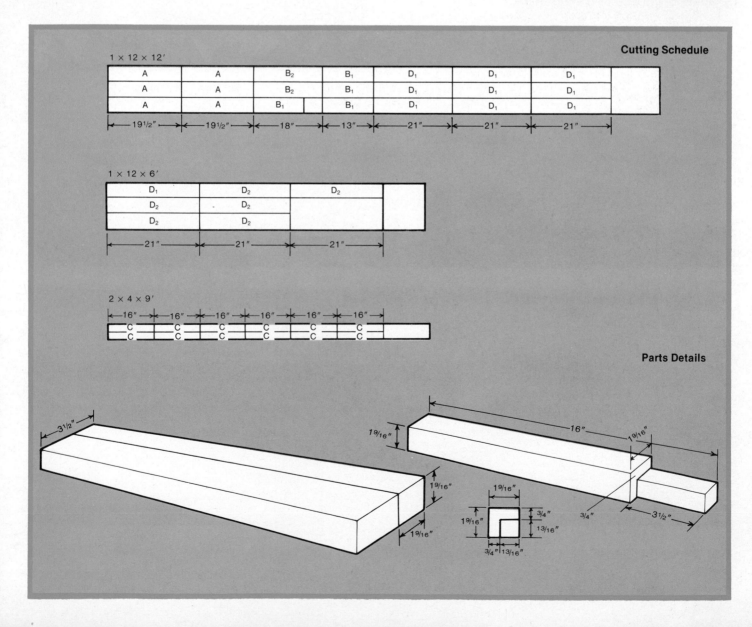

Cutting Schedule

1 × 12 × 12'

A	A	B₂	B₁	D₁	D₁	D₁	
A	A	B₂	B₁	D₁	D₁	D₁	
A	A	B₁		B₁	D₁	D₁	D₁	

19½" 19½" 18" 13" 21" 21" 21"

1 × 12 × 6'

D₁	D₂	D₂	
D₂	D₂		
D₂	D₂		

21" 21" 21"

2 × 4 × 9'

16" 16" 16" 16" 16" 16"

| C | C | C | C | C | C |
| C | C | C | C | C | C |

Parts Details

Purchase the redwood and the hardware according to the shopping list. Then, check out the cutting schedule and decide how you're going to handle it, based upon a personal choice of methods and the tools available to you.

STEP 1
CUTTING PROCEDURES

If you have a radial saw, use it to crosscut the two 1 × 22-inch boards and the one piece of 2 × 4-inch lumber. Otherwise, a portable saw, jigsaw, or handsaw will do the job. Next, make the rip cuts to get the pieces to the correct width, and trim the only B1 that comes along with two B2's to length.

Note that the upper section of all legs is rabbeted down to sit in the corners formed by the sides and ends, allowing the main part of the leg to be flush with the outer faces of these other parts when secured.

This rabbeting is done most easily by gang sawing—that is, clamping all the legs together in a group either on the radial or table saw.

Before cutting, check the exact thickness of your side and end pieces; this thickness is precisely the amount of wood that you should remove from the leg tops.

STEP 2
ASSEMBLING THE TABLES

Start the assembly of open box frames by marking in pencil the locations of the screw holes near the ends of the various sides. Then, with the side placed over the ends in exact position, drill the screw holes with a combination bit. Drive the screws.

Clamp the legs in place with the frame-held square. Drill a second set of holes on each side of the corner into the leg, and drive the screws home. Use the same marking, drill, and fastening methods for the top boards, but allow them to overhang the sides and ends by about 3/4 inch.

ASSEMBLING THE FRAMES AND LEGS

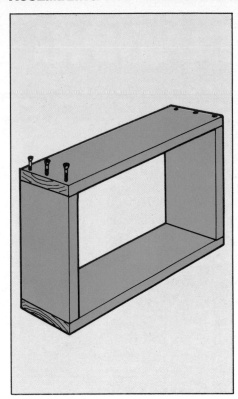

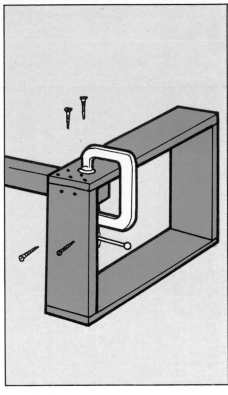

1. Overlap the ends with the sides. Drill three holes at each corner with a combination bit, and drive the screws home.

2. Clamp the rabbeted portion of a leg inside each box corner. Drill holes and drive screws into the leg from two sides.

FASTENING THE TOP BOARDS

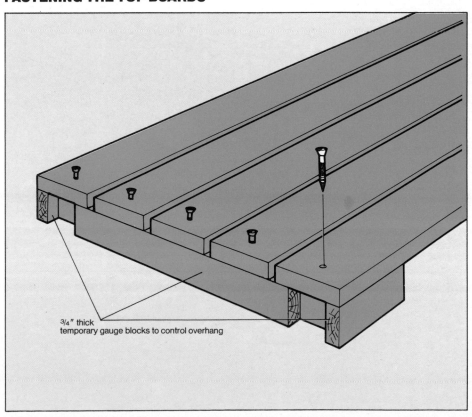

3/4" thick temporary gauge blocks to control overhang

Place the top boards on the frame, and control the overhang with gauge boards. Hold the frame square, drill holes, and drive screws.

LARGE STANDING PLANTER

Our large standing planter is basically a four-post rectangular tower, with four pairs of support arms at varying heights and directions.

This project displays the beauty of redwood in a contemporary design. It also accommodates a generous amount of flowers in a relatively small space because of its essentially vertical configuration. Another advantage of this planter is its versatility. For example, instead of building just four boxes, build eight. Then, a greater variety of flowers or small plants may be displayed, by alternating the boxes on a deck or on the ground with those on the tower's support arms.

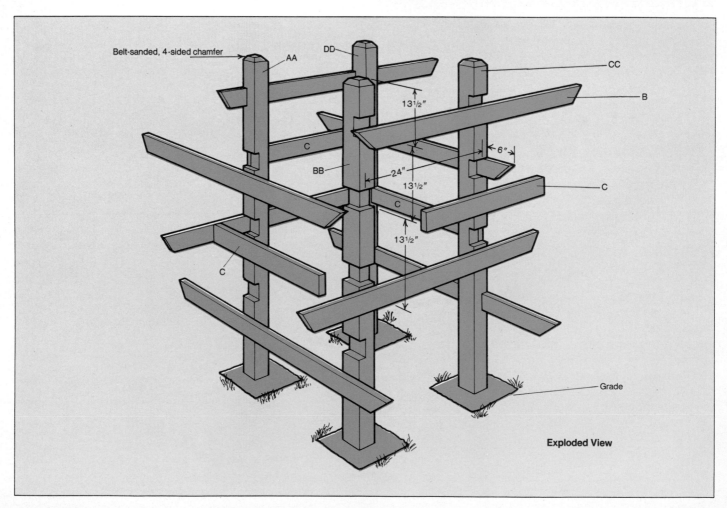

Belt-sanded, 4-sided chamfer · AA · DD · CC · B · C · BB · 6" · 24" · 13½" · 13½" · 13½" · C · C · C · Grade

Exploded View

BILL OF MATERIALS

Qty	Size	Material
2	4×4×12'	Construction heart redwood (ConHR)
5	2×4×8'	Clear heart redwood (ClrHR)
1	5/4×12×8'	Clear heart redwood
2	1×8×16'	Clear heart redwood
1	1/2×4×4'	CDX plywood
10d		Oval head galvanized nails
88	#8×11/2"	Flat head, Phillips head, stainless steel wood screws

PARTS LIST

Part	Name	Qty	Description
A	Post	4	31/2"×31/2"×72", ConHR
B	Arm	8	11/2"×31/2"×48", ClrHR
C	Stretcher	4	11/2"×31/2"×24", ClrHr
D	Box side	8	3/4"×71/4"×48", ClrHR
E	Box end	8	11/16"×8"×71/4", ClrHR
F	Box bottom	4	1/2"×8"×443/4", CDX ply
G	Cleat	8	11/16"×11/16"×24", ClrHR
H	Cap	8	11/16"×11/16"×91/2", ClrHR

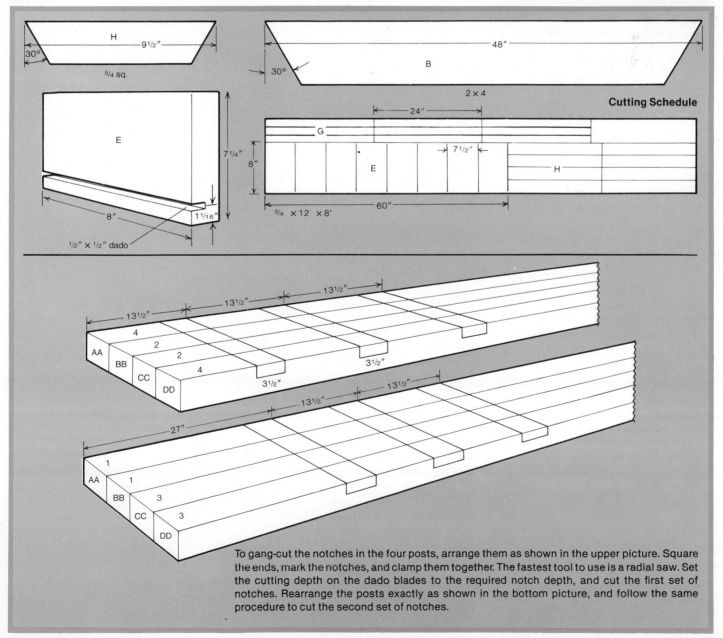

To gang-cut the notches in the four posts, arrange them as shown in the upper picture. Square the ends, mark the notches, and clamp them together. The fastest tool to use is a radial saw. Set the cutting depth on the dado blades to the required notch depth, and cut the first set of notches. Rearrange the posts exactly as shown in the bottom picture, and follow the same procedure to cut the second set of notches.

STEP 1
PREPARING THE POSTS, ARMS, AND STRETCHERS

The tower is constructed with 4 × 4 posts, and 2 × 4 stretchers and arms. The major effort required is the precision gang-notching of the posts. This work may be done with a portable saw for the crosscuts and a chisel for removing the waste, but it's far more efficient to use a dado setup on a radial saw.

In either case, note that the 4 × 4s are arranged in only two ways, so mark the notches with the posts clamped together in gangs. Some of your 4 × 4s may require trimming so that the butt ends are squarely aligned and the gang is flush against the fence. Also, be sure that the dado blade's path matches one end line of the first set of notches and that the radial saw post is adjusted for the correct depth of cut, nominally 1½ inches.

Pull the saw through the first cut, move the ganged posts laterally for the next cut, and pull the saw through it. Finish up the first set of notches in this manner, and then cut the remaining two sets of the first gang arrangement: 4–2–2–4 faces up, in that order.

Now, set up for the second set of notches: 1–1–3–3 faces up, in that order, and make the cuts using the same technique. Complete the posts by belt-sanding a four-sided 45° chamfer on the top of each post.

Switch your radial saw over to a single blade, and trim to length all the stretchers. Then miter both ends of all the arms.

STEP 2
ASSEMBLING THE TOWER PARTS

Lay out the posts in pairs on a work surface, with the common notches facing up. Note that the points on the posts that will receive arms alone are notched on one face only. The points at which both an arm and a stretcher will be attached will be notched on two adjacent faces.

Note also that when working with a pair of posts (for example, posts BB and CC, faces 2), the topmost and

ASSEMBLING THE TOWER

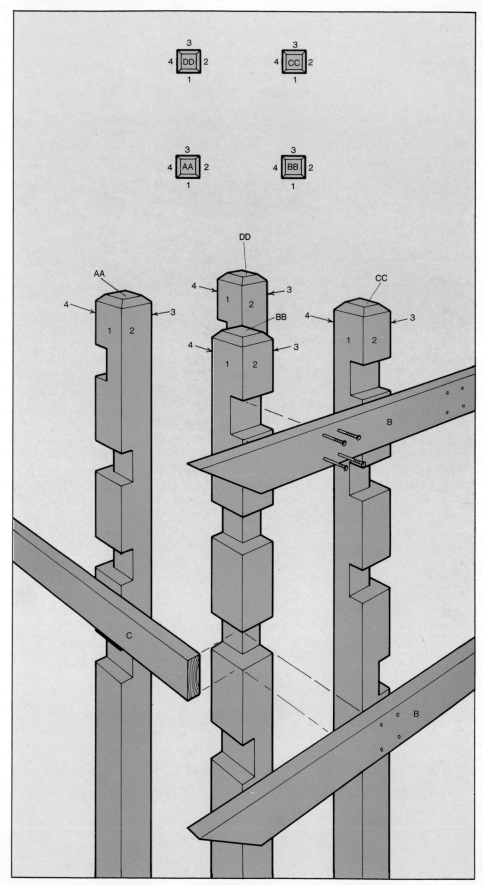

Keep the posts, which have already been gang-notched and chamfered at the top, in sequence and proper orientation so that the arms and stretchers will fall in their proper place.

EXPLODED VIEW OF BOX

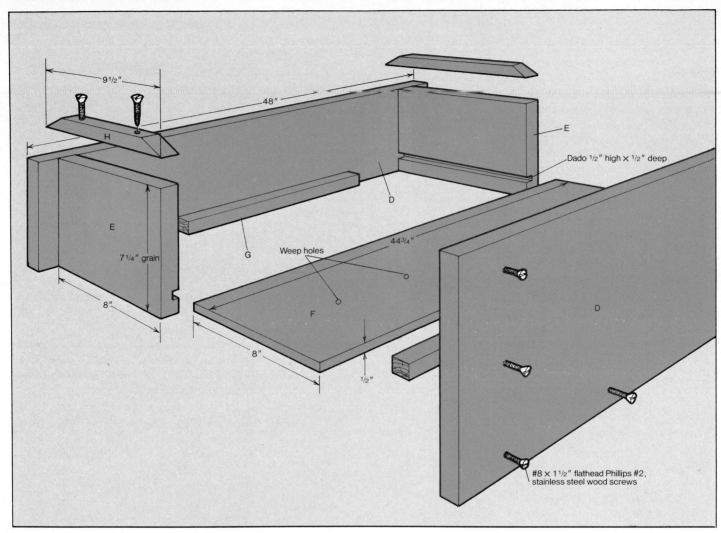

9½″

48″

H

E

Dado ½″ high × ½″ deep

E

7¼″ grain

D

8″

G

Weep holes

44¾″

F

8″

½″

D

#8 × 1½″ flathead Phillips #2,
stainless steel wood screws

Isometric drawing of flower box shows that shelf is supported on its ends by dadoes, and along its sides by cleats. Note cap strip attached to top of ends, covering grain.

bottommost notches receive arms, while the mid-height notches receive a stretcher. Also, the uppermost arm overhangs mainly to the right, while the lowermost arm overhangs mainly to the left. The uppermost arm will become the top level and the lowermost arm the third level; the stretcher is on the second higher level and is at right angles to the first and third level arms.

Assemble the arms to the posts with oval head, galvanized nails. Do the same with posts AA and DD faces 4. Pay careful attention to the orientation of the arms.

Then, with the two sub-assemblies propped up on edge, add the stretchers and arms joining them together—that is, AA–DD to BB–CC.

STEP 3
SETTING THE TOWER

Decide how deep the post will go into the ground, and paint the below-grade portion with Cuprinol #10. Dig the post holes, and drop some 5/8–3/4-inch stone into them. Set the tower in place, adjust the height with stone, and check that adjacent post faces are plumb with a level. Backfill the post holes, and tamp down the dirt.

An alternate method is to mix up two 80-pound bags of dry-mix concrete (each bag has enough cement, sand, and aggregate to make .6 cubic foot of concrete when combined with water). Then backfill the post holes with the concrete, forming collars that taper up at grade level to shed water. Allow at least 24 hours for the concrete to set.

STEP 4
BUILDING THE BOXES

Cut out all box parts according to the Materials and Parts Lists. Machine the dadoes in the box ends, and check the fit with the box bottoms. Cut out the cleats and caps, and then bevel the cap ends.

Use stainless steel screws to assemble the boxes. Since they are flat head screws, pre-drill all screw holes with a combination bit that makes the pilot hole, clearance hole, and countersink in one pass.

Fasten one side to both ends. Then, slide the bottom into the dadoes until it's flush with the first side, and install the second side. Center the cleats between the ends, at the bottom-side intersection, and clamp them. Screw in the cleats. Add the caps and drill weep holes in bottom.

ASSEMBLING A BOX

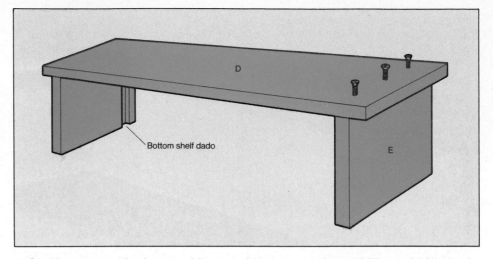

1. Start box construction by assembling one side to two ends by pre-drilling and driving stainless steel screws. Allow overhang at both ends.

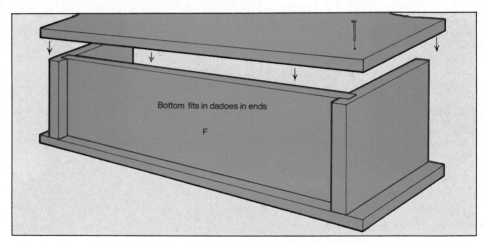

2. Before the second side is attached, slide the bottom in place. After assembly, all planter bottoms should have weep holes drilled in them to drain excess water.

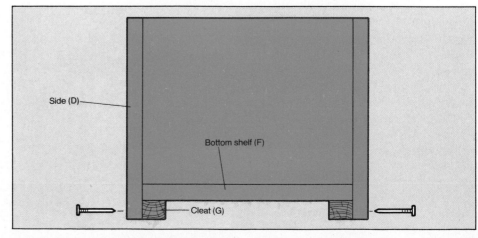

3. Drive screws through the side pieces into the cleats to support the long dimension from end to end. It's not necessary to screw the bottom to the cleats.

JUNGLE GYM

The little folks around your house will get a lot of enjoyment out of this backyard playground combination. The possibilities are endless, with two slides, one cleated ramp, one seesaw, four ladders, two platforms, and an overhead trussed walkway. You can install climbing ropes or nets, rings or swings beneath the walkway.

The structure is built with standard, readily available lumberyard wood products and hardware. It's basically two towers, constructed of 4 × 4s and 2 × 4s, connected by the trussed walkway. The entire structure rests on concrete footings and is stabilized by the slides, which are bolted to it at one end; the slide feet also rest on concrete footings.

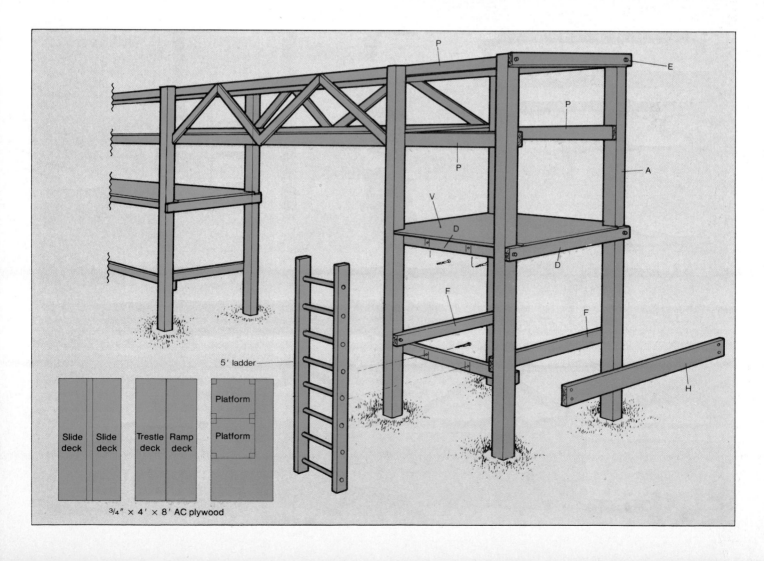

5' ladder

Slide deck | Slide deck

Trestle deck | Ramp deck

Platform

Platform

³/₄" × 4' × 8' AC plywood

BILL OF MATERIALS

Qty	Size	Material	Qty	Size	Material	Qty	Size	Material
8	4×4×12'	Pressure-treated lumber (P/T)	1	3/4×8'	Pine 1/2 round molding	56	3/8×5"	Carriage bolts, washers, nuts
11	4×4×6'	Pressure-treated lumber (P/T)	7	1×36"	Maple dowel	4	3/8×6 1/2	Carriage bolts, washers, nuts
1	2×8×12'	Douglas fir	2	#4	Stanley door pulls	120	#8×2"	Flat head, Phillips head, hardened assembly screws
7	2×4×14'	Douglas fir	1	1/2×16"	Galvanized pipe (n.p.t.)	—	10d	Oval head, galvanized nails
2	2×4×12'	Douglas fir	2	1/2"	Floor flanges (n.p.t.)	—	8d	Oval head, galvanized nails
6	2×4×10'	Douglas fir	1	18' length	24-inch wide aluminum flashing	4	#12×1"	Flat head screws
9	2×4×8'	Douglas fir				4	1/4×2"	Flat head bolts, washers, nuts
1	5/4×4×9'	Oak	22	3/8×3 1/2"	Carriage bolts, washers, nuts			

PARTS LIST

Part	Name	Qty	Description	Part	Name	Qty	Description	Part	Name	Qty	Description
A	Tower post	4	3 1/2"×3 1/2"×12', P/T	I	Ramp rail	2	1 1/2"×3 1/2"×8', fir	R	Trestle deck	1	3/4"×24"×8', A-C plywood
B	Seesaw post	1	3 1/2"×3 1/2"×6', P/T	J	Ramp deck	1	3/4"×23"×8', A-C plywood	S	5' ladder side	4	1 1/2"×3 1/2"×5', fir
C	Temporary cross-member	8	1 1/2"×3 1/2"×31", fir	K	Ramp cleat	9	1 1/16"×1 1/16"×23", oak	T	Rung	20	1" diameter × 11 7/8", maple dowel
D	Platform supports	8	1 1/2"×1 1/2"×31", fir	L	Slide rail	4	1 1/2"×3 1/2"×10', fir	U	3' ladder side	4	1 1/2"×3 1/2"×3', fir
E	Upper cross-member	2	1 1/2"×3 1/2"×31", fir	M	Slide deck	2	3/4"×22 1/2"×8', A-C plywood	V	Platform	2	3/4"×31"×34", A-C plywood
F	Lower cross-member	4	1 1/2"×3 1/2"×31", fir	N	Slide deck nosing	4	3/4"1/2 round molding, pine	W	Seesaw	1	1 1/2"×3 1/2"×9', fir
G	Lower 5' ladder support	2	1 1/2"×3 1/2"×31", fir*	O	Slide surface	2	22 1/2"×108", aluminum flashing	X	Seesaw adjustment cleats	6	1 1/16"×1 1/16"×7 1/2", oak
H	Inner seesaw trunnion support	1	1 1/2"×5 1/2"×31", fir	P	Trestle beam	4	1 1/2"×3 1/2"×158", fir				
				Q	Trestle bracing	8	1 1/2"×2 3/4"×36 3/8", fir**				

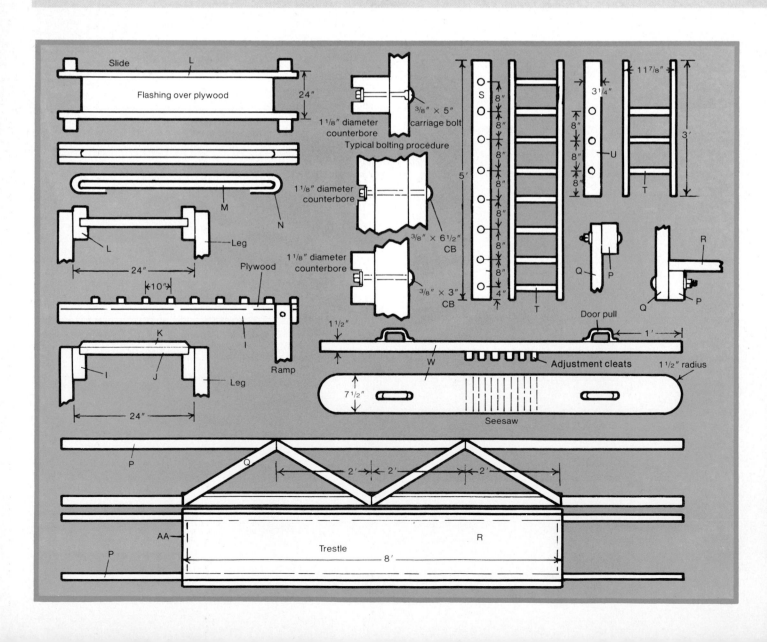

Qty	Size	Material
14	5/16 × 3″	Lag bolts, washers
1	bundle	1 × 2 furring (eight 8′ pieces)
15	80-lb. bags	Dry concrete mix
5	5-gal. buckets	5/8–3/4″ stone
2	gallons	Stain

Part Name		Qty	Description
Y	Feet, slide, and ramp	6	1½″ × 3½″ × 4′, P/T
Z	Seesaw trunnion	1	18″ wide overall, Galvanized iron
AA	3′ ladder top support	2	1½″ × 3½″ × 21″, fir*
BB	3′ ladder spacers	2	1½″ × 3½″ × 8″, fir*

*Make from temporary supports after towers are installed.
**Rip 2¾″ wide pieces from 2 × 4 dimensional lumber. Fit exact-length and miter angle to P pieces, with Ps laid out parallel at exact spacing.

STEP 1
BUILDING THE TOWERS

Build up each tower on saw horses, one side at a time, to limit the amount of heavy lifting you have to do. To begin this assembly, position the two 12-foot-long posts on the horses, parallel to each other, and 24 inches apart from inside face to inside face. In this position, the post faces that are up will be the inside faces when the assembly is complete.

There are three 31-inch-long 2 × 4s needed for each pair of posts: (1) one temporary cross-member (C) flush with the top; (2) one temporary cross-member (C) whose bottom edge is 24 inches down from the top; and (3) one platform support (D) whose top edge is 48¾″ down from the top.

Mark the locations for these pieces on the posts. Then clamp or tack-nail them in place, while checking that the assembly is square. Next, drill ³/₈-inch-diameter bolt holes with the aid of a drill guide. Turn the assembly over, and counterbore the holes in the 4 × 4s ¾ inch deep, using a 1⅛-inch spade bit. Doing this will keep the hardware out of the kids' way. Then install the bolts. Nail scrap cross-bracing between the posts on the unoccupied ends.

Repeat the entire procedure described above, making three more

BUILDING THE TOWERS

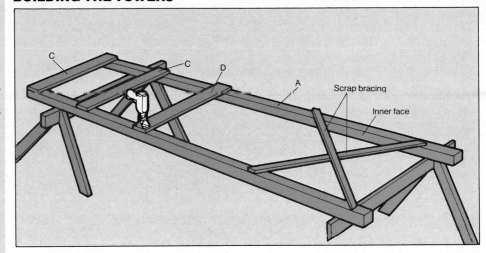

1. Build the towers half at a time. Place a pair of posts on saw horses, parallel to each other, with the ends squared up. Then mark, position, clamp, drill, and bolt the cross members and supports in place. Add the × bracing.

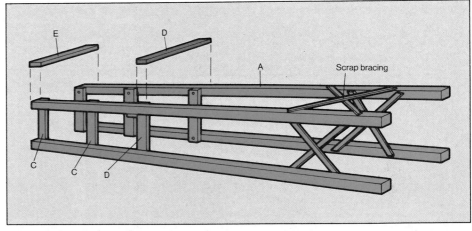

2. Place these halves on edge on the horses, two at a time, parallel to each other, and with the ends squared up and the insides facing each other. Mark, clamp, drill, and bolt the joining members in place. Stabilize the assembly with × bracing.

ASSEMBLING THE TRESTLE

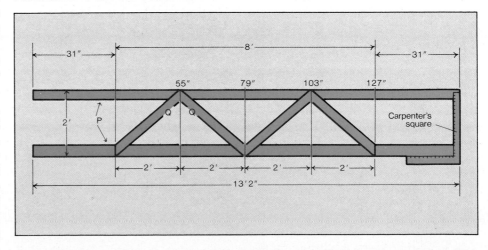

1. Place two beams on the horses, parallel to each other and with their ends squared up. Mark off the positions of the triangular bracing on both beams. Then fit, clamp, drill, and bolt the bracing to the beams.

subassemblies. Then set two of these subassemblies on edge on the horses, with the insides facing each other.

Join the two subassemblies by adding, in the same manner as before, the upper cross-member (E) at the top and the third platform support (D) and the lower cross-member (F) to the inner post faces, with the cross member's top edge 82 inches from the top. Then rotate the complete assembly, and add the last (D) and the last (F), also on the inner post faces. There is no second (E).

Add scrap cross-bracing to the remaining two planes not yet braced, and nail the platform to its supports (D) to stabilize the assembly. Now, install the lower 5′ ladder support (G), with its top edge flush with the bottom edges of the lower cross-members (F).

Repeat the entire operation to build the second tower. Note that the towers will eventually face each other, so install both ladder supports (G) at the rear, opposite the slides.

STEP 2
BUILDING THE TRESTLE

Position a pair of trestle beams (P) on the horses, parallel to each other and 24 inches apart from outer edge to outer edge. Square up the ends, and mark off the 2-foot increments on the beam faces, starting 31 inches in from either end. When completed, the 31-inch sections of the beams will fit between the tower posts and will be bolted to them.

Rip 12 feet of 2 × 4 to a width of 2¾ inches. Then cut this into four lengths approximately 36 inches each. Set the miter gauge on the table saw at 40½°, and trim both ends of each piece so that the miters are parallel. Then fit each piece in the triangular truss pattern by trimming it back with the miter gauge at the same setting. This should occur at about 33⅞ inches overall length. When the fitting's done, clamp, drill, and assemble the trestle side with ⅜ × 3½-inch carriage bolts, nuts and washers. Make another trestle side in the same way. Then nail the trestle deck to the upper edges of the

ASSEMBLING THE TRESTLE (CONTINUED)

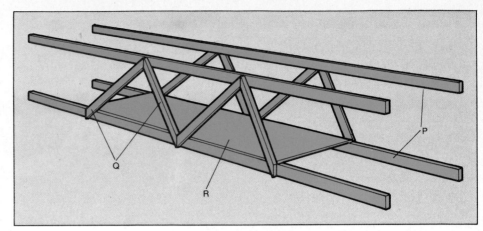

2. Stand a pair of trestle sides on edge on the horses with the insides facing each other and the ends squared up. Place the trestle deck between them and on top of the lower beams. Nail the deck to these beams.

MAKING THE RAMP

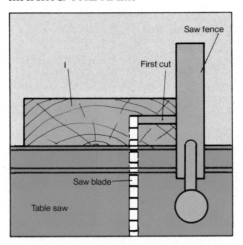 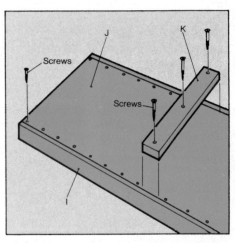

1. The ramp deck sits in rabbets machined in the rails. Cut these rabbets in two passes for each rail on the saw.

2. Place the deck in the rabbets, and center it. Assemble with screws. Position the cleats on the deck, and screw them in.

MAKING THE SLIDES

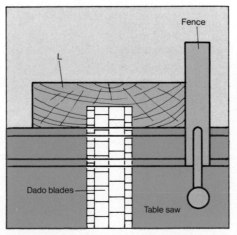 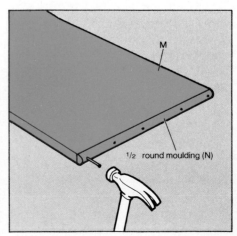

1. Machine the grooves in the slide rails using a dado blade or wobble dado. Keep the depth very accurate.

2. Nail pieces of ¾-inch half round molding to the ends of the slide deck. Trim these nosing ends flush.

lower trestle beams, lining up the deck ends with the 31-inch marks.

STEP 3
MAKING THE RAMP

Machine 1-inch-wide by ⁷/₈-inch-deep rabbets in the 2 × 4 rails. Screw the deck to the rails. Now, saw out the oak cleats, and bevel their ends. Mark the cleat locations on the ramp deck, and position them. Finally, drill through them into the deck with a combination bit, and screw the cleats in place.

Cut a pair of feet to length from pressure-treated wood, and clamp them to the lower ends of the rails. Drill holes and install the feet using ³/₈ × 3¹/₂-inch carriage bolts, nuts, and washers. Note that the overall width of the ramp from outer rail face to outer rail face must be 24 inches so that it will fit exactly between the posts of the tower.

STEP 4
MAKING THE SLIDES

The total width of the slides from outer rail face to outer rail face must be 24 inches to fit between the posts of the towers; the slide deck itself is 22¹/₂ inches wide. Therefore, machine dadoes in the 2 × 4 slide rails that are ³/₄ inch deep and ¹³/₁₆ inch wide.

Next, nail pieces of ³/₄-inch half round molding to the top and bottom edges of the ³/₄ plywood slide decks. Since the slide decks are to be surfaced with 23¹/₂-inch-wide aluminum flashing, order it 24 inches wide, and cut ¹/₂ inch off one edge with a utility knife, guided by a straight edge.

Align the flashing with the slide deck, and roll 5 to 6 inches of it around one end on to the back side; then staple or tack it in place. Stretch it out, roll it around the other end, and staple it.

Now, with one end of the rails lying flat on a work surface and the dado facing up, start the slide deck into the dado, and advance it until it's centered on the rail. Do the same with the second rail, and compress the rails in place with bar or pipe clamps.

Next, drive galvanized, oval head

MAKING THE SLIDES (CONTINUED)

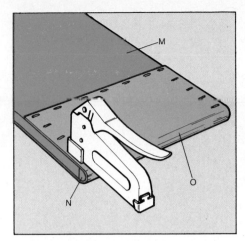

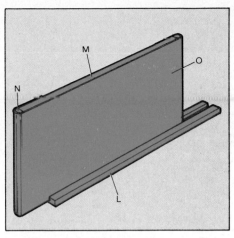

3. Place the pre-cut flashing on the deck, and roll it around the ends. Nail or staple it in place on the underside.

4. Slide the combined deck and its aluminum surface into the machined grooves in the slide sides.

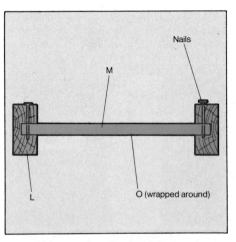

5. Cross-section view shows how nails driven through rail edge and deck lock these parts together in an assembly.

BUILDING THE LADDERS

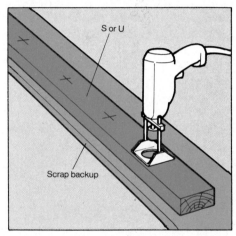

1. Mark the rung positions on the ladder sides. Mount a drill in a guide and, against scrap backup, drill the holes.

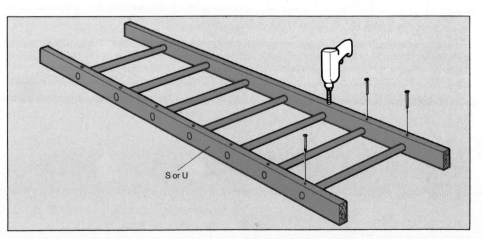

2. Insert the rungs flush with the outer faces of the sides. Cross drill and drive nails to lock rungs in place.

nails into the rail edge, through the slide deck, and into the rail on the other side of the dado, locking the assembly together. Add the legs as you did before for the ramp. Repeat this entire procedure to build the second slide.

STEP 5
MAKING THE LADDERS

There are two 5-foot ladders and two 3-foot ladders; both sizes are constructed in exactly the same way. Lay out the hole centers for the rungs on all 2 × 4 ladder sides as follows: (1) on the 5-foot ladder, make the first hole center 4 inches from the end and the other hole centers every 8 inches; (2) on the 3-foot ladder, make the hole centers every 8 inches.

Drill these holes using a 1-inch-diameter bit, assisted by a drill guide to keep the holes perpendicular to the surface. Saw the rungs from dowel, and assemble the ladders. The 11^7/$_8$-inch rung length allows three rungs to be obtained from each 3-foot dowel.

Then drill ^{1}/$_8$-inch-diameter pilot holes through the sides at each rung, and drive in galvanized, oval head nails to lock the rungs in place.

STEP 6
BUILDING THE SEESAW

The seesaw can be made of Douglas fir or ^{6}/$_4$ or ^{8}/$_4$ oak, depending on the size of the people who will be using it. For large kids or adults, use the oak and switch to ^{3}/$_4$-inch n.p.t. (normal pressure and temperature) pipe and flanges. But for small kids, those weighing about 60 pounds, the fir and ^{1}/$_2$-inch n.p.t. pipe and flanges should be fine.

Round off the seesaw ends, and, if you wish, customize the shape by slightly necking down the area where a small child will sit. Be sure to break all corners (sand and/or plane the edges smooth for handling), and sand the surface smooth to remove splinters.

Saw out the adjustment cleats from ^{5}/$_4$ oak. Then, lay the seesaw on a work surface, face up, and mark the

LAYING OUT THE GROUND PLAN

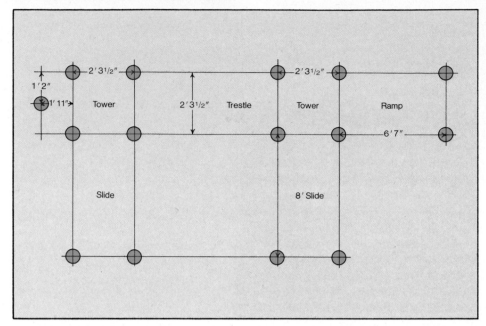

Use stakes and mason's cord to lay out the locations of the post holes. Drive a stake in the ground at each intersection, marking the hole centers. Dig the holes down to the frost line.

SETTING THE POSTS

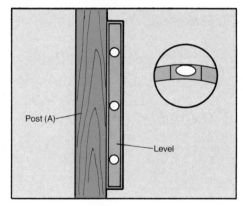

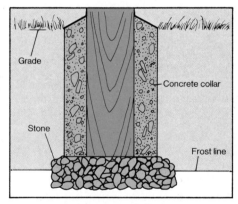

1. Place posts in the holes on top of 4 to 6 inches of stone. Check for plumb on adjacent faces with level, and brace the posts in place.

2. Backfill the plumbed and braced posts with concrete. The collars should taper at the top to shed water.

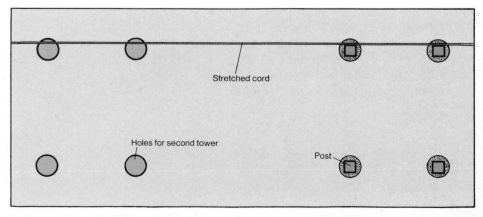

3. To align the tower posts, stretch a cord from the farthest tower post, past and just touching second post, and on past the other tower locations. This will let the trestle fit between the towers without bending the beams.

locations for these cleats. The centerline is blank, and three cleats are attached to the seesaw on either side, separated by a 7/8-inch gap (larger for 3/4-inch pipe).

Clamp the cleats in position, drill holes with a combination bit, and drive the screws home. Finish up by installing door pulls for handholds.

Note that both the pipe and its flanges are supported by a separate 4 × 4 post on the outboard side and a 2 × 6 trunnion support on the inboard side. Fitting these parts is best done after the towers, trestle, ramp, and slides have been installed.

STEP 7
STARTING THE INSTALLATION

Drive in stakes, and stretch mason's cord between them so that the intersections of the cords are over the post hole centers. Then drive a stake into each of these centers and remove the cords.

Use a rented post-hole digger to excavate each of the fifteen holes down to the frost line in your area. (If you return the rental tool promptly, you may be able to take advantage of a half-day rate.) Drop about 6 inches of 5/8-inch stone into each hole, and keep a bucket of stone handy in case you need to adjust the post height.

Now, remove the scrap bracing from one of the towers, and, with some help, place the bottoms of the posts into the first four-hole group. Check the posts for plumb by placing a level in the vertical position against adjacent faces on the posts, while your helpers add or remove stone to accommodate the adjustment.

The top ends of the slide and ramp rails may need minor changes in length or miter trimming in order to fit neatly between the posts before bolting. The feet may also require some trimming to adjust the heights of the slide or ramp over them.

When the tower is plumbed and all slide and ramp adjustments have been made, backfill the appropriate holes with concrete, forming collars. These collars should taper up at grade to shed water. Allow all concrete to cure for 2 to 3 days.

ERECTING THE TOWERS AND SLIDES

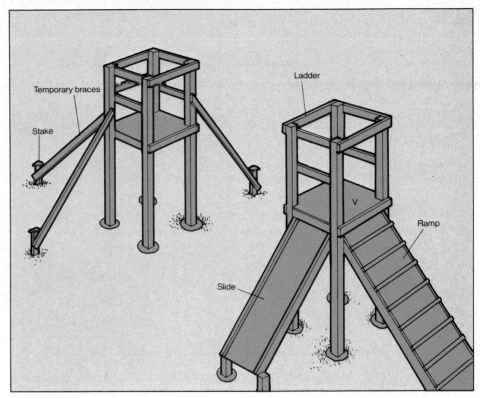

1. Stabilize the first tower with the ramp and the slide assemblies. Then adjust the second tower for alignment, height, plumb, and distance from the first tower. Brace it in position, recheck it, and backfill the holes.

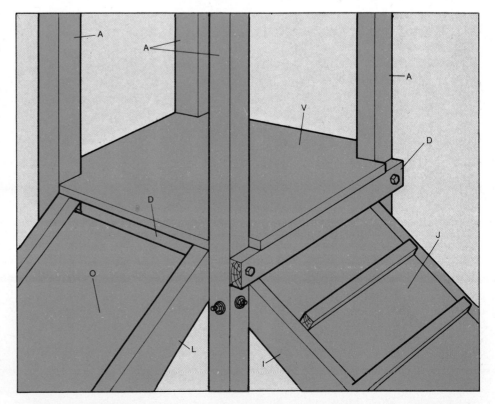

2. This close-up shows how the slide and ramp are joined to the first tower just underneath the platform. After fitting these parts and bolting them to the posts, trim back the ends of the rails that protrude past the posts.

STEP 8
INSTALLING THE SECOND TOWER

Erecting the second tower is a bit more difficult because it must conform to the position, height, and orientation of the first. So, with your helpers, set the second tower in place and check its alignment relative to the first tower with the cord as shown in the drawing. Check and correct the stone level to accommodate the plumb attitude of the tower posts. Hang a line level on the cord between the towers to check that they are at the same height. Finally, make sure that there are exactly 8 feet between the towers at the 7- and 9-foot levels for fitting the trestle. Do this critical work slowly. Then lock the tower in place with stakes and braces, and backfill the holes with concrete. Allow the concrete to cure.

STEP 9
INSTALLING THE TRESTLE, SECOND SLIDE, SEESAW, AND LADDERS

Install the second slide, making trim and height adjustments as before. Bolt on the inner seesaw trunnion support, and install the seesaw post, pipe, and floor-flange assembly. Backfill this post and the second slide's feet with concrete. Allow curing time.

Before lifting the trestle up to the towers, remove the temporary crossmembers (C) from the tower tops. Then trim two of these crossmembers to 21-inch lengths. These are the upper ladder supports. Screw them (AA) in place under both trestle deck ends, between the beams.

You'll need some help to raise the trestle into position; once it's in place, clamp the beams to the posts in exactly the same position the Cs occupied. Drill through the beams from the existing holes in the posts, and bolt the beams to the posts.

Lag-bolt the 5-foot ladders to the lower ladder supports at the bottom and to the platform supports at the top. Set the 3-foot ladder side ends on the platform, and sandwich the ladder spacer (BB) between the post

ADDING THE TRESTLE

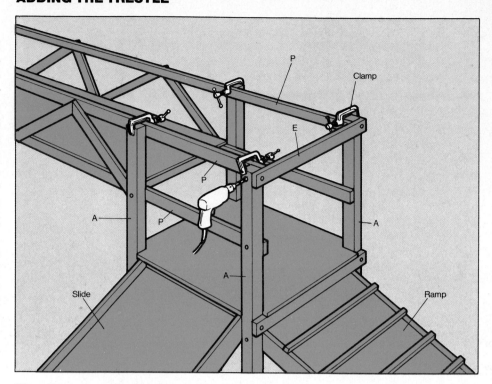

When the concrete footings have set, remove the temporary cross members from the tower tops. With a helper, lift the trestle assembly, and clamp it where the temporary cross members were. Drill and bolt the beams to the posts.

INSTALLING LADDERS

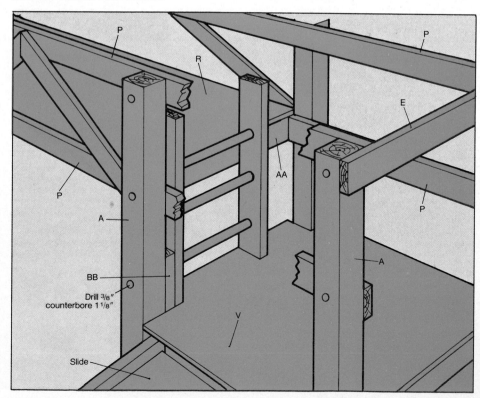

Install the upper ladder support at the end of the trestle deck. Then install the 3-foot ladder and its spacer. Lag-bolt both the ladder support and the platform to the ladder. Carriage-bolt the ladder side and its spacer to the post.

and the ladder side. Drill and bolt them together. Then, lag-bolt the upper parts of the 3-foot ladders to the supports (AA), and run a lag bolt up through the platform into the end of the other ladder side.

If you have larger kids, add a pair of vertical posts for extra-firm support under the trestle center; set the posts in concrete and bolt them to the trestle at the top. Paint or opaque-stain the entire structure for appearance. When the kids try out the slides for the first time, have them sit on a foot-square piece of waxed paper; this will make the slide a bit slicker.

Rings, knotted ropes, landing nets, and swings are available in the larger toy-store chains. Attach this additional equipment to the trestle according to the instructions provided; they usually call for eyebolts or screweyes.

INSTALLING LADDERS AND SEESAW

1/2″ NPT pipe and two flanges, 18″ wide overall

B

18″

H

The 5-foot ladder is lag-bolted to the lower ladder support near the bottom and to the platform support at the top. The seesaw pipe and flange assembly is attached to the outboard post and to the trunnion support on the tower.

GLOSSARY

Abrasive Material used for smoothing, polishing, lapping, etc., as sandpaper.

Air-dried Lumber that has been dried by exposure to air, usually in the open, without artificial heat.

Along the grain In the same direction as the grain; in plywood, the same direction as the grain of the face ply, usually the long dimension. Plywood is stronger and stiffer along the grain than it is across the grain.

Back The side of a plywood panel having the lower-grade veneer.

Band saw Saw consisting of an endless toothed steel band passing over two wheels.

Bevel To cut edges or ends at an angle to make smooth mating joints between pieces.

Bit Removable drill or boring tool for use in a brace or drill press.

Bleeding The seeping of resin or gum from lumber.

Board A term generally applied to lumber 1 inch thick and 2 or more inches wide.

Board foot Unit of lumber measurement: 1 foot × 1 foot × 1 inch.

Bond To glue together, as veneers are "bonded" to form plywood. Pressure can be applied during the process to keep mating parts in proper alignment.

Bow The distortion in a board that deviates from flatness lengthwise but not across its faces.

Brace Piece of lumber or metal used to support or position another piece or portion of a framework.

Breaking corners In woodworking, planing or sanding a tiny radius on edges that are sharp or inconvenient to handle.

Butt joint A joint formed by abutting the squared ends or ends and faces of two pieces. Because of the inadequacy and variability in strength of butt joints when glued, they are not generally glued.

Caulking Material filled into seams, joints, or crevices to make a watertight seal.

Chalk line Also called **snap line**. A chalked string used to make a straight line on a surface by holding the string taut against the surface and snapping it to transfer the chalk.

Chamfer The flat surface created by slicing off the square edge or corner of a piece of wood or plywood.

Clear lumber A term including the higher grades of lumber. It is sound and relatively free of blemishes.

Cleat Wedge-shaped block fastened to a surface to serve as a check or support.

Combination square Adjustable device for testing squareness of carpentry work, consisting of a pair of straightedges fixed at right angles to one another.

Commons A term describing the ordinary grades of knotty lumber.

Countersinking To position the head of a screw or bolt so as to be flush with or below the surface.

Cove Concave surface or molding.

Crook A distortion of a board in which there is a deviation edgewise from a straight line from end to end of the board.

Crossband (cores) In plywood, the layers of veneer whose grain direction is at right angles to that of the face plies; they minimize shrinking and swelling.

Cross lamination In plywood manufacture, the placing of consecutive layers at right angles to one another to minimize shrinkage and increase strength.

Cup A curve in a board across the grain or width of a piece.

Dado A joint formed by the intersection of two boards; one is notched with a rectangular groove to receive the other.

Dimension lumber A term generally applied to lumber 2 to 4 inches thick and 2 or more inches wide.

Dovetail Tenon broader at its end than at its base; a joint formed of one or more such tenons, fitting tightly within corresponding mortises.

Dowel Also **dowel pin**. A pin, usually round, fitted into holes in adjacent pieces of wood to align them or prevent slippage.

Dressed lumber Lumber after shrinking from the green dimension and being surfaced with a planing machine, usually 3/8 or 1/2 inch smaller than the nominal (rough) size; for example, a 2 × 4 stud actually measures 1 1/2 × 3 1/2 inches.

Drill press Drilling machine having a single vertical spindle.

Eased edges A term used to describe slight rounding of edge surfaces of a piece of lumber or plywood to remove sharp corners.

Epoxy A synthetic resin used in some paints and adhesives because of its toughness, adhesion, and resistance to solvents.

Eyebolt Bolt or screw having an eye or opening at one end.

Face The wide surface of a piece of lumber; the side showing the better quality or appearance on which a piece is graded.

Finish A term including the higher grades of sound, relatively unblemished lumber. Also, a material applied to protect and enhance the appearance of wood.

Finished size The net dimensions after surfacing.

Gable The triangular part of a wall under the inverted V of the roof line.

Gang saw Saw having several parallel blades for making simultaneous cuts.

Good-one-side Plywood that has a

higher-grade veneer on the face than on the back; used where only one side will be visible. In identifying these panels, the face grade is given first.

Grade The designation of the quality of lumber or plywood.

Grain The direction, size, arrangement, appearance, or quality of the fibers in wood.

Grout Thin, coarse mortar used in masonry joints and narrow cavities to form adjoining objects into a solid mass.

Gusset Plate or wedge used to join structural members.

Hacksaw Saw for cutting metal, consisting of a narrow, fine-toothed blade fixed in a frame.

Hardwoods The botanical group of broad-leaved trees such as oak or maple.

Jig saw Narrow saw, mounted vertically in a frame for cutting curves and other complicated lines.

Joint The junction of two pieces of wood or veneer.

Kerf A slot made by a saw; the width of the saw cut.

Kiln-dried Wood that has been dried in ovens by controlled heat and humidity to specified limits of moisture content.

Knot The portion of a branch or limb that has been surrounded by subsequent growth of the wood of the tree trunk.

Lap To position two pieces so that the surface of one extends over that of the other.

Loose knot A knot that is not held firmly in place by growth or position and cannot be relied upon to remain in place.

Loosened or raised grain A small section of the wood that has been loosened or raised, but not displaced.

Lumber The product of the saw and planing mill not further manufactured than by sawing, resawing, passing lengthwise through a standard planing machine, crosscutting to length, and matching.

Lumber-core Plywood construction in which the core is composed of lumber strips and outer plies are veneer.

Miter joint A joint formed by fitting together two pieces of lumber or plywood that have been cut off on an angle.

Moisture content The amount of water contained in wood, usually expressed as a percentage of the weight of oven-dried wood.

Mortise Notch, groove, or slot made in a piece of wood to receive a tenon of the same dimensions.

Oven-dried wood Wood that has been dried so completely that it is without any moisture content.

Panel faces Outer veneers of a plywood panel.

Pawl Pivoted bar adapted to engage with teeth of a ratch wheel to prevent movement or impart motion.

Ply A single veneer in a glued plywood panel.

Plywood A panel made of three or more layers of veneer joined with glue and usually laid with the grain of adjoining plies at right angles. To secure balanced construction, an odd number of plies is almost always used.

Preservative Any substance that, for a reasonable length of time, will prevent the action of wood-destroying fungi and borers, and other destructive insets when the wood has been properly coated or impregnated with it.

Rabbet A joint formed by cutting a groove in the surface along the edge of a board, plank, or panel to receive another piece.

Radial saw Cantilevered circular saw adjustable at various angles to the length of the work and to the perpendicular.

Resaw To reduce the thickness or width of boards, planks, or other material by cutting into two or more thinner pieces on a resaw.

Saw kerf Grooves or notches made when cutting with a saw. Also, the piece of wood removed by the saw in parting the material into two pieces.

Seasoning Removing the moisture from green wood in order to improve its serviceability.

Select lumber The higher grades of sound, relatively unblemished lumber.

Softness The property of wood that is indicated by a relative lack of resistance to cutting, denting, pressure, or wear.

Softwoods The botanical group of trees that have needle or scalelike leaves. Except for cypress, larch, and tamarack, softwoods are evergreen. The term has no reference to the actual hardness of the wood.

Solid-core Plywood composed of veneers over a lumber core.

Spiked knot A knot cut approximately parallel to its long axis so that the exposed section is definitely elongated.

Split A lengthwise separation of the wood, due to the tearing apart of the wood cells.

Spokeshave Cutting tool having blade set between two handles for dressing curved edges of wood and for rounding and shaping.

Surfaced lumber Lumber that has been planed or sanded on one or more surfaces.

Tenon Projection formed at the end of a piece of wood for insertion into a mortise of the same dimensions.

Toe nail Driving nails into corners or other joints at an angle.

Tongue-and-groove A carpentry joint in which the jutting edge of one board fits into the grooved edge of a mating board.

Twist A distortion caused by the turning or winding of the edges of a board so that the four corners of any face are no longer on the same plane.

Veneer A thin layer or sheet of wood.

Warp Any variation from a true or plane surface. The term covers **crook, bow, cup, twist,** and any combination of these.

Yard lumber Lumber of all grades, sizes and patterns; intended for ordinary construction and general building purposes.

INDEX

Abrasives, 15
A-C paneling, 40, 50, 58
Acrylic server, 63
Alkyd primer, 51
Allen key, 16
Aluminum flashing, 47
Aluminum guide, 12
Aluminum nails, 23
Aluminum oxide paper, 15
Asphalt shingles, 58, 62
Assembly screws, 17
Audubon Society, 43
Awls, 19

Backfilling, 45
Backgammon, 30
Backyard furniture. See
    Furniture, outdoor
Band saw, bench-top, 10
Barbecue, 63-69
Bar unit, 38-42
Beads, cutting, 14
Belt, tool, 19
Belt, sander, 15
Benches:
    bench, perimeter, 34-37
    planter, sitting, 81-84
    tree surround, 117-122
Bench-top band saw, 10
Bench-top drill press, 16
Bench-top vises, 9
Bevel cuts, 10-12, 15
Bevel-planing, 24
Bin, firewood, 89-92
Birdhouse, 43-47
Bit, combination, 16, 95, 136,
    146, 152
Bit, core-box, 14
Bit, roller-guided, 65
Bit, spade, 16
Bits, boring, 16
Bits, router, 14
Bits, self-piloted, 14
Blade face, 10
Blades, saw, 10-12
Block plane, 13
Bolted supports, 20
Bolts:
    carriage bolts, 45, 50, 55, 69,
        116, 150
    galvanized bolts, 17
    hanger bolts, 116
    stiffener bolt, 116
    lag bolts, 55, 154
Bow saw, 10
Bracing, triangular, 20
Breaking corners, 13
Burlap rags, 57
Butcher block, 63

Cabinets:
    barbecue, 63-69
    bar unit, 38-42
    garbage storage, 48-51
    potting unit, 52-57
Canvas sling chair, 25-29
Carbide blades, 19
Carbide-tipped router bits, 14
Card games, 30
Carpenter's square, 22, 33, 54,
    60
Carriage bolts, 45, 50, 55, 69,
    116, 150
Cart, barbecue, 63-69
Casters, 41, 50
Caulk, redwood, 23
Caulking, 47, 57
C clamps, 9
Cement, contact, 32

Cement, veneer, 32
Centering dogs, 16
Chairs:
    deck chair, 93-96
    slat chair, 129-132
    slat chaise, 133-138
    sling chair, 25-29
Chaise, slat, 129, 133-138
Chalk line, 24, 62
Checkers, 30
Chess, 30
Children's gym, outdoor, 147-155
Chip pockets, 32
Chisel, hollow, 28
Chisel, rotating. See Routers
Chisels, 13, 19
Chuck key-safety lock, 16
Chute (radial saw), 10, 18
Circles, cutting, 11-12
Clear heart redwood. See
    Redwood
Cleats, 50, 67, 72-73, 146, 152
Climbing ropes, 147
Coarse-toothed blades, 11
Combination bit, 16, 95, 136,
    146, 152
Combination square, 27
Compass, 61
Compression nuts, 76
Conduit. See EMT conduit
Constantine's, 31, 53
Contact cement, 32
Contoured seat bench, 34-37
Copper chromium arsenate, 78
Cordwood. See Firewood
    storage bin
Core-box bit, 14
Corner jigs, 14
Corners, breaking, 13
Countersinking screws, 36, 67,
    72, 87, 116, 136, 146, 149
Coves, 14
Crosscutting, 10
Cross-grain sanding, 15
Cross-head screws, 17
Cuprinol #10, 146
Curves, cutting, 10
Cutter head, 15
Cutters, dado, 10
Cutting into knots, 12
Cutting metal, 11
Cutting problem material, 11

Dado blades, 28, 46, 75, 132
Dado cutters, 10
Dadoes, 14
Deck furniture. See Furniture,
    outdoor
Decking, diagonal, 85
Decorating workpiece edges, 14
Diagonal decking, 85
Dimensioned lumber, 12
Disk sander, 54
Doghouse, 58-62
Dogs, centering, 16
Dogs, plastic, 9
Double-decked planter. See
    Sandbox
Douglas fir, 44, 49, 124, 148, 152
Dovetail templates, 14
Dowels, 94
Drawknife, 13
Drill bits, 16
Drill chuck, 10, 18
Drill guides, 16
Drill press, 16
Drill-press vises, 16
Drill-storage index, 16
Duckboards, 78-80

Edge guide, 12
Edges, belt-sanding, 92
Edges, decorating, 14
Edges, routing, 28
Electrical parts, 17
Embossing, 14
EMT conduit, 70
Engraving, 14
Epoxy mortar, 57
Expanded polystyrene foam
    (EPS), 60
Exterior-finish paint, 17, 42
Exterior metal primer, 17, 51, 56
Extruded polystyrene foam
    (EPS), 60
Eyebolts, 154
Eye protection, 18

Featherboard, 36
Felt, 62
Felt, impregnated, 58
File, 13
Filler. See Putty
Fine-tooth blades, 11
Finger, router, 14
Firewood storage bin, 89-92
Flashing, aluminum, 47
Flat head screws, 136, 146
Flexible rule, 27
Floor, multi-layered, 58
Footrest, chair, 93
Formica, 10
Frames, surface-embossing, 14
Fret saw, 14
Furniture, outdoor:
    barbecue, 63-69
    bar unit, 38-42
    bench, perimeter, 34-37
    deck chair, 93-96
    game table, 30-33
    lighting enclosure, 70-77
    picnic table, 113-116
    planter, sitting, 81-84
    planter, standing, 142-146
    potting unit, 52-57
    sandbox, 85-88
    slat chair, 129-132
    slat chaise, 133-138
    sling chair, 25-29
    tables, nest of, 139-141
    tree surround, 117-122
    umbrella table, 20-24
    wishing well, 123-128

Gables, 47, 61, 127
Galvanized bolts, 17
Galvanized metal cans, 48
Galvanized nails, 37, 46, 58, 91
Gang-sawing, 21, 75, 80, 91, 126,
    141
Garbage unit, 48-51
Garden lighting, 70-77
GFI breaker, 72
Glue, waterproof, 37
Grain, sanding, 15
Grit marks, 15
Grout float, 57
Grouting, 57
Guide, rip-sawing, 12
Guide fence, 12
Guides, drill, 16
Guide/work table, 12
Gussets, 127

Hacksaw, 76
Half-lap joints, 22, 27, 131
Half-sheet orbital pad sander,
    15
Hanger bolts, 116

Hardware, 17
Hardwood panel, cutting, 11-12
Hardwoods, 15
Hasps, 17, 42, 51, 57
Herringbone pattern, 20
Hex nut, 45
Hickey. See Tubing bender
High-carbon blades, 13
High-lead assembly screws, 17
Hinges, 17, 42, 51, 69, 115, 135
Hinge screws, 8
Hip roof, 123
Hold-downs, 10
Hole saw, 16, 24, 41
Hollow chisel, 28
Horses, metal, 8

Impregnated felt, 58
Inlays, 12
Insulation, polystyrene, 58

Jigs, corner, 14
Jig saw, 11, 12, 28, 42, 54, 60
Joinery work, 13
Jointing, 15
Joints, half-lap, 22, 27, 131
Jungle gym, 147-155

Kerf, 19
Kickback in saws, 12, 19
Knife, utility, 60, 62
Knock-down-design chair, 25
Knots, cutting into, 12

Ladders, 147
Lag bolts, 55, 154
Laminate, 33
Laminates, plastic, 14
Lighter-duty belt sander, 15
Lighting, outdoor, 70-77
Linseed oil putty, 51
Lock, chuck key-safety, 16
Lock dogs, 88
Lounger, backyard. See Deck
    chair
Louver assemblies, 70-77
Lumber, dimensional, 12
Lumber, pressure-treated, 58-62,
    117

Mah jongg, 30
Mahogany, 30
Mandrels, 16
Maple, 19
Marquetry, 30
Masks, safety, 18
Metal, cutting, 11
Metal hardware, 42
Metal horses, 8
Metal paint, 17
Metal primer, exterior, 17, 51
Miter gauge, 10
Miter joint, 10, 12, 24, 28, 47, 75,
    83
Mortar, 57
Mortises, 14, 27, 28
Multi-layered floor, 58
Muslin, 29

Nailers, 24, 40, 56, 60
Nailing, zig-zag pattern, 91
Nails, galvanized, 37, 46, 58, 91
Nails, oval-head, 37, 46, 91
National pipe thread, 65
Nipples, pipe, 55
Notches, 10
n.p.t. See National pipe thread

Oak, 65, 67, 93, 152

Octagonal tree surround, 117-122
Oil primer, 51
Orbital pad sander, 15
Outdoor furniture. See Furniture, outdoor
Outdoor lighting, 70-77
Oval-head nails, 37, 46, 91

Pad sander, 15
Paint, metal, 17
Paneling:
 A-C, 40, 50, 58
 hardwood, 11-12, 15
 particleboard, 30
 plywood, 12
 T1-11, 17, 40, 42, 50, 51, 126-128
Pan screw, 69
Pantographic letters, 14
Particleboard, 30
Patio furniture. See Furniture, outdoor
Patio lighting, 70-77
Pawls, anti-kickback, 10, 18
Perimeter bench, 34-37
Phillips head screws, 17
Picnic table, 113-116
Pilot hole, 54
Pilotless bits, 14
Pipe nipples, 55
Pipe straps, 55
Planer, 10
Planes, 13
Planter, double-decked. See Sandbox
Planters:
 sandbox, 85-88
 sitting planter, 81-84
 standing planter, 142-146
 tree surround, 117-122
 wishing-well planter, 123-128
Plastic, cutting, 11
Plastic laminates, 14
Platen, 11-12
Platforms, 147
Playground, backyard, 147-155
Plug cutter, 16
Plugging screw holes, 36
Plunge-cutting, 11-12
Plywood, 12
Pocket cuts, 11-12, 40, 56, 65
Polystyrene slab, 58
Portable saw, 11-12, 60
Post-hole digger, 125, 152-153
Potting unit, 52-57
Preservative, wood. See Copper chromium arsenate
Pressure-treated lumber, 58-62, 78, 89, 117

Primer, alkyd, 51
Problem-material cutting, 11
Protractor, saw, 12
Punch, 23
Putty, 23, 42, 56
Putty, linseed oil, 51

Quill crank, 16

Rabbets, 14
Radial saw, 10, 18, 60
Rafter square, 22, 33, 54, 60
Ramp, 147
Rasps, 13
Recesses, 14
Recreation-area lighting, 70-77
Red oak, 64, 94
Redwood, 30, 36, 52, 53-57, 70-77, 81-84, 117, 129, 133, 142
Redwood caulk, 23
Rip fence, 10, 15
Ripping, 10
Ripping stock, 18
Rip-sawing guide, 12
Roller-bearing guided bits, 14, 54, 65
Rolling barbecue cart, 63-69
Roof, hip, 123
Roofs, 43-47, 58-62, 123-128
Roof shingles, cutting, 11-12
Routers, 12, 14, 54, 65
Routing edges, 28
Rule, flexible, 27
Rungs, ladder, 151-152

Safety, power-tool, 18-19
Safety, saw, 12
Sandbox, 85-88
Sanding, cross-grain, 15
Sandpaper, aluminum oxide, 15
Sawbucks, 89
Saw horse, 8
Saws, 10-12
 band saw, bench-top, 10
 bow saw, 10
 fret saw, 28
 hacksaw, 76
 hole saw, 16, 24, 41
 jig saw, 11, 12, 28, 42, 54, 60
 portable saw, 11-12, 60
 radial saw, 10, 18, 60
 table saw, 10, 19, 60
Screweyes, 56, 154
Screw holes, counterboring. See Countersinking screws
Screw holes, plugging, 36
Screws, 17
Screws, countersinking. See Countersinking screws
Scribing, 13

Scroller blade, 11-12
Seat bench, contoured, 34-37
Seesaw, 147
Self-piloted bits, 14
Semi-transparent stain, 17
Server, acrylic, 63
S hooks, 51
Shank drills, 16
Shaper. See Routers
Shaper tables, 14
Shaping wood, 13
Sharpened tools, 19
Sheet metal, 45
Shingles, asphalt, 58, 62
Short-circuiting, danger of, 18
Skirt trim, 24
Slat chair, 129-132
Slat chaise, 129, 133-138
Slats, 34-37, 94
Slats, redwood, 129
Sleepers, 80
Slides, 147
Smoothing wood, 13
Snack tables, 139-141
Socket wrench, 92
Spade bit, 16
Spar varnish, 93
Splintering, 29, 68, 75
Spokeshave, 13
Spruce, 40
Square, carpenter's, 22, 33, 54, 60
Stain, 17, 47
Stainless-steel nails, 23
Standing planter, 142-146
Stanley's Surform® tools, 13
Starter holes, 11-12
Steamship deck chair. See Deck chair
Steel blades, 13
Stiffener bolt, 116
Storage bin, 89-92
Straps, pipe, 55
Stretchers, 27
Suction feet, 9
Suppliers, hardware, 17
Supports. See Saw horses
Supports, bolted, 20
Surface-embossing frames, 14
Swings, 147

Tables:
 game table, 30-33
 nest of tables, 139-141
 picnic table, 113-116
 umbrella table, 20-24
Table saw, 10, 19, 60
Table-top pattern, 20
Tack-nailing, 37
Taper jig, 10

Tempered steel blades, 13
Templates, dovetail, 14
Tenoning jigs, 10
Tenons, 14, 27
Termites, 91
Test-fitting wedges, 28
Tiles (American Olean Quarry Natural), 57
Tile top, 57
T1-11 paneling, 17, 40, 42, 50-51, 126-128
Tool belt, 19
Tools, sanding, 15
Tools, stationary. See Radial saw, Table saw
Torque, 19
Trammels, 11-12, 14
Triangular bracing, 20
Trim, skirt, 24
Trowel, 57
Truss head screw, 69
T slots, 12
Tubing bender, 76
Tubing cutter, 76
Twist bit, 16

UF sealed connector, 72
Universal jig, 10, 28
Ultra-fine blades, 11
Urethane varnish, 30-33, 51
Utility knife, 12, 19, 60, 62

Vaportight lighting fixtures, 70-77
Varnish, 47
Varnish, urethane, 30-33
Veneer cement, 32
Veneers, 30
Vises, 8-9
Vises, drill press, 16
V jaws, 16
V miters, 10

Walkways, wooden, 78-80, 147
Waterproof glue, 37
Wedges, test-fitting, 28
Wheels, 65, 93, 137
White pine, 39, 44, 49, 124
Wing nuts, 45, 47, 116
Wishing-well planter, 123-128
Wood, pressure-treated, 89
Wooden walks, 78-80
Wood preservative. See Copper chromium arsenate
Work table, 8
Worm-gear driven saws. See Portable saws
Wrench, socket, 92

Yoke, 10

METRIC CHARTS

Sizes: Metric cross-sections are so close to their nearest Imperial sizes, as noted below, that for most purposes they may be considered equivalents.

Lengths: Metric lengths are based on a 300mm module which is slightly shorter in length than an Imperial foot. It will therefore be important to check your requirements accurately to the nearest inch and consult the table below to find the metric length required.

Areas: The metric area is a square metre. Use the following conversion factors when converting from Imperial data: 100 sq. feet = 9.290 sq. metres.

METRIC SIZES SHOWN BESIDE NEAREST IMPERIAL EQUIVALENT

mm	Inches	mm	Inches
16 × 75	⁵⁄₈ × 3	44 × 150	1³⁄₄ × 6
16 × 100	⁵⁄₈ × 4	44 × 175	1³⁄₄ × 7
16 × 125	⁵⁄₈ × 5	44 × 200	1³⁄₄ × 8
16 × 150	⁵⁄₈ × 6	44 × 225	1³⁄₄ × 9
19 × 75	³⁄₄ × 3	44 × 250	1³⁄₄ × 10
19 × 100	³⁄₄ × 4	44 × 300	1³⁄₄ × 12
19 × 125	³⁄₄ × 5	50 × 75	2 × 3
19 × 150	³⁄₄ × 6	50 × 100	2 × 4
22 × 75	⁷⁄₈ × 3	50 × 125	2 × 5
22 × 100	⁷⁄₈ × 4	50 × 150	2 × 6
22 × 125	⁷⁄₈ × 5	50 × 175	2 × 7
22 × 150	⁷⁄₈ × 6	50 × 200	2 × 8
25 × 75	1 × 3	50 × 225	2 × 9
25 × 100	1 × 4	50 × 250	2 × 10
25 × 125	1 × 5	50 × 300	2 × 12
25 × 150	1 × 6	63 × 100	2¹⁄₂ × 4
25 × 175	1 × 7	63 × 125	2¹⁄₂ × 5
25 × 200	1 × 8	63 × 150	2¹⁄₂ × 6
25 × 225	1 × 9	63 × 175	2¹⁄₂ × 7
25 × 250	1 × 10	63 × 200	2¹⁄₂ × 8
25 × 300	1 × 12	63 × 225	2¹⁄₂ × 9
32 × 75	1¹⁄₄ × 3	75 × 100	3 × 4
32 × 100	1¹⁄₄ × 4	75 × 125	3 × 5
32 × 125	1¹⁄₄ × 5	75 × 150	3 × 6
32 × 150	1¹⁄₄ × 6	75 × 175	3 × 7
32 × 175	1¹⁄₄ × 7	75 × 200	3 × 8
32 × 200	1¹⁄₄ × 8	75 × 225	3 × 9
32 × 225	1¹⁄₄ × 9	75 × 250	3 × 10
32 × 250	1¹⁄₄ × 10	75 × 300	3 × 12
32 × 300	1¹⁄₄ × 12	100 × 100	4 × 4
38 × 75	1¹⁄₂ × 3	100 × 150	4 × 6
38 × 100	1¹⁄₂ × 4	100 × 200	4 × 8
38 × 125	1¹⁄₂ × 5	100 × 250	4 × 10
38 × 150	1¹⁄₂ × 6	100 × 300	4 × 12
38 × 175	1¹⁄₂ × 7	150 × 150	6 × 6
38 × 200	1¹⁄₂ × 8	150 × 200	6 × 8
38 × 225	1¹⁄₂ × 9	150 × 300	6 × 12
44 × 75	1³⁄₄ × 3	200 × 200	8 × 8
44 × 100	1³⁄₄ × 4	250 × 250	10 × 10
44 × 125	1³⁄₄ × 5	300 × 300	12 × 12

METRIC LENGTHS

Lengths Metres	Equiv. Ft. & Inches
1.8m	5′ 10⁷⁄₈″
2.1m	6′ 10⁵⁄₈″
2.4m	7′ 10¹⁄₂″
2.7m	8′ 10¹⁄₄″
3.0m	9′ 10¹⁄₈″
3.3m	10′ 9⁷⁄₈″
3.6m	11′ 9³⁄₄″
3.9m	12′ 9¹⁄₂″
4.2m	13′ 9³⁄₈″
4.5m	14′ 9¹⁄₃″
4.8m	15′ 9″
5.1m	16′ 8³⁄₄″
5.4m	17′ 8⁵⁄₈″
5.7m	18′ 8³⁄₈″
6.0m	19′ 8¹⁄₄″
6.3m	20′ 8″
6.6m	21′ 7⁷⁄₈″
6.9m	22′ 7⁵⁄₈″
7.2m	23′ 7¹⁄₂″
7.5m	24′ 7¹⁄₄″
7.8m	25′ 7¹⁄₈″

All the dimensions are based on 1 inch = 25 mm.

LUMBER

NOMINAL SIZE (This is what you order)	ACTUAL SIZE (This is what you get)
Inches	Inches
1 × 1	³⁄₄ × ³⁄₄
1 × 2	³⁄₄ × 1¹⁄₂
1 × 3	³⁄₄ × 2¹⁄₂
1 × 4	³⁄₄ × 3¹⁄₂
1 × 6	³⁄₄ × 5¹⁄₂
1 × 8	³⁄₄ × 7¹⁄₄
1 × 10	³⁄₄ × 9¹⁄₄
1 × 12	³⁄₄ × 11¹⁄₄
2 × 2	1³⁄₄ × 1³⁄₄
2 × 3	1¹⁄₂ × 2¹⁄₂
2 × 4	1¹⁄₂ × 3¹⁄₂
2 × 6	1¹⁄₂ × 5¹⁄₂
2 × 8	1¹⁄₂ × 7¹⁄₄
2 × 10	1¹⁄₂ × 9¹⁄₄
2 × 12	1¹⁄₂ × 11¹⁄₄